ST/CTC/149

United Nations Conference on Trade and Development
Programme on Transnational Corporations

Environment Series No. 4

Environmental Management in Transnational Corporations

Report on the Benchmark Corporate Environmental Survey

United Nations   New York, 1993

Note

The Transnational Corporations and Management Division of the United Nations Department of Economic and Social Development serves as the focal point within the United Nations Secretariat for all matters related to transnational corporations and acts as secretariat to the Commission on Transnational Corporations, an intergovernmental subsidiary body of the United Nations Economic and Social Council. The objectives of its work programme are to further the understanding of the nature of transnational corporations and of their economic, legal, political and social effects on home and host countries and on international relations, particularly between developed and developing countries; to secure effective international arrangements aimed at enhancing the contribution of transnational corporations to national development goals and world economic growth; and to strengthen the negotiating capacity of host countries, particularly developing countries, in their dealings with transnational corporations.

The report *Environmental Management in Transnational Corporations* is part of TCMD's *Environment Series*. Previous publications in this series include *Transnational Corporations and Industrial Hazards Disclosure* (ST/CTC/111), *Climate Change and Transnational Corporations* (ST/CTC/112) and *International Environmental Law: Emerging Trends and Implications for Transnational Corporations* (ST/CTC/137). In the near future, two additional publications of the *Environment Series* will be released: *Technology Transfer: Options for Sustainable Development* and *Improving Liability Measures for Addressing Transfrontier Pollution.*

The term "country" as used in this volume also refers, as appropriate, to territories or areas; the designations employed and the presentation of the material do not imply the expression of any opinion whatsoever on the part of the Secretariat of the United Nations concerning the legal status of any country, territory, city or area or of its authorities, or concerning the delimitation of its frontiers or boundaries. In addition, the designations of country groups are intended solely for statistical or analytical convenience and do not necessarily express a judgement about the stage of development reached by a particular country or area in the development process.

The following symbols have been used in the tables:

Two dots (..) indicate that data are not available or are not separately reported. Rows in tables have been omitted in those cases where no data are available for any of the elements in the row;

A dash (—) indicates that the item is equal to zero or its value is negligible;

A blank in a table indicates that the item is not applicable;

A slash (/) between dates representing years, e.g., 1988/89, indicates a financial year;

Use of a hyphen (-) between dates representing years, e.g., 1985-1989, signifies the full period involved, including the beginning and end years.

Reference to "dollars" ($) means United States dollars, unless otherwise indicated.

Annual rates of growth or change, unless otherwise stated, refer to annual compound rates.

Details and percentages in tables do not necessarily add to totals because of rounding.

The material contained in this study may be freely quoted with appropriate acknowledgement. Comments should be sent to the Director, Transnational Corporations and Management Division, United Nations Department of Economic and Social Development, United Nations, Room DC2-1220, New York NY 10017, United States. Telephone: (212) 963-2990; Fax: (212) 963-2146; Telex: 661062 UNCTNC.

ST/CTC/149

UNITED NATIONS PUBLICATION

Sales No. E.94.II.A.2

ISBN 92-1-104422-7

Transnational corporations (TNCs) are frequently the repositories of scarce technical skills for the preservation and enhancement of the environment and they conduct activities in sectors that have an impact on the environment. The way in which TNCs globally manage their assets and the environmental impact of their processes and products is therefore of crucial importance for sustainable development.

This report presents the results of the Benchmark Survey on Corporate Environmental Management (BMS). The survey was conducted by the United Nations Conference on Trade and Development (UNCTAD) Programme on Transnational Corporations.* The survey collected data on companies with operations in more than one country and with annual sales in excess of $US1 billion. Its primary objective was to measure the current state of international corporate environmental management. The preliminary statistical findings of this study have already identified priorities and stimulated discussions on TNCs and sustainable development, most notably during the United Nations Conference on Environment and Development (UNCED). The data collected in the BMS provided the background for a 46-page report of the Secretary-General entitled: Recommendations of the Executive Director (E/C.10/1992/2). In this report to the Economic and Social Council, The Programme on Transnational Corporations consolidated existing standards and practices of the most progressive TNCs and suggested corrective steps that other TNCs might undertake to achieve the same level of environmental excellence. The Benchmark Survey also enabled the Programme on Transnational Corporations to make recommendations on specific issues discussed at UNCED, such as atmospheric pollution, biodiversity and toxic chemicals issues (UNCTC, 1991).

The Benchmark Survey results are intended to inform decision makers on the state of corporate environmental management, and on the expectations that the corporate community has of the international system. It is hoped that a better understanding of these matters will help sustain and encourage further dialogue between the business community and policy makers on how corporate management of the environment can be improved, and how laws and regulations can be established in the post-UNCED era. Moreover, it is hoped that a broader understanding of corporate environmental management can help choose the regulatory frameworks that most effectively induce environmentally friendly responses from TNCs investing in developing countries. The survey report is also directed towards decision makers in the corporate community. By disseminating ideas of improved environmental management and innovative sustainable development programs, it is hoped that corporations not yet as engaged in environmental protection will be inspired to incorporate environmental concerns into their decision-making.

The current report combines both the final statistical findings of the Benchmark Survey as well as an analysis of material from policy statements, annual reports, brochures, and the like supplied by TNCs participating in the survey. UNCTAD would like to express its gratitude to the executives of TNCs who responded for their contribution to this ambitious project.

UNCTAD would also like to recognize the five research institutions that took part in the complex process of data collection and analysis. These are the Centre for Technology, Environment and Development

---

* In the past the Programme on Transnational Corporations was carried out by the United Nations Centre on Transnational Corporations (UNCTC) (1975-1992) and by the Transnational Corporations and Management Division of the United Nations Department of Economic and Social Development (TCMD/DESD) (1992-1993).

at Clark University (United States); the Department for the Conservation of Human Resources at Columbia University (United States); the Centre for Environmental Management and Planning at Aberdeen University (United Kingdom); the Institute for Environmental Management at the European Business School (Germany); and the Nomura Research Institute (Japan). These five centres serving the regions targeted vigorously pursued follow-up that enhanced the response rate measurably. They also actively participated in joint discussions in an effort to bring their analyses of regional data into closer alignment with one another. All these contributors to the survey are, of course, not responsible for any errors and mistakes that may be present in this report.

The following staff of UNCTAD's Programme on Transnational Corporations drafted this report: Harris R. Gleckman, Michael W. Hansen, Anna Theofilopouiou, Olive Wahome and Lloyd Wright. The report was produced for publication by Melanie Beth Oliviero, Louise Rankin and Bennett Olson.

Finally, UNCTAD would like to express its appreciation to the Government of the Netherlands for its generous financial support of the project.

Carlos Fortin
Deputy to the Secretary-General
United Nations Conference on Trade and Development
Director-in-Charge
Programme on Transnational Corporations

New York, August 1993

Boxes
page

(List of boxes cont'd.)

Text Figures

page

(List of text figures cont'd.)

Text Tables

page

BAUM	Bundesdeutscher Arbeitskreis für umweltbewußtes Management e.V. (German Environmental Management Association)
BCSD	Business Council for Sustainable Development
BMS	Benchmark Survey on Corporate Environmental Activities
CEFIC	Conseil Europeen des Federations de l'Industries Chimique
CMA	Chemical Manufacturers' Association
DESD	Department of Economic and Social Development
EH&S	Environment, Health and Safety
EPA	Environmental Protection Agency (United States)
FAO	Food and Agriculture Organization
FDI	foreign direct investment
GATT	General Agreement on Tariffs and Trade
GEMI	Global Environmental Management Initiative
ICC	International Chamber of Commerce
ILO	International Labour Organisation
ISO	International Organization for Standardization
LDC	Less developed countries
MDSS	Material and data safety sheets
MITI	Ministry of International Trade and Industry (Japan)
NGO	Non-governmental Organization
OECD	Organisation for Economic Co-operation and Development
R & D	research and development
SARA	Superfund Amendment and Reclamation Act (United States)
TCMD	Transnational Corporations and Management Division (DESD, United Nations)
UNCED	United Nations Conference on Environment and Development
UNCTC	United Nations Centre on Transnational Corporations
UNEP	United Nations Environment Programme
UNIDO	United Nations Industrial Development Organization
WCED	World Commission on Environment and Development

A. CORPORATE MANAGEMENT AND THE ENVIRONMENT

"We have already begun the transition to a new era in which environmental issues will increasingly drive our economic life. The transition to economically sound and sustainable development is as imperative for the continued viability of our economy as it is for our environmental security. Every business that impacts on the environment must accommodate the fact that the environment will have an important impact on its business".[1]

A profound transformation has occurred in the corporate management of environmental and occupational matters during the last decade. Numerous corporations have taken up the challenges of an age where environmental concerns are among the most salient on the political agenda and are enthusiastically engaged in managing their environmental impacts. A 1991 study from McKinsey & Company reported that 92 per cent of the 400 firms surveyed agreed with the statement, "The environmental challenge is one of the central issues of the 21st century" (McKinsey & Co., 1991, p. 4). Further, at the February 1990 World Economic Forum, a global business advisory group, 650 industry and governmental leaders ranked the environment as the number one challenge facing business (Cahan and Smith, 1990). Many corporations select members of their boards with special environment, health and safety (EH&S) responsibilities and formulate elaborate environmental policies and programmes. Those policies often go far beyond regulatory requirements and reflect substantial investments by corporations.

Overall, companies now allot an average of 1.1 to 2 per cent of sales revenues to environmental expenditures and often over 25 per cent of their net income (after tax); in the case of the United States car industry the amount can be as high as 65 per cent (Booz-Allen & Hamilton, 1991, p. 8). In 1989, Texaco, Inc. supported its environmental policies by investing some $354 million, including capital expenditures for air, water and solid waste pollution abatement.[2] Bayer AG has announced that it spends 20 per cent of its manufacturing costs on environmental protection. One of the largest manufacturers of chloroflurocarbons (CFCs), Imperial Chemical Industries (ICI), has committed $100 million to the search for alternatives to CFCs. DuPont estimates that by the turn of the century, it will have invested $1 billion in developing and marketing alternatives to CFC gases. In 1989, Minnesota Mining and Manufacturing Company (3M) developed new environmental goals which included a 70 per cent reduction in air emissions by 1993, at a price of $175 million, and a 90 per cent reduction of all emissions by 2000. Numerous other examples of corporate EH&S initiatives could be given.[3]

This phenomenon of corporate greening has been called "corporate responsiveness", "responsible care", "corporate self-regulation", "good corporate citizenship", "product stewardship", "precautious management", "proactive management" or "corporate voluntarism". The Benchmark Survey was undertaken to measure and evaluate that activity as it is anchored in corporate management policies and practices.

As more and more corporations engage in environmental management, the supporting industry has expanded rapidly. The international industry that provides environmental services and equipment has grown at a stunning pace and is becoming a major, if not the major, business opportunity of the future. The industry is now valued at $300 billion annually, with the potential to double by the end of the century (Smart, 1992, p. 90). The bulk of this industry is involved in producing and selling pollution-fighting equipment. But the service sector has also been profiting from the corporate search for knowledge and advice on environmental matters. Thus, consultant firms such as Arthur D. Little and the McKinsey Company have played a central role in developing new green concepts and in applying them to daily corporate routines. Simultaneously, specialist magazines, journals and newsletters dealing solely with corporate environmental management and responsibility are mushrooming;[4] business schools and economics departments are increasingly offering programmes in corporate environmental management;[5] and the academic literature in the field continues to grow.[6]

Industrial associations and related groups seek to coordinate and facilitate corporate environmental initiatives by setting industry-wide standards and by disseminating information on innovative practices. Corporate charters and guidelines on environmental issues such as the International Chamber of Commerce (ICC)'s "Business Charter on Sustainable Development", the Japanese industry association Keidanren's "Global Environmental Charter", or the Chemical Manufacturers Association (CMA)'s "Responsible CARE Program" are being adopted by more and more firms,[7] and conferences on corporate environmental management are held regularly. New business organizations have been created that are devoted solely to this issue, such as the Business Council for Sustainable Development (BCSD), the Global Environmental Management Initiative (GEMI) or the German Environmental Management Association (known by its German acronym, BAUM).

B. CORPORATE MANAGEMENT AND SUSTAINABLE DEVELOPMENT

The emerging field of corporate environmental activism has a profound significance for the international discussions on sustainable development. Sustainable development challenges the international community to find ways of social, economic and political cooperation that meet the development imperative without exhausting the environment or the natural resource base. In that process TNCs can play a key role because they can function simultaneously as major engines of development and as a means to improve the global environment.

The importance of TNCs for development becomes evident when one considers their pivotal role in the global economy. According to United Nations estimates, TNCs invested $234 billion in 1991 outside their home country. Ninety-five per cent of those investments come from the most industrialized countries. Nearly one quarter of foreign direct investment (FDI) goes to developing nations, including newly industrialized countries. The annual sales of the 350 largest TNCs amount to one third of the industrialized world's GNP and exceed by several hundred billion those of the developing world. Seventy per cent of world trade is controlled by TNCs. Ninety per cent of all technology and product patents world-wide are held by TNCs, but only 6 per cent of the world's 3.5 million patents are held by TNCs located in developing countries. Obtaining access to TNC capital, technology and know-how is an essential element in the development strategy of many countries, and increasingly, countries around the world seek to attract TNCs through trade and investment liberalization.

Similarly, the potential of TNCs to alter the environment is extensive. TNCs possess the technologies and research and development (R&D) capabilities that will likely provide the solutions to many environmental problems of today. On the other hand, TNCs also have the potential to affect the environment adversely. General assessments indicate that more than 50 per cent of global greenhouse gas emissions are generated by TNCs. The bulk of biotechnological research world-wide is financed by TNCs, and TNCs are extensively involved in natural-resource exploitation activities such as oil drilling, mining, and forestry. The impact of TNCs on the environment in developing nations has aroused particular concern. Claims that TNCs exploit differences in environmental regulations, relocate production where the regulatory requirements are lowest, and employ double standards--one set for industrialized countries, and another in developing nations--have been raised by a number of sources. Events such as the Bhopal catastrophe in India involving Union Carbide, European corporations' export of hazardous and highly toxic waste to West African nations, and the forestry practices of Japanese corporations operating in South-East Asia, have tended to foster unease about TNC's activities in developing nations. Thus, a Gallup poll conducted in the summer of 1992 found that 35 per cent of the world's population agreed that multinational corporations were "a great deal responsible for the environmental degradation in developing countries".

Given the potential of TNCs to affect both development and environment, it is not surprising that corporate management issues came to play a central and often controversial role at the United Nations Conference on Environment and Development (UNCED) held in Rio de Janeiro from 3 to 14 June 1992.

C. BUSINESS DISCUSSIONS AT THE UNITED NATIONS CONFERENCE ON ENVIRONMENT AND DEVELOPMENT

In June 1992, government officials, politicians, environmentalists, business representatives and researchers from all over the world gathered in Rio de Janeiro at UNCED. With more than 30,000 participants and 10,000 journalists in attendance, this was the largest United Nations conference ever held. Prior to the conference, two years of deliberations had been held in the Preparatory Committees for UNCED, where numerous background documents were presented, and where intense negotiations on the principles of sustainable development took place. The conference concluded by endorsing a 500-page, 40-chapter "Agenda for the 21st century" (Agenda 21). Agenda 21 is an extremely comprehensive compilation of non-binding recommendations, spanning subjects from the protection of different environmental media such as water, air and land, and the role of non-governmental groups such as those representing women, business or indigenous people in sustainable development, to organizational and institutional matters related to the implementation of Agenda 21. Recommendations for business and industry, including TNCs, are made throughout its 40 chapters, particularly in a separate chapter on business and industry.[8]

Several groups took part in the discussions on business and environment. Governments and the different intergovernmental organizations of the United Nations which deal directly with industrial matters, such as the United Nations Industrial Development Organization (UNIDO), the International Labour Organisation (ILO), and the United Nations Environment Programme (UNEP), as well as the Transnational Corporations and Management Division of the Department of Economic and Social

Development (TCMD/DESD) (now UNCTAD, Programme on Transnational Corporations) were pivotally involved.

Non-governmental organizations (NGOs) also took an active part in the discussions. At the Global Forum, a gathering parallel to UNCED, more than 5,000 environmental and grassroots organizations from all over the world assembled. A series of treaties were drafted, among them a treaty entitled "Democratic Regulation of TNC Conduct", which outlines the basic responsibilities for corporations and TNCs, as well as basic principles for the cooperation of NGOs, on that issue in the future.

Representatives from the business community also participated in the UNCED process. The ICC lobbied for its Business Charter for Sustainable Development and for its numerous sectoral- and industry-specific environmental policies and programmes. Another organization, the Business Council for Sustainable Development (BCSD), played a central role in the UNCED process. The BCSD is an association of 50 or more CEOs from environmentally leading corporations around the world. It was founded and partly sponsored by the Swiss industrialist, Stephen Schmidheiny, pursuant to a request from the Secretary-General of UNCED. Its role in the process was to advise the Secretary-General of UNCED on business and industry matters and to stimulate the interest and involvement of the international business community in UNCED.

In addition to business associations, several individual corporations were active in the process, either through their affiliation with a business organization or through individual participation in conferences, exhibitions, publishing activities, and the like.

TCMD/DESD participated in the business discussions leading up to UNCED. It was soon realized that although business self-regulation was widely seen as an essential element in sustainable development, in fact very little was known of corporate management in relation to sustainable development issues, apart from anecdotal evidence and public relations campaigns from well-organized and well-financed business groups.[9] That was particularly true for business activity in developing countries. In order to explore that unknown transnational dimension and measure corporate involvement in sustainable development management, TCMD/DESD undertook the project known as the Benchmark Survey on Corporate Environmental Management. This report concludes the analysis of the Benchmark Survey results.

D. THE BENCHMARK SURVEY DESIGN

The questionnaire was developed in the summer of 1990 with input from government officials, business executives, environmental groups and academics. The respondents were asked to answer more than 200 questions related to more than 20 different sustainable development topics. The four response categories were: "yes", "no", "no answer" or "data not available at headquarters". In addition, the respondents were encouraged to expand on their answers, and to attach documentation, if available.[10]

The questionnaire covered four broad areas. The first dealt with background information on the enterprise. The second covered corporate environmental policies and programmes. The third covered the environmental management structures and techniques of the respondents. The last section asked the respondents to place their activities in the context of the subjects of UNCED and the United Nations system in general.

The questionnaire was mailed to 794 TNCs with sales over $1 billion, based on information from the Lotus One-Source Database. The mailing took place between November 1990 and May 1991 and was directed to the chief executive officer of each firm, with a copy to the chief environmental official if one could be identified.[11]

Responses to the Benchmark Survey continued to arrive during 1991, and by the end of the year twenty-seven per cent (210) of the 794 firms with sales over $1 billion targeted by the Survey had responded. Of those responding, 169 filled out the questionnaire, whereas the remaining 41 TNCs preferred to send informative material only. Apart from statistical analysis of the questionnaire data, the material attached to the questionnaire enabled more qualitative analysis of individual corporation's policies and practices.

In order to permit statistically significant data analysis, the sample was divided into three **geographic regions**: North America, Europe and Asia;[12] four **industrial sectors**: agricultural products (food processing, forestry, and pharmaceuticals) at 24 per cent of the firms, extractive processing (chemical and oil corporations) at 31 per cent, finished products (manufacturing of durables) at 36 per cent, and the service sector at 9 per cent; and, finally, into three equally large divisions **grouped by sales**: the bottom third at $1 - 2.3 billion, the middle third at $2.3 - 4.9 billion, and the top third at $4.9 billion and more in terms of annual sales. Figure 1 shows the distribution of the sample of 169 respondents across regions, sales and sectors.[13]

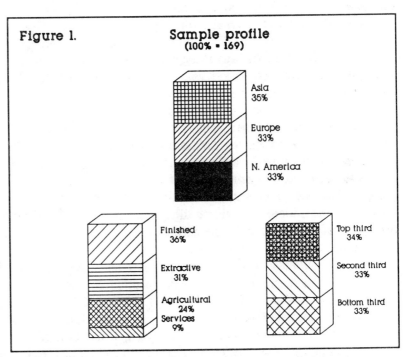

Source: TCMD/DESD Benchmark Survey, 1990-1991.

The material that the respondents attached to the questionnaires consisted of annual or company reports, written statements of environmental management principles or philosophies, and public relations brochures about environmental measures implemented by the company. Those materials were useful in assessing the mission and self-perception of the companies as well as their responses to what they perceived as important public issues. A second group of materials, such as corporate environmental health and safety manuals, internal memoranda, business guidelines or direct written replies, were more reflective of internal corporate policies and implementation systems and were therefore interpreted accordingly.

Generalizations beyond the sample must be made with caution. Most likely the sample does not represent the total population of TNCs with sales over $1 billion. That there is a systematic bias in the sample is indicated by the significant differences in response rates. As figure 2 shows, whereas the overall response rate was 21 per cent, Asian firms, 95 per cent of which are Japanese, were significantly more responsive than their European and North American counterparts. Looking at industrial sectors, 40 per cent of the targeted extractive-based-sector TNCs responded, but only 14 per cent of the service TNCs did so. There was a tendency for the larger the corporations to be more responsive. Finally, the analysis is clearly biased in favour of European, Japanese and North American TNCs. Only one developing country TNC (from India), of eight targeted, provided data.

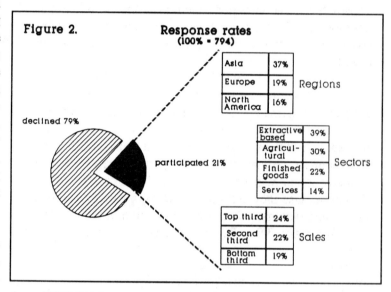

Source: TCMD/DESD Benchmark Survey, 1990-1991.

Another factor that must be kept in mind before generalizing the findings is that the survey data are subjective in nature. The data do not necessarily reflect the actual state of TNC environmental management, but rather the way TNCs perceive themselves, or want to be perceived by the world. Moreover, cultural differences have most likely influenced the way in which the respondents have interpreted and responded to the questions.

It should also be noted that the subsequent analysis of individual corporations is biased in favour of European, and especially North American, corporations which provided more supplemental materials than the Japanese ones. Another factor in reporting is that Asia-based corporations were strongly inclined to request anonymity, whereas two thirds of the Europe-based corporations and half of the North America-based corporations agreed to have their names used for the Benchmark Survey report. A more in-depth analysis of the methodology problems of the survey can be found in Annex B.

E. OUTLINE FOR THE REPORT

The UNCED recommendations on sustainable development set forth in Agenda 21's 40 chapters can be divided into three main categories: (a) recommendations for specific participants in the process; (b) recommendations pertaining to specific environmental problems; and (c) recommendations for sustainable development decision-making. Into the first category fall recommendations for the involvement of groups such as women, farmers or indigenous people. Agenda 21 also contains a specific chapter on business and industry (30), outlining the management responsibilities of corporations in implementing sustainable development objectives. Into the second category fall recommendations referring to specific environmental problems. Those recommendations are stated in Agenda 21 chapters on issues such as waste management, biotechnology and management of toxic substances. Numerous recommendations directed towards business can be found throughout the chapters dealing with these issues. Finally, the third category of recommendations addresses the issues of who is to decide the objectives and policies, on which criteria decisions should be made, who is to participate, and who is to pay. The recommendations on sustainable development decision-making are stated in chapters on international institutional arrangements, international cooperation, and integrating environment and development in decision-making.

Following the structure of Agenda 21, this report will have three parts. Part One will look into generic management practices and the practices and policies of TNCs. Part Two will examine corporate management in relation to seven specific environmental issues discussed at UNCED: protection of the atmosphere, the environmentally sound management of toxic chemicals and hazardous wastes, protection of freshwater resources, protection and management of land resources, protection of oceans, environmentally sound management of biotechnology, and conservation of biodiversity. Those issues have been chosen because they are assumed to have particular relevance for TNCs. The chapters of Parts One and Two will have a statistical analysis section, a section with examples illuminating the statistical findings, and a summary. For each theme discussed, a selection of relevant Agenda 21 recommendations will be cited.

Part Three will conclude the analysis of Part One and Part Two and outline how corporations, in cooperation with governments and international organizations, can further integrate sustainable development objectives in corporate decision-making.

Notes

[1] Interview with Maurice Strong, Secretary-General of UNCED, conducted by the Business Council for Sustainable Development, 1992.

[2] Unless otherwise stated, all figures given in dollars are United States currency.

[3] In recent years numerous compilations containing examples of corporate EH&S innovativeness have been published. Some of the most interesting recent titles are; J.O. Willums and U. Goluke (ICC), *From Ideas to Action: Business and Sustainable Development*, (Oslo, Gyldendal, 1992); B. Smart, *Beyond Compliance: A New Industry View of the Environment*, (USA, World Resources Institute, 1992); S. Schmidheiny (BCSD), *Changing Course: A Global Business Perspective on Development and the Environment*, (Cambridge, Massachusetts, MIT Press, 1992); Business International, *Managing the Global Environmental Challenge*, (New York, 1992). Good background articles are "Cleaning up: a survey of industry and the environment", *The Economist*, September 8, 1990; "The greening of corporate America", *Business Week*, April 23, 1990.

[4] See, for example, *Tomorrow: The Global Environment Magazine*, *Haz-News*, the series of environmental newsletters by Business Publishers, Inc., *Business and the Environment*, or *Resources: The Magazine on Environmental Management*.

[5] For example, the Stern School of Business of New York University, the Center for Environmental Management, Tufts University, the Institute for Environmental Management, European Business School, London School of Economics, Clark University and Harvard Business School all have faculty and programmes specializing in environmental management.

[6] Refer to the bibliography for selected readings.

[7] Keidanren's Global Environmental Charter has 4,000 Japanese corporate subscribers; The German Environmental Management Association's (BAUM) Code of Practices has 320 corporate sponsors; ICC's Business Charter for Sustainable Development has more than 1000 corporate subscribers; and the Chemical Manufactures Association's (CMA) Responsible CARE Program has 191 United States subscribers.

[8] The Agenda 21 chapter on business and industry can be found in Annex E.

[9] Although studies on corporate environmental management do exist, they tend to emphasize activities in the most industrialized nations and to focus on perceptions among corporate managers. Generally, the examination of the international and developing-country aspects of corporate EH&S management are negligible. Examples of surveys on corporate responses to the environmental challenge include: Deloitte & Touche, *The Environmental Transformation of United States Industry: A Survey of US Industrial Corporations' Environmental Strategies, Management Policies and Perceptions.* (Stanford, Stanford University Graduate School of Business Public Management Program, 1990); M. Flaherty and A. Rappaport, *Multinational Corporations and the Environment: A Survey of Global Practices.* (MA, Center for Environmental Management, 1991); Keidanren, *Towards Preservation of the Global Environment. Results of a Follow-up Survey on the Subject of the Keidanren Global Environmental Charter* (Tokyo, 1992); McKinsey & Company, *The Corporate Response to the Environmental Challenge.* (Amsterdam, 1991).

[10] The full questionnaire can be found in Annex A.

[11] Originally 1,000 corporations were identified. Eventually that number shrank to 794 because of: (a) recent mergers and takeovers; (b) identified companies that were affiliates of companies already targeted; and (c) the impossibility of locating the company.

[12] The North American region includes eight non-United States corporations (from Canada); the European region includes two Australian and one New Zealand corporation; and, for all practical purposes, the Asian region is Japanese, as only one non-Japanese Asian corporation (from India) with sales over $1 billion participated in the survey by contributing statistically significant data.

[13] For more information on the profile of the sample, see Annex B on methodology.

PART ONE

PART ONE: CORPORATE ENVIRONMENTAL MANAGEMENT: POLICIES, PRACTICES AND REGULATIONS

UNCED addressed generic corporate management issues in a separate chapter on business and industry as part of Agenda 21 (reproduced here in Annex E). The chapter has two sections, one that deals with "cleaner production" and one that deals with "responsible entrepreneurship". Briefly, the chapter calls for corporations to establish world-wide corporate policies on sustainable development (30.22); to report annually on their environmental records (30.10); to promote awareness among employees (30.14); to foster openness and dialogue with employees and the public (30.26); to facilitate the transfer of clean technology to developing countries (30.22); and, in general, to ensure ethical and responsible management of products and processes (30.26).

The chapters of Part One of this report relate to Agenda 21's recommendations for generic corporate management by focusing on four central aspects of corporate environmental management: the philosophy, principles and internal rules guiding EH&S management in the corporation (chapter I); the external rules and principles influencing corporate environmental management (chapter II); the organizational structure established to implement the EH&S policies and programmes (chapter III); and the actual practices and tools enabling management to implement EH&S policies and programmes (chapter IV).

CHAPTER I.

CORPORATE POLICY STATEMENTS, POLICIES AND PROGRAMMES

This analysis of the policy aspect of corporate environmental management is derived from responses to the questionnaire as well as from policy statements, policy directives and programme descriptions provided as attachments to the questionnaire. The analysis will distinguish between policy statements (section A), and policies and programmes (section B). There is no clear or commonly acknowledged distinction between policy statements, policies and programmes. Tentatively, policy statements can be defined as general expressions of the corporate EH&S philosophy directed towards the public and the employees, whereas policies and programmes are issue-specific behavioural guidelines of varying specificity aimed at the operational levels of the corporation.

A. POLICY STATEMENTS AND CORPORATE PHILOSOPHIES

Agenda 21:

"Recognize environmental management as among the highest corporate priorities and as a key determinant to sustainable development (30.3)

A corporation's recognition of its EH&S responsibilities will often be stated in a published policy statement. A generalized environmental policy statement is an important indicator of a corporation's environmental commitment. It sends a message from top management to the stakeholders that the corporation is committed to environmental protection, and it outlines the principles for subsequent environmental activities of the corporation. The audience may include employees, investors, politicians, regulators, stockholders, peer companies, consumers and environmental groups.

1. Statistical findings

The survey found that 43 per cent of all respondents had a published international policy statement. As seen in figure I.1, 70 per cent of the North American respondents had a formal published international policy statement. In 1974, before the latest surge in corporate greening, a study among 516 United States corporations found formal environmental statements in 40 per cent of the corporations (Lund, 1974). That suggests that the development of EH&S policy statements has a long history in North America. In comparison, only 18 per cent of the Asian and 41 per cent of the European respondents to the Benchmark Survey had such statements, indicating that European, and particularly Asian, corporations have less of a tradition of making public policy statements on EH&S issues.

TNCs in the top-third sales group were almost twice as likely to have a policy statement as TNCs in the bottom-third sales group (58 per cent versus 30 per cent). The extractive-based sector was by far the sector that more often issues such statements (60 per cent). That North American corporations, corporations in the extractive-based sector and the largest corporations were more likely to be engaged in EH&S management is a finding recurring throughout the subsequent analysis and will be discussed in the concluding chapter of Part One.

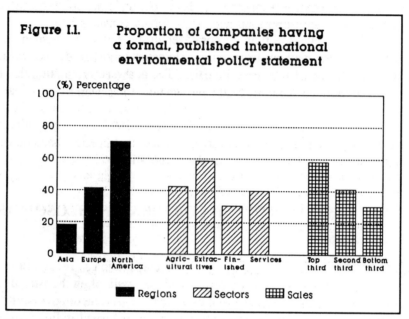

Figure I.1.   Proportion of companies having a formal, published international environmental policy statement

Source: TCMD/DESD Benchmark Survey, 1990-1991.

2. Examples of corporate policy statements and philosophies

The environmental policy statements that were submitted with the questionnaires tend to be recent; most were developed in the mid-1980s. They consist primarily of corporate principles that express in fairly general terms the fundamental attitudes and activities of the corporation with regard to the environment. The pattern that emerged from the review of the documentation indicates that in many instances, the principles of a particular corporation are first communicated to staff internally. They then become material included in brochures and annual reports intended for the public. The following analysis will focus on three aspects of corporate policy statements: (a) the discourse; (b) the content; and (c) the statements outlining specific targets for EH&S performance.

(a) *The discourse of corporate policy statements*

One of the principal characteristics of the corporate policy statements submitted by respondents to the Benchmark Survey is the very distinct language or discourse that has evolved to express corporate environmental orientations and principles in official documents. By far the most common observation is that the language used to project the environmental health and safety components of transnationals' identity is rather general. It consists of phrases such as "environmental excellence", "environmental leadership", "environmental stewardship", "long-term environmental commitment", "environmental challenges", "environmentally responsible", "success", "innovative", "first", and "pioneering". What is notably absent is the discourse common to the international development community--terms such as "sustainable development", "appropriate technology", "host country"; or, common to risk managers-- "feasible" and "acceptable"; or to environmental activists-- "green consumerism".

The text of a CEO's letter printed in a special environmental issue of a company journal is particularly illustrative of the preferred transnational discourse. In the excerpts from that text (presented below), the transnational's identity has been withheld and emphasis has been added to certain words and phases.

> "In my judgement, every company has an <u>obligation</u> to ensure that its business operations pose <u>no significant risk</u> to human health or the environment. That's something that we as citizens of this country and as the members of the world community have a <u>right</u> to expect. At [corporate name], protecting the environment is a serious <u>commitment</u> we've had for a long time. It's a <u>commitment</u> we view as especially important. I'm <u>proud</u> to say that [corporate name] has a <u>very solid record</u> of <u>positive environmental stewardship</u> over the years. We conduct routine environmental self-audits at our facilities, we've established a corporate-wide <u>environmental excellence</u> award for outstanding <u>environmental commitment and achievement,</u> and we've assigned an environmental manager to each region of the country where we have operations. But the <u>success</u> we've already <u>achieved</u> isn't enough. Each of us has a responsibility to continuously search for ways to enhance our environmental performance, prevent environmental problems, and correct any problems that occur. As employees of [corporate name] our <u>challenge</u> is to <u>continue our commitment</u> to <u>sound environmental management and practices,</u> each and every day. Ultimately, we are <u>responsible</u> for the quality of our own environment. To underscore this <u>commitment,</u> you'll be seeing more about the <u>environmental issues</u> facing our company in future articles and publications. As you read this issue of [journal name], I hope you'll feel as good as I do about [company name]'s environmental values, practices, and <u>accomplishments</u> and that you'll share this information with family and friends. Whether we're reforesting our timberlands, preserving or enhancing wildlife habitat, protecting air and water quality near our facilities, or minimizing the waste we generate [company name] has an <u>environmental record</u> every employee can be <u>proud</u> of. But its a <u>record</u> we have to <u>continue</u> making even better."

(b) The content of the policy statements

With regard to the content of the policy statements submitted by the responding TNCs, it was found that the level of detail varied. Decentralized companies and companies that operated in more than one industrial sector tended to produce very general, all-encompassing statements such as "will operate in an environmentally friendly manner", or "will pursue best environmental practice", and to specify that it was the responsibility of individual subsidiaries to formulate policies and programmes appropriate to their specific operations and activities. More centralized companies, or those operating in single sectors, tended to produce more detailed statements specifying what was to be achieved, by whom and when. In general, the statements covered the following issues: a definition of environmental protection (preventive, integrative, international validity); research and development; aspects of process and product safety; health protection; production technology; environmental protection technology; control and environmental information instruments; responsibility of employees; environmental management practices; environmental protection measures; emergency plans; information to the public; and relations with customers.

The statements generally included references to a certain standard that the corporation seeks to meet. Thus, the following standards were commonly set forth in policy statements:

- Compliance with existing regulations and laws.
- Highest standard.
- Best contemporary practice.
- Environmentally responsible manner.
- A high degree.
- Reduce adverse effects to a practicable minimum.
- Without unacceptable effects to the environment.
- Minimize environmental consequences.
- Ensure activities continue on a sound basis environmentally.
- Technically feasible, financially possible and ecologically justifiable.
- Highest practically achievable standards.
- Have the least possible long-term impact on the environment.
- Ecologically motivated, technically possible and economically reasonable.
- Be a good citizen within the local community in which it operates.
- Best environmental practice.

In stating their principles, almost all the corporations referred to technical aspects of environmental protection and to the protection of environmental media (air, water, soil, noise and waste). In that context, the emphasis is on environmental protection as an integrated part of production according to the latest developments in technology. Thus, the statements focused on issues such as changes geared to environmental protection in the production process or in the products themselves. Organizational or personnel aspects were subordinate to those. At best, reference was made to persons or institutions entrusted with tasks linked to environmental protection.

An illustrative example of the issues covered by the policy statements was provided by **Akzo N.V.**[1] In a 12-page pamphlet entitled "Corporate rules of conduct concerning safety, health and the environment", the Board of Management acknowledged that it recognizes environmental management as among the highest corporate priorities and as a key determinant of sustainable development. It is thus committed to establishing policies, programmes and practices for conducting operations in an environmentally sound manner. Those policies, programmes and practices should be integrated fully into each business as an essential element of management in all its functions and should be continually improved, taking into account technical developments, scientific understanding, consumer needs and community expectations, with legal regulations as a starting point, applying the same environmental criteria internationally. The company undertakes to educate, train and motivate employees to conduct its activities in an environmentally responsible manner and to assess any new activity or project, as well as any decommissioned facility or site, for its environmental impact. Products or services that are developed should have no undue environmental impact and be safe in their intended use; they should be efficient in their consumption of energy and natural resources. They should be recycled, reused or disposed of safely. Customers, distributors and the public should be advised and educated in the safe use, transportation, storage and disposal of products. Facilities should be developed, designed and operated taking into consideration the efficient use of energy and materials, the sustainable use of renewable resources, the minimization of adverse environmental impact and waste generation, and the safe and responsible disposal of residual wastes. Research should be conducted or supported on the environmental impacts of raw materials, products, processes, emissions and wastes associated with the enterprise and on the means of minimizing such adverse impacts. The company is committed to modifying the manufacture, marketing or use of products or services or the conduct of activities, consistent with scientific and technical understanding, in order to prevent serious or irreversible environmental degradation. Finally, **Akzo** undertakes to encourage wider use of the principles by its contractors and suppliers by requiring improvements in their practices to make them consistent with those of the enterprise.[2]

The following analysis of the content of corporate policy statements will focus on six types of statements: (a) statements of an integrated approach to EH&S questions; (b) statements indicating that the corporation seeks a leadership role in the EH&S area; (c) statements indicating that corporations have a precautions approach to the environment; (d) statements indicating a clear orientation towards community and stakeholder expectations; and (e) statements that stress compliance and safety. Finally, the section will provide a separate analysis of the policy statements submitted by Japanese corporations, as they share a distinct approach.

(i) Integrated approaches

Most statements addressed issues related to prevention of accidents and pollution. However, it seems that a change in orientation towards a more strategic and proactive approach could be under way in some corporations. Thus, in North America, respondents frequently justified corporate efforts in the area of EH&S in a way that seems to reflect a shift among the leading corporations towards viewing the cost of the EH&S as long-term investment central to successful business ventures. Hence, phrases such as "safety pays" and safety is "good business" were found in the statements. **Amoco Corporation's** statement that "environmental leadership produces business leadership" was perhaps the most direct. **Company Z** noted how its "unwavering determination" to health safety and the environment "will play a major role in the Company's success in the 1990s".[3] **Noranda Inc.** went as far to say that "a change in corporate culture would be necessary to face the environmental challenge of the 1990s and the twenty-first century". Perhaps the most thoughtful insight was provided by the Statement of Financial Objectives section in the **B.F. Goodrich Company's** Annual Report. After stating that "Narrow focus on short-term goals must not be given priority over actions that build greater shareholder value over the longer term", the report continued:

> "The company's strong commitment to strict compliance with environmental regulations creates an on-going need for an appropriate level of financial support for environmental projects at various plant locations. Such obligations are a fact of life in American industry today, and management believes that it is to the benefit of the shareholders to fund such liabilities from a growing -- rather than a shrinking -- sales and asset base."[4]

Similarly, the **Pennzoil Company** made a public commitment to give environmental, safety, and health accountability equal importance with financial standards when evaluating managerial performance, and to provide sufficient resources to ensure that those policies are carried out. More specifically, the board of directors and executive officers of the **Pennzoil Company** have committed themselves to a policy to:

"(a) protect the environment and natural resources wherever the company operates or conducts business; (b) provide a safe and healthful workplace for employees, and concurrently maintain equal safeguards to protect neighbors of our facilities; (c) produce and market commodities and products that meet high quality standards and are safe and free of unacceptable risks to consumer health and safety; ...It shall be the company's policy to comply with all applicable federal, state and local regulations".[5]

An Australia-based participant corporation that requested anonymity recognized, in its environmental policy, "that an active concern for the environment is an integral part of good business practice". It acknowledged sustainable development and recognized "that development and use of resources are accompanied by changes in the natural environment, the built environment and the socio-economic environment", hence management will "continue to assess the impact on the environment of its existing activities and at all stages of new project planning an development".[6]

Similarly, several corporations suggested in their corporate principles that environmental protection has economic potential (lower costs, increased proceeds) and can therefore be deemed an opportunity. Three European companies (**Cultor Ltd.**, **Imperial Chemical Industries [ICI]**, and **Enso-Gutzeit OY**), for example, recognized the market advantage in reducing their impact on the environment, "by stepping up environmental protection and minimizing environmental consequences of operations, a company also stands to gain significant competitive edge ... We must recognize the fact that our work is also judged on the basis of its impact on Nature ... A satisfactory environmental performance is fundamental to a successful business strategy".[7]

In a few cases, there were explicit references to the notion of proactive environmental protection, in other words, seeking to avoid environmental degradation from the outset and to establish long-term application of environmental measures. The **Gechem/Recticel N.V.** management stated that it ensures that "...all plants shall... exhibit a proactive policy towards new environmental issues".[8] **Company Y** intends to "...strive to anticipate future environmental, health, and safety risks and regulatory requirements, and have a proactive approach to dealing with them whenever appropriate...".[9] Some corporations directly stated that they seek to influence EH&S regulation. **Chevron Corporation** said it will "...seek opportunities to participate in the formulation of safety, fire, health and environmental legislation, regulation or policy issues that may significantly impact our business. Work actively with the appropriate government agencies to ensure timely, reasonable and cost effective solutions for issues wherever possible...".[10] **Caterpillar Inc.** also stated its intention to "...offer, where appropriate, constructive ideas for change in the law".[11]

(ii) Leadership

Some corporations have policy statements that indicate their aim at becoming environmental leaders:

Toyota Motor Corporation stated that "although we are at the forefront in environmental activities, we are not satisfied with the present state of affairs. We will continue to search for new ways to take the protection of the environment to ever higher levels".[12] Also that "Our basic principle in environmental management is to emit no pollutants" and to "create plants that are environmentally sound, with due regard for the greater good of the community".[13]

AB Volvo's "Group Environmental Policy" is illustrative of a progressive corporate policy statement, indicating that the corporation seeks a leadership role to:

- "Develop products and marketing products with superior environmental properties and which will meet highest efficiency requirements.
- Opt for manufacturing processes that have least possible impact on the environment.
- Participate actively in, and conducting our own research and development in the environment field.
- Select environmentally compatible and recyclable material in connection with the development and manufacture of our products and when we purchase components from our suppliers.
- Apply a total view regarding the adverse impact of our products on the environment.
- Strive to attain a uniform, world-wide environmental standard for processes and products."[14]

Similarly, **Company V** recognized its responsibility to protect air, water, and land resources and is committed to being a world-wide environmental leader. The company believes that environmental protection and sound business management are mutually achievable objectives. The company stated that it is committed to the following principles: to preserve health, safety and a sound environment; to operate its facilities in compliance with applicable environmental requirements; to work constructively with government bodies and the public to preserve precious environmental resources; to monitor the performance of its operations to ensure proper environmental performance; to devote research and technological resources to improve the environmental performance of its processes and products; to continue its efforts to minimize releases to the environment; to expand its role as a leader in recycling to conserve resources and energy; to conduct educational and instructional programmes to ensure that its employees know, understand and comply with environmental laws and regulations; and to provide public information on its operations and their relation to the environment.

(iii) Preventive and precautionary management

Many of the respondents expressed a preventive and precautionary approach in their policy statements, and stress product stewardship:

Thorn EMI plc has adopted the following environmental principles:

- "Use, whenever possible, and commercially sound, earth resources which can be replaced in a lifetime.
- Prevent pollution at source whenever and wherever possible.
- Conserve natural resources by the use of energy management, recycling and other appropriate means.

●   Ensure that the Company's facilities and products meet and
        sustain the regulations of all Government environmental
        agencies."[15]

In addition, all **Thorn EMI plc** companies are required to formulate and make public a statement on their own environmental policy. Those individual policies refer to the above corporate policy, but they identify more closely with the workplace operation and management structure of the companies concerned. That should include consideration of the following issues:

"Energy consumption, recycling, packaging, environmental impact of products and services, product/service promotion in an era of increasing environmental concern, chemical discharges (into air, sewer) and transport."[16]

Waste Management, Inc. is typical of other North American examples that reflect similar philosophies. Its policy stated that the company is committed to protecting and enhancing the environment and to updating its practices in light of advances in technology and new understandings in health and environmental science. Prevention of pollution and enhancement of the environment are the fundamental premises of the company's business. The company believes that all corporations have a responsibility to conduct their business as stewards of the environment and to seek profits only through activities that leave the earth healthy and safe. The company also believes that it has a responsibility not to compromise the ability of future generations to sustain their needs. The principles of that policy are applicable to the company throughout the world. The company is committed to taking actions on a continuing basis in furtherance of those principles.

For **Boehringer Ingelheim GmbH**, environmental protection measures should be based on the principle of precaution. Such measures for environmental protection must be drawn up in accordance with scientific principles, the state of technology and environmental protection legislation. The company's principles of environmental protection stated that the aim of all measures is to avoid contamination of the water, soil and atmosphere, as well as to protect the environment from noise, shock and radiation pollution, taking into consideration the state of technology and the proportionality of resources. All employees are thus committed to following that objective. Laws and official provisions must be observed at all times. Company guidelines or regulations going beyond those must also be observed. Superiors and the technically competent bodies are obliged to develop greater employee awareness of environmental protection by providing information and instruction. All employees are personally responsible for environmental protection in accordance with their knowledge and ability. They must know the specifications applicable in their field of activity and adhere to them carefully. Staff and the general public must be properly informed.[17]

Ciba-Geigy Ltd. stated in its "Principles for environmental protection in production" that the company endeavours to solve potential environmental problems at their origin. To that end, products are reportedly manufactured using production procedures compatible with the needs of the environment. Whenever possible, reusable materials are recycled into a production process. For the elimination of by-products and wastes, technologies which limit the impact on the environment to an acceptable minimum are used. Every employee, in the context of his or her duties, carries a personal responsibility for environmental protection. That is encouraged through training and instruction.[18]

Company X stated in its corporate environmental policy that:

> "...it will continue to recognize and exercise its responsibility to: solve its own environmental pollution and conservation problems; prevent pollution at the source wherever and whenever possible; develop products that will have a minimum effect on the environment; conserve natural resources through the use of reclamation and other appropriate methods; assure that its facilities and products meet and sustain the regulations of all federal, state and local environmental agencies; assist, wherever possible, governmental agencies and other official organizations engaged in environmental activities".[19]

Another approach is exemplified by **Oryx Energy Co.**, which reported that it has established an environmental policy composed of ten principles, which among other issues, pledges to:

> "Exercise stewardship in the use of the earth's resources. The Company will manage its operations to make them compatible with the global environment: the land, air, and water and the human and other life forms found there. This commitment underlies our resolve to take responsibility for our actions and participate in the search for balanced solutions...".

> "Make health, safety and environmental concerns an integral part of corporate decision-making. Health, safety and environmental goals need not conflict with the Company' economic goals. Both are to be woven into the Company's decision-making fabric and used prominently in measuring the performance of all employees--especially management."[20]

The company undertakes to minimize health and safety risks through the use of proper contingency planning, well-trained personnel, and properly maintained equipment. Although the creation of waste material is an inevitable part of the exploration and production business, the company states it will strive to minimize the amount of waste created, especially if that waste is dangerous. The company believes a polluter should be accountable for the harm it causes. If the company causes harm, it responds accordingly--including remedial action where appropriate.

(iv) Stakeholder orientation

An emphasis on outreach to customers, suppliers and the general public is reflected in several corporate policy statements. **Ciba-Geigy Ltd.**'s "Principles for environmental protection in production", for example, recognizes protection of the environment as an important and determining factor in the manufacture of the company's products. Employees, customers and the public are informed about measures for the protection of the environment. Open cooperation with the relevant public authorities is sought and fostered.[21]

That sentiment appears across all three of the regions surveyed. The Japan-based **Yamaha Motor Co. Ltd.**, for example, stated that one of its five corporate policies is "coping with the need for global environmental protection--responding to expectations of society by actively applying ourselves to the task of protecting the irreplaceable gifts of human life, health and the environment".[22]

Based on its fundamental philosophy of existing and prospering side by side with the local community, **Toyota's** basic approach to the environmental measures it needs to take to fulfil its social responsibilities as a corporate citizen is structured around the three main precepts given below.

- "To promote environmental measures with a mind to remaining 'a company trusted by the local community'.
- Always to set farseeing targets and to promote forward-looking environmental measures.
- To promote environmental measures for the industry as a whole, to be taken in concert with related companies rather than unilaterally."[23]

Texaco, Inc., United States-based, designated its long-standing policy as "compliance plus". It reported that when it comes to the environment this approach is active, not reactive, and has resulted in many accomplishments. It claimed that "although we are proud of our record, we know we must challenge ourselves to meet and exceed the public's ever-increasing expectations for the future".[24]

Company M, New Zealand-based, stated in its annual report that "we aim to meet or exceed reasonable community expectations for environmental standards affecting our businesses. We intend to plan and act ahead of legislation on environmental issues". It added that "managing environmental issues responsibly and in accord with reasonable community expectations is central to [company name]'s long-term business strategy".[25]

Further discussion of corporate policies that are oriented towards the public and neighboring communities appears below in chapter VI, section B on public relations.

(v) Compliance and safety orientation

Borden, Inc's company policy included a compliance pledge that is illustrative of the numerous references to compliance found in the statements:

"...complying with applicable environmental laws and regulations while generating internal initiatives, programmes and procedures that address the letter and spirit of those laws and regulations".

Company W's environmental policy is to assure the company's compliance with all applicable federal, state and local environmental laws and to provide for and stress employee education in environmental compliance and workplace safety. It is the company's intention to give the highest priority to environmental compliance and workplace safety.

Corporations that have operations with a high safety-risk tend to focus more explicitly on health and safety issues in there policy statements. For example, **Amoco Corporation** and its subsidiaries support the goals for adhering to high standards of environmental quality, product safety, and providing a workplace that protects the health and safety of its employees and the communities surrounding their facilities. In accordance with these goals, **Amoco's** corporate policy is:

"To conduct activities in a manner consistent with appropriate safety, health, and environmental considerations; to manufacture and market products and furnish user information on them in a manner consistent with appropriate safety, health, and environmental considerations; to establish and maintain corporate controls, including periodic reviews; to assure that the Company's policy is being properly implemented and maintained; to work with all levels of government in the furtherance and development of appropriate public policies supportive of environmental quality, product safety, and occupational health and safety; to comply with applicable environmental quality, occupational health and safety, and product safety laws and regulations; to build and operate facilities in a manner to protect the health and safety of employees and of individuals in the surrounding communities; to safeguard employees' health through appropriate medical programmes".[26]

The same goals are echoed in policy statements of TNCs based outside North America. United Kingdom-based **Company Q**, for example, states that:

"It is the general policy of the company, as a major international mining company, that all operations and activities of Group companies should exemplify best contemporary practice in respect of the environment, health and safety. Every Group company's expected to build from a foundation of compliance with the legal, regulatory and consent requirements to the governmental authorities in the countries in which its operations and activities are conducted. In pursuance of this general policy, it is the responsibility of every Group company to formulate its own environmental policy and plan appropriate to its operations and activities, and to designate a senior executive with responsibility for ensuring that the policy and plan is implemented at all sites. Responsibility for environmental matters is given to a senior manager of each site."[27]

Also included are guidelines on the principles to be incorporated into each company's policy, and information on: best contemporary practice, environmental impact work, mine closures, monitoring policy implementation, the group's head office responsibilities and personnel resources.

In accordance with the United Kingdom-based **Unilever plc** policy guidelines, companies are required to do all that is practicable to:

- "Develop products and packaging which are environmentally acceptable.
- Operate their factories in an environmentally responsible manner to ensure the health and safety of their employees and of those people living within the vicinity of their operations.
- Design, operate and maintain processes and plants so that they satisfy, at the minimum, all national and local environmental legislation.
- Establish and maintain procedures for the environmental auditing, monitoring and control of all their operations.
- Establish and maintain close working relationships with all relevant government and local authority environmental agencies and third parties.
- Together with central Unilever advisory services, continuously reassess operating processes with respect to their environmental effects.
- Ensure that all employees at every level and function are aware of their environmental responsibilities and that they are appropriately trained, motivated and involved."[28]

In addition, there are guidelines that help local management to apply the policies and a range of technical and scientific support services available on a world-wide basis.[29]

The chapter on the relationship between corporate EH&S policies and practices and environmental regulation (chapter II, section A) will expand on the compliance aspects of policy statements submitted in response to the survey.

(vi) Japanese policy statements

The Asian (Japanese) respondents to the Benchmark Survey, as a group, employ such means as distribution of public relations material, corporate summaries, annual reports, and press releases in order to make their mission and philosophy widely known to the outside world. Within the company, they publicize their policies by means of broadcasts, company reports, and transmissions via corporate headquarters. Some firms set up Environment Months, during which various events are held to make mission and philosophy material available.

In the past, Japanese companies have tended to be inactive in the field of overseas publicity. As internationalization advances and they become increasingly aware of its importance, however, they engage more frequently in overseas publicity. Japan-based companies with international operations, as well as those companies which export their products overseas, and others which care active in foreign countries, produce English-language versions of their corporate summaries and, sometimes, of their annual reports. The most enthusiastic firms set up international communications departments to deal with official corporate reports. Recently, corporations in the industrial and the financial sectors have also begun to publicize their philosophy in connection with environmental problems.

Among the Japan-based participant corporations, corporate commitment to sustainable development and environmental development manifests itself in a number of ways: (a) by pledging that one's own products and commodities are environment-friendly and by developing new environment-friendly commodities; (b) by promising to minimize the negative effects of a company's production processes and overall business activities on the environment; (c) by aiming to fulfil social responsibilities in relation to disposal of waste products and recycling; and (d) by fostering the protection of agricultural, forest and marine resources.

The following examples illustrate some of the Japanese participants' philosophy toward sustainable development and environmental protection. A major chemical manufacturer uses the term "maintaining safety" to mean "maintenance of safety, protection of environment and maintenance and improvement of industrial hygiene" collectively. Hence, the company's "...corporate goal is to contribute to the social development and welfare of mankind. To achieve these social responsibilities, the company must always give priority to maintaining safety based on a fundamental respect for human life ... Protection of the environment is a high-priority concern of [company name] ... the branch offices as well as factories of [company name] are carrying out the reduction of wastes and energy conservation with implementation programmes. [company name] is reducing CFCs at the level exceeding the reduction target in accordance with the Montreal protocol".[30]

In another instance, one of the Japanese participants stated that "we always focus considerable attention on preserving the environment in response to the public's confidence ... we have a complete safety structure in place, and always act with the greatest possible care of the prevention of accidents and preservation of the environment, always keeping in mind, 'No safety, no production'". Environmental preservation "...is done in order to fulfill social responsibility as a business concern and is aimed at attaining harmonized growth as a member of the community".[31]

(c) Setting specific EH&S targets

Several of the responding corporations have precise targets for their future environmental performance in their policy statements. Targets are used to motivate employees and will sometimes be backed by performance and compensation reviews that measure individual contributions. The targets draw heavily on widely publicized topics such as waste management and minimization, CFC reduction, and pollution control. Typically, they are presented as a percentage reduction of a given pollution level from a base year.

The pattern of setting specific targets for EH&S performance varies among the regions. In North America, there are numerous examples of policies establishing specific targets. This is less the case with the Asia-based (Japan) respondents, which offer few examples of explicit targets. For Europe, there is a striking absence of concrete targets in the policy statements.

Where explicit policies do exist, they are exemplified by the **Amoco Chemical Company**, a subsidiary of the Amoco Oil Company, which announced during 1990 a long-term goal of eliminating hazardous waste from more than 60 facilities that the chemical company operates world-wide. Similarly, it designated 1988 as the base year for measuring progress in waste reduction, and it has set a goal of 50 per cent decrease in disposed refinery waste by 1994.

Box I.1. Merck's EH&S objectives

This United States-based pharmaceutical corporation has pledged not only to meet at least 50 per cent reductions by 1995 under the EPA 33-50 program, but also to reduce all environmental releases of toxic chemicals by 90 per cent for all Merck manufacturing facilities world-wide (Sarokin, 1992).

Although not as explicit, **Georgia Gulf Corporation's** goal "is a long-term downward trend in the amount of water generated and pollutants released" at all facilities. **Company E**, Japan-based, plans for a 20 per cent cut in the use of electricity and oil by March 1994. **Raychem Corporation**, United States-based, has the following five-year Environmentally Compatible Operational Goals, using calendar year 1989 as the base year:

- Reduce water consumption by 20 per cent.
- Increase energy use efficiency by 20 per cent.
- Reduce nonhazardous waste disposal by 30 per cent.
- Reduce hazardous waste disposal by 40 per cent.
- Reduce solvent emissions by 50 per cent.
- Reduce ozone depleting emissions by 90 per cent.

- Completely eliminate the use of CFCs.
- Decrease the weekly percentage of employee one-passenger automobile commutes by 20 per cent.

Many Japanese corporations have set up goals for the phasing out of CFC gases. For example, **Toyota Motor Corporation** has set the following goal for new vehicles:

- Place air conditioners containing HFC-134a refrigerant by 1994.
- Start conversion process for refrigerant in 1992.
- Provide service centers world-wide with recovery/recharge equipment to prevent CFC escape into the atmosphere by 1991.[32]

As noted, the Europe-based corporations appear to be less specifically committed programmatically to environmental goals. For example, the Swiss chemical company **Ciba-Geigy Ltd.** points out that it does not pursue any global environmental objectives but concentrates on special measures for particular manufacturing plants, affiliates and production lines. The German automobile concern **BMW AG** (Bayerische Motoren Werke) has a similar approach; "...we have no specific targets, but a continuing review of technology and processes...". Environmental objectives are, however, at least implicit in environmental programmes of Europe-based TNCs and, above all, in corporate principles, primarily as technology-linked projections. On the other hand, there are no references to the development of objectives within the framework of strategic planning or control. Still, five corporations based in Europe do point out that they are developing programmes of environmental targets.

3. Summary

Some corporations have given EH&S questions serious consideration, and have formulated often elaborate and exacting EH&S principles. Many statements are rather trivial, referring to compliance with regulations stating that EH&S protection is an important principle etc. But some corporations have at least acknowledged in their principles and objectives that EH&S policies should be an integrated part of overall business strategy, that the responsibilities of the corporation are global, and that the corporation has responsibilities to the public as well as to its employees. Although a policy statement may be nothing but a public relations exercise, an international public commitment stated by the corporation may also be of some consequence for the corporation. It makes it possible for the public around the world to hold corporations accountable for their EH&S pledges.

North American corporations are leading significantly in that area, indicating that corporate headquarters in the region have assumed more responsibility for EH&S policies than those in Europe and Asia. The regional differences also suggest that formulating EH&S statements is a North American exercise which has only recently been taken up in Europe and Asia (Japan).

The trend of supplementing EH&S policy statements with concrete objectives and time-frames is a positive one. It enables the public to evaluate and compare the EH&S achievements of corporations. However, standardization of target-setting and ways of evaluating success in reaching those targets have to be developed in order to enable the public to assess the outcomes.

B. POLICIES AND PROGRAMMES

Environmental policies are internal codes of conduct setting targets and standards for environmental protection in the corporation on specific issues such as water, energy, safety and waste. They are often the first step in launching programmes and management activities to address specific issues. Programmes are more detailed operational guidelines on how the corporation can implement the objectives expressed in corporate policies. Without corporate-wide policies and programmes, EH&S issues do not gain the benefits of shared knowledge and expertise, and control with regard to affiliates will tend to be ad hoc and piecemeal.

1. Statistical findings

(a) Policy use

> **Agenda 21:**
>
> "Increase self-regulation, guided by the appropriate codes, charters and initiatives, integrated into all elements of business decision-making and planning" (30.26).
>
> "Incorporate cleaner production policies in operations and investments" (30.12).
>
> "Undertake programmes for improved environmental awareness and responsibility at all levels to make these enterprises dedicated to the task of improving environmental performance based on internationally accepted management practices" (30.14).

The Benchmark Survey questionnaire provided a list of 23 specific policies that go beyond national requirements which TNCs may apply throughout the corporation. These are policies on issues such as air, water and soil pollution, health and safety, waste disposal, and sustainable development. Generally, the respondents seem to make extended use of corporate policies: 75 per cent have policies in place; one fifth reports having over 15 such policies; and the average respondent has 5.2 company-wide policies.

Figure I.2 shows a breakdown of the percentage of firms that have one or more such policies. There are significant variations among the corporations across regions and sectors. European corporations, corporations that process agricultural raw materials, and smaller corporations are the least likely to have in place any of the 23 specific company-wide policies listed in the questionnaire, whereas North American and Asian corporations, corporations in the extractive-based and finished-goods sectors, and corporations with high sales are most likely to have such policies.[33]

(b) Corporate policy priorities

Table I.1 groups corporate policies and programmes into five main categories and shows the percentage of respondents having such policies and programmes. The data indicate that energy-related policies and programmes occupy a central position in the corporate agenda. Clearly, the repeated energy crises of the seventies and early eighties have made corporations keenly aware of the importance of stable energy supplies and of the savings to be obtained from energy-conserving activities. Somewhat surprisingly, North American corporations are significantly more involved in those activities than other regions (annex table D.1). The relatively

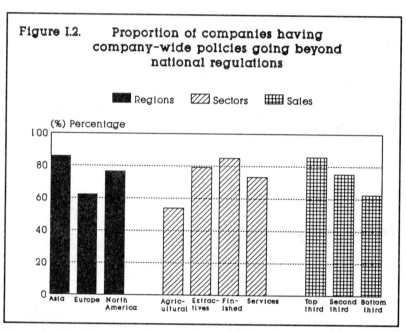

Source: TCMD/DESD Benchmark Survey, 1990-1991.

higher energy prices in Europe and Japan would lead one to believe that these regions would be more strongly motivated to have activities in this field.

Health- and safety-related policies and programmes are more widely adopted than those pertaining to the environment in general. The reason could be that health and safety issues have a longer regulatory history, and policies to that effect may be more established in TNCs. Mr. Bjorn Stigson, head of AB Flakt and a member of the Business Council for Sustainable Development, notes this historical difference: "We treat nature like we treated workers a hundred years ago. We included then no cost for the health and social security of workers in our calculations, and today we include no cost for the health and security of nature."[34] Furthermore, health and safety may be perceived to have a more direct impact on operations since employee welfare and productivity are directly related, and liabilities are easier to anticipate. In contrast, environmental issues might be viewed as externalities whose importance declines beyond the factory gate. Firms in the top-third sales group are considerably more likely to undertake programmes in accident prevention and health and safety than the bottom-third group (60-80 per cent vs. 35-55 per cent). Large corporations have more extensive operations, face greater legal consequences, and possess the needed managerial and financial resources to undertake such programmes. Interestingly, the service sector, which in most cases trails behind other the sectors, is leading on accident prevention policies and worker health and safety (see annex table D.1).

In terms of typical environmental issues such as air, water or waste, table I.1 indicates that waste issues are of particular concern to the responding companies. Soaring expenses for clean-up and waste

Table I.1. Corporate policy priorities:
Corporate activities on EH&S and sustainable development

Higher-priority areas	Percentage of respondents
Energy-related activities	
R&D for energy efficient production	70.7
Policies for securing energy supplies	67.7
Polices for conserving non-renewable resources	54.4
Energy conservation	54.0
Health and safety activities	
Worker health and safety	67.5
Accident prevention	60.3
Emergency preparedness	58.0
Hazard assessment procedures	56.9
Traditional environment activities	
Water quality/pollution	48.1
Air quality/pollution	47.2
Noise pollution	41.1
Soil quality/pollution	31.2
Waste/disposal-related activities	
Recycling	84.5
Waste-handling procedures	56.3
Waste-disposal policies	51.6
Waste-reduction technologies	48.7

Lower-priority areas	Percentage of respondents
Genuine sustainable development activities	
Afforestation programmes	40.4
R&D for greenhouse gas generation reduction	39.0
Renewable energy sources	22.0
Preservation of endangered species	15.8
Conservation of biodiversity	10.1
Policies for protection of wetlands/rainforests in LDCs	9.2

Source: TCMD/DESD Benchmark Survey, 1990-1991, (see annex table D.1).

treatment are likely explanations for that finding.[35] Eighty-five per cent of the respondents recycle; in North America it is more than 95 per cent. (annex table D.1) Fewer companies have policies and programmes related to air, water, soil and noise pollution. Asian (Japanese) TNCs are significantly more inclined to have policies on air, water and noise than European and North American corporations. Close to 70 per cent of the Japanese respondents have such policies, but only 40 to 50 per cent of the North American corporations and 20 to 30 per cent of the European corporations have them, depending on the activity in question. The difference probably reflects the salience of those issues in densely-populated Japan. In the case of soil contamination, however, North America-based firms are more inclined to have a policy than Asia- and Europe-based firms; a finding that could be related to the strict United States Superfund legislation.

(c) Sustainable development programmes

> **Agenda 21:**
>
> "Be encouraged to establish world-wide corporate policies on sustainable development" (30.22).
>
> "Have a special role and interest in promoting cooperation in technology transfer and in building a trained human resource pool and infrastructure in developing countries"

The Brundtland Commission defined sustainable development as the process of meeting the needs of the present without compromising the ability of future generations to meet their own needs. Although the precise implications of sustainable development for corporate management are still rather obscure, it seems clear that sustainable development requires increased focus on environmental problems related to the global commons such as the rainforest or the oceans, as well as on environmental problems related to the development process.

Table I.1 indicates that, in general, less than 20 per cent of the respondents are engaged in activities aimed at protecting the global commons; activities such as R&D programmes for renewable energy, policies for the protection of the rainforests; or programmes for the protection of biodiversity. The low priority given to sustainable development activities is reflected in the corporate policy statements. As shown in the previous section, only a few references to sustainable development are made in those statements. There are some exceptions however; almost one third of the respondents have policies and programmes for greenhouse gas reduction, and more than 40 per cent have afforestation programmes. The latter findings suggest that the intense international discussions on greenhouse gases, ozone layer depletion, and destruction of forests have influenced corporate priorities and helped garner corporate attention.

In general, the largest corporations, those in the extractive-based sector and corporations from the North American region, are most likely to have activities related to the global commons. One notable exception is that the finished-goods sector and European corporations are leading in R&D to reduce the amount of greenhouse gas generated.

As shown in table I.2, most of the corporations from Asia (Japan), Europe and North America have environment-related activities in developing countries. Fifty-four per cent of the respondents indicated that they have one or more of 13 developing-country activities mentioned in the questionnaire. Whereas approximately 60 per cent of the Asian (Japanese) and North America corporations engage in those activities in developing countries, less than 40 per cent of the European companies engage in such activities. That might indicate that the North American and Asian corporations are more global in their character than their European counterparts. Approximately 60 per cent of the corporations in the extractive-based and finished-goods sectors have environment-related activities in developing countries. Seventy per cent of the largest corporations have environment-related activities in developing countries, but only 40 per cent of the smallest TNCs do. The most common developing-country activities aimed at protecting the environment are related to the monitoring of pollution, support for local infrastructure, and toxic-education programmes.

Table I.2. Developing country issues

Activities of corporations in developing countries on specific aspects of the UNCED themes

Higher-priority aspects	Percentage of respondents
Has provisions for infrastructure etc. for workforce	48.7
Monitors disposal of generated hazardous wastes	47.8
Has toxic-education programme for workforce & community	40.5
Monitors its stacks for air-emission components	36.6
Uses CFCs or related products in plants	27.4

Lower-priority aspects	Percentage of respondents
Has plants near drinking water supplies	16.0
Release effluents into oceans off developing countries	14.3
Holds land for safety zones	13.6
Has wetlands & rainforest protection programmes	9.2
Surveys biological species on undeveloped land	8.7
Has products hazardous to drinking water supplies	3.4
Markets any genetically engineered products	2.6
Practices mono-cropping or clear-cutting	1.7

Source: TCMD/DESD Benchmark Survey, 1990-1991.

One particularly dismal finding is that between 20 and 30 per cent of the respondents reported repeatedly that data are insufficient at headquarters to answer specific questions on their developing-country activities. That finding suggests that the flow of information between plants in developing countries and corporate headquarters is inadequate. The observation was confirmed in a study conducted by McKinsey & Co., which found that most CEOs outside the third world itself are not certain that the level of knowledge in their industry is adequate to deal effectively with relevant developing countries' environmental issues (McKinsey & Co., 1991, p. 14). Decentralized structures, lack of affiliate communications, bureaucratic problems, sometimes even language problems, contribute to a lack of awareness at corporate headquarters about the environmental performance of developing-country operations. The lack of basic public infrastructure to monitor environmental performance at the local level in developing countries makes it all the more imperative for corporate headquarters to monitor closely the environmental performance of their developing-country affiliates.

2. Examples of corporate policies and programmes

The responding firms supported their commitments to environmental health and safety objectives with numerous examples of accomplishments, policies and programmes, both recent and on going, and, to a lesser extent, to agendas for the future. Generally, the policies are technical and detailed, dealing with specific EH&S problems. Most of those policies and programmes will be displayed in the analysis in Part Two of corporate activities related to specific environmental problems. To give an overview of the approaches that can be implemented by policies and programmes, the following section will set out **Union Carbide's** rather exhaustive list of possible programmes.

Union Carbide pledges that programmes will be implemented and maintained which are equal to or better than the

> **Box I.2. Japanese afforestation programmes in developing countries**
>
> One of the most popular sustainable development activities identified through the Benchmark Survey, is afforestation programs; in some cases linked with greenhouse gas reduction programs. Thus Toyota reports that it has reduced its emissions of CO_2 worldwide by off-setting emissions in Japan with tree planting projects in South America. Both Mitsubishi Paper Mills and Daio Paper have announced afforestation projects in Latin America. Oji Paper and Honshu Paper have undertaken such projects in Southeast Asia, including an 11,000 hectares project by Honshu in Papua New Guinea.
>
> *Source:* TCMD/DESD, Benchmark Survey, 1990-1991.

competition's and provide reasonable assurance that the corporation complies with all applicable governmental and internal health, safety and environmental requirements. There must be programmes in place designed to address reasonably foreseeable emergency situations at **Union Carbide** locations and to provide appropriate hazard and emergency response information to local communities. Programmes must exist for independent contractors at **Union Carbide** locations and provide reasonable assurance that their work is performed in compliance with applicable health, safety and environmental requirements. Programmes must also exist for independent off-site contractors and provide reasonable assurance that the processing and storage performed in their work for **Union Carbide** is in compliance with applicable health, safety and environmental requirements.

Moreover, there must be programmes that address employee information and training, visitor safety, communications and internal reporting and follow-up. Programmes must also provide reasonable assurance that operational hazards are identified, significant episodic incidents are avoided and operational safety requirements are considered in evaluating business decisions. The programmes must cover all phases of operational life, from conceptualization, design and construction through operation and decommissioning. There must be programmes which enable employees to perform their work-related responsibilities safely, to protect employees exposed to potentially hazardous work conditions, and to protect employees required to enter confined spaces. Other programmes must exist which are designed to protect the safety of employees working on or in close proximity to equipment with the potential for unexpected operation, movement, release of energy, or release of hazardous materials. Still other programmes for employees must be in place designed to protect them from overexposure to physical, chemical and biological agents in the workplace and from overexposure to noise in the workplace. There must be programmes that provide reasonable assurance that respiratory-protective equipment is maintained and used properly when provided as part of an overall programme to protect employees from overexposure to chemical or biological agents in the workplace. Programmes for employees must exist that are designed to protect them from reproductive hazards in the workplace. In addition, affirmative programmes must be designed to protect the embryo-fetus in the workplace. Programmes must also exist that provide reasonable assurance that product safety and distribution safety risks are properly evaluated and controlled. There must be communications programmes which provide reasonable assurance that the known hazards of **Union Carbide's** products, together with relevant health, safety and environmental protection information, are communicated to potentially affected persons in a timely man-

---

Box I.3. Shell's Sustainable Development Policies

The Europe-based oil corporation, Shell, has developed a conceptual framework for sustainable management of an industrial enterprise. In 1990, Shell Canada adopted a "Sustainable Development Policy" in place of its previous "Environmental Policy". The new policy recognizes that the concept of sustainable development needs clarification, but that nevertheless environmental sustainability is an essential goal which can only be achieved by integrating environmental and economic decision-making. Furthermore, the corporation acknowledges that even if there are substantial gaps in scientific knowledge about climate change, there is enough indication of potential environmental risk to make it prudent to adopt appropriate precautionary measures.

Source: TCMD/DESD, Benchmark Survey 1990-1991.

---

ner. Programmes must exist for air emissions resulting from normal operations at **Union Carbide** locations that provide reasonable assurance that they are properly characterized and controlled. Programmes must also exist to provide reasonable assurance that all **Union Carbide** locations have programmes to minimize waste and that waste management practices do not affect adversely the health or safety of employees or the public, or the environment. There must also be programmes which provide reasonable assurance that **Union Carbide** locations do not have an adverse effect on groundwater as a result of their operations.

3. Summary

Most respondents, particularly those from North America and Asia, have established practical measures to ameliorate environmental problems through policies and programmes. Some corporations cover a broad range of problems with their policies and programmes. Others have no company-wide policies and programmes in place.

The analysis clearly shows that the respondents concentrate their efforts in areas where the costs and liabilities are high. Thus, a high proportion of the respondents have policies and programmes in areas such as accident prevention, waste reduction and energy conservation. Traditional environmental problems such as air, water and soil pollution are frequently addressed by the respondents although there are notable variations. Genuine sustainable development programmes are only cursorily addressed. About half the corporations report that they engage in any of the thirteen LDC activities. Only a small fraction of those actually have specific LDC policies and programmes. This suggests that corporate orientation towards the particular problems in LDCs is minimal.[36]

Even if relatively few corporations have specific policies and programmes for protecting the global commons, it seems that the public debate on greenhouse gases and afforestation has had an impact on the corporate agenda which has been translated into specific corporate responses.

Notes

[1] For further information about the corporations that have participated in the BMS, see annex C, which details the regional, sectoral and sales data for all the respondents.

[2] Akzo N.V., *Corporate Rules of Conduct Concerning Safety, Health and the Environment.*

[3] For those companies that requested anonymity, an arbitrary letter has been assigned for reference throughout this report. An identification of them under their assigned code can also be found in annex C.

[4] B.F. Goodrich Company (The), *Annual Report 1989*, p. 27.

[5] Pennzoil Company, *Corporate Policy Manual*, Effective date 1 August 1990, pp. 800-1.

[6] Environmental policy statement, 1983.

[7] Material submitted in support of responses to the BMS questionnaire.

[8] Gechem/Recticel N.V., *Management Declaration on Environment and Safety*, Brussels, 1990.

[9] Material submitted in support of responses to the BMS questionnaire.

[10] Chevron Corporation, *Strategic Management in the Environmental Era*, p. 5.

[11] Caterpillar Inc., *A code of worldwide business conduct and operating principles*, Revised, 1 May 1985, p. 12.

[12] Toyota Motor Corporation, *Toyota and the environment*, p. 24.

[13] Toyota Motor Corporation, *Overview of Environmental Measures at Toyota*, slide A-6.

[14] AB Volvo, *Volvo Group Environmental Policy*, 1989.

[15] Thorn EMI plc, *Policies Manual*, Tech 39, Revision 4, January 1991.

[16] ibid.

[17] Boehringer Ingelheim, *Annual Report 1989*.

[18] Ciba-Geigy Ltd., *Principles for Environmental Protection in Production*, Approved by the Executive Committee on May 23, 1984.

[19] Material submitted in support of responses to the BMS questionnaire.

[20] Oryx Energy Company, *Oryx and the Environment.*

[21] Ciba-Geigy Ltd., *Principles for Environmental Protection in Production*, Approved by the Executive Committee on 23 May 1984.

[22] Letter dated 21 February 1991, from Tadao Oguri, Manager, Corporate Planning Division, Yamaha Motors.

[23] Toyota Motor Corporation, *Toyota Plant Environmental Measures*, 1990, p. 1.

[24] Texaco Inc., *Texaco & the Environment*, 22 April 1990.

[25] Material submitted in support of responses to the BMS questionnaire.

[26] Amoco Corporation, *The Environment at Amoco*, p. 1.

[27] Material submitted in support of responses to the BMS questionnaire.

[28] Unilever plc, *Unilever and the Environment*, July 1990.

[29] Ibid.

[30] Company's *Annual Report 1990*.

[31] Material submitted in support of responses to the BMS questionnaire.

[32] For additional examples of corporate targets for phasing out CFC gases, see chapter VI on protection of the atmosphere.

[33] A study of United States-based corporations conducted by Tufts University found that 95 per cent of the responding corporations had a written EH&S policy in place (Flaherty and Rappaport, 1991). The difference between the findings of the Benchmark Survey and this survey can be explained by differences in the types of questions.

[34] *The Economist*, 8 September 1990.

[35] For example, landfill costs for hazardous waste went from around $80 a ton in the early 1980s, to around $255 a ton by the end of the decade, with the main increase in treatment rather than dumping. According to OECD figures, the price of landfills for asbestoses in Europe grew tenfold during the eighties, (*The Economist*, 8 September 1990).

[36] See also chapter III.B on international EH&S organization for findings on corporate policies for developing nations.

CHAPTER II.
ENVIRONMENTAL REGULATIONS AND INTERNATIONAL GUIDELINES

Much of the management literature views corporate environmental management as the result of executive decisions alone. Whatever merit such accounts may have, they tend to disregard the fact that corporate management does not take place in a vacuum but is strongly influenced by regulatory frameworks, international guidelines and public pressure. This chapter of the Benchmark Survey Report will analyse the relationship between national regulation, international guidelines and corporate EH&S activities.

A. NATIONAL REGULATION

In order to deal with the environmental problems related to industrial production, different countries have chosen markedly different regulatory strategies. Moreover, differences in political culture and political systems contribute to creating different conditions of production in different regions. Those factors produce significant differences in the regulatory environment of a corporation.

The United States regulatory process has often been described as highly legalistic and contentious. The thrust of United States environmental regulation has been to restrict administrative discretion as much as possible and to establish uniform standards. At the same time, United States environmental authorities rely heavily on taking corporations to court in order to ensure compliance. Huge fines awarded by the courts have further contributed to making United States' environmental regulation contentious. The adversarial approach of the United States has led to widespread dissatisfaction with environmental regulations in the United States business community, providing a platform for attempts to roll back environmental regulations in the 1980s.

Even though it is difficult to generalize about European environmental regulation, it seems that the regulatory environments in European countries like Britain, Germany, the Netherlands and the Scandinavian countries have common features, especially after the European Community Commission's efforts to harmonize environmental regulations by issuing numerous directives in recent years. European environmental regulation appears to be characterized by a much closer and more cooperative relationship between regulators and representatives of industry than is the case in the United States. Environmental regulation is seldom enacted before industrial consent has been reached, and enforcement of environmental regulations is less adversarial than is the case in the United States. Voluntary agreements and corporate self-regulation play a much more dominant role in European environmental regulation. Furthermore, European regulators have tended to use environmental regulation as a way of supporting national industrial strategies.

As is the case in Europe, Japanese environmental regulation is relatively cooperative and consensual. After having observed many environmental accidents, e.g., at Minimata, Yokkaichi and the Kurobe River, the Japanese society reached a consensus regarding environmental protection which led to the establishment of the Japanese Environment Agency. However, the relative success of Japanese environmental protection has in many ways been driven by a low-energy, technology-based and service-oriented industrial strategy initiated by the powerful Japanese Ministry of International Trade and Industry (MITI). In recent years, MITI, in cooperation with the Japanese industrial association, Keidanren, has actively sought to utilize environmental issues strategically and to move Japan towards a conservation-oriented society.[1] Thus, the Japanese Environment Agency must share responsibility for environmental protection with several other ministries, including MITI. The Japanese regulatory process also seems more diffuse than in the United States, where the powerful Environmental Protection Agency (EPA) plays a leading role in environmental protection, and compared to Europe and the United States, grass-roots groups are far less active. Finally, technological fixes, rather than regulatory solutions to environmental problems, have historically played a central role in Japanese environmental protection.

1. Statistical findings

The survey findings repeatedly show a close relationship between regulation in the home country of the corporation and corporate EH&S practices. Respondents were asked which of the following factors had prompted change in company-wide environmental policies and programmes: consumer protests, negative media publicity, potential legal costs, home-country environmental regulation, host-country environmental regulations, accidents at their firm, and accidents at other firms. The results are summarized in figure II.1. Sixty-two per cent of the respondents indicated that the development of EH&S laws and regulations in the home country had motivated changes in environmental policies and pro-

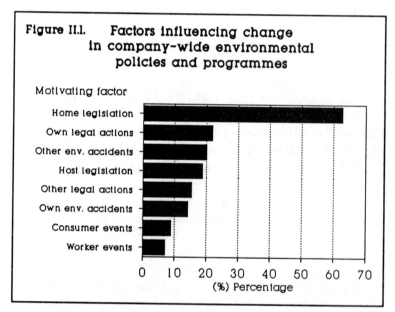

Figure II.1. Factors influencing change in company-wide environmental policies and programmes

Source: TCMD/DESD Benchmark Survey, 1990-91.

grammes. That finding is consistent with the results of a survey conducted among 98 United States corporations by Tufts University (Flaherty and Rappaport, 1991). The survey identified government laws and regulations as the most influential factor in the development of corporate environmental policies.[2]

The importance of national regulations in influencing corporate environmental management is further supported by the Benchmark Survey's finding of differences between the EH&S practices depending on the location of corporate headquarters. As seen in figure I.1, North American and Asian corporations were significantly more inclined to have environmental policies and programmes than their European counterparts.[3] Also, the content of corporate management varied across those three regions; TNCs in different regions seemed to concentrate on different EH&S aspects. The explanation likely rests with differences in the nature of the regulatory environment in the three regions.

Overall, more than 20 per cent of the respondents stated that environmentally-related legal actions involving the company influenced change in environmental programmes and policies. One third of the North America-based corporations cited legal action as influential, but only 18 per cent of the Japanese and ten per cent of the European corporations found it so. The litigious nature of the North American business environment may be responsible for this sensitivity to legal actions. A survey conducted by Booz-Allen & Hamilton in 1991 among 220 United States business executives confirmed that environmental policy in United States corporations in most cases was driven by threat, that is, fear of lawsuits or criminal prosecution, rather than by the opportunity to enhance the benefits of strategic environmental planning (Booz-Allen & Hamilton, 1991).

In Europe, accidents and malfunctions with ensuing environmental damage were the second most frequently cited reason for change in EH&S policies. Major accidents, such as the ones at Bhopal, Seveso and Basel, appeared to have influenced the EH&S programmes of many companies in the region. For example, **Sandoz International Ltd.**, a Switzerland-based firm, attributed the change of its entire corporate policy to the 1986 accident at its Basel plant. However, smaller-scale incidents at particular TNC subsidiaries, such as leaking storage tanks, also seemed to have played an important role in the establishment of EH&S policies in several corporations.

In general, the respondents reported a relatively minor role for consumer- and worker-related events in determining environmental policy. However, a Belgium-based firm, which requested anonymity, reported that staff had instigated change by objecting to asbestos materials in the workplace, and **Degussa AG**, German-based, cited Greenpeace campaigns against the use of CFCs as decisive in shaping its environmental policy.

2. Examples of corporate compliance activities

That the observance of EH&S regulation is a central aspect of business management is confirmed by analysis of the policy statements. Here, many corporations make explicit reference to compliance to regulation. Thus, expressions such as the following were common:

- Take every necessary step to comply with relevant laws, regulations and codes of practice.
- Help its customers to meet regulatory guidelines ... meet its own regulatory requirements.
- Meet and sustain the regulations of all government environmental agencies ... in accordance with the law of the countries where their activities are situated.
- Comply with all statutory obligations.
- Conform to regulations.

The North America-based respondents were most likely to state explicitly their policy of complying with all applicable national and local standards of countries hosting foreign affiliates. For example, it was the policy of **Arco** (Atlantic Richfield Company) to "comply with all laws and regulations and government safety, health and environmental protection", while **Borden, Inc.'s** company policy included "complying with applicable environmental laws and regulations while generating internal initiatives, programmes and procedures that address the letter and spirit of those laws and regulations".

Another electronics concern, **Company Y**, maintained a corporate policy that was more explicit: "Comply with all federal, state and local environmental health and safety laws and regulations in all countries in which we do business" and "adopt our own corporate standards for protection of human health and the environment in those areas where [the company] believes that current laws and regulations either don't exist or are inadequate".[4]

Cargill Inc. stated that it would comply with all local, state and other government agency laws and regulations regarding reporting of spills or releases to the environment. **Cargill** managers were responsible for knowing and complying with the reporting requirements that were applicable to their facilities. In addition, complaints and inspections by outside agencies and enforcement notifications must be reported internally. All major plant modifications or expansions and new plants must be designed to comply with existing and projected environmental regulations. Compliance with all applicable statutes and regulations governing polychlorinated biphenyls (PCBs) was required by **Cargill** of all its divisions, departments and subsidiaries.

At **Pennzoil**, programmes and operating procedures to assure compliance with all applicable regulations and standards were developed and implemented while proper cooperation was given to federal, state and local regulatory agency personnel.

At **Oryx**, the guiding principle was that reasonable laws established reasonable compliance standards in protecting health, safety and the environment. The company had to be as willing to go beyond weak standards as it was to challenge unreasonable standards. **Waste Management Inc.** stated that it was committed to complying with all legal requirements and to implementing programmes and procedures to ensure compliance. Those efforts were to include the training and testing of employees, the rewarding of employees who excelled in compliance, and the disciplining of employees who violated legal requirements.

The purpose of **Tenneco's** Environmental Compliance Programme was to ensure that the requirements of the company's Environmental Affairs Policy and of applicable environmental laws and regulations were known and understood. In addition, their specific applicability to the company's various facilities and operations was to be properly perceived, and appropriate procedures for monitoring compliance were to be established and employed by each of the company's operating units.

Finally, reporting to ensure compliance with local, national and international laws and regulations, as well as with the company's own policy, was a central requirement of health, safety and environmental performance in such corporate examples from Europe as **Elkem**, or the approach typified by **Boehringer Ingelheim**, which stated that laws and official provisions must be observed at all times and that company guidelines or regulations going beyond them must also be observed.

Some corporations referred explicitly to international compliance in their policy statements. The interpretation of international compliance varied between those policy statements which used the home-country laws and regulations as the company standard and those which pledged to honour all applicable laws wherever the corporation had operations. For example, it was the policy of **Company U** to protect human health, safety and the environment at all locations world-wide in a manner equivalent to that provided at United States locations. This policy applied to all activities of the corporation, including design, construction, production and distribution of its products and services.

In contrast, **Cargill Inc.** indicated that its policy was to conduct all operations world-wide in a manner that promoted environmental quality; each **Cargill** facility was to comply with all relevant environmental protection laws and regulations of the community, state and country in which it operated.

Company U's policy was to "conduct all operations, including the sale and distribution of products and services, in compliance with all applicable environmental laws, regulations and standards". The company's goals extended even further to "adopt appropriate standards to protect people and the environment where laws or regulations do not exist or may be inadequate".[5] **White Consolidated Industries, Inc.** made a similar commitment to "establish and maintain programmes to assure that environmental laws and regulations applicable to its products and operations are known and obeyed; adopt its own standards where laws or regulation may not be adequately protective, and adopt, where necessary, its own standards where laws do not exist".[6] In the case of **Pennzoil Company**, if the company believed that existing laws and regulations were not adequately protective, that risks were unacceptable, or if it found that proper regulations were nonexistent, it might develop more demanding company environmental, safety, and health standards.[7]

3. Summary

Many corporate policy statements and policies indicated that compliance with governmental regulations had a high priority on the corporate agenda. Chapter IV, section A, below will look further into compliance-oriented management by analysing different management practices and tools that corporations utilize to ensure compliance.

The analysis clearly demonstrates that a strong relationship exists between corporate EH&S activities and the home country of the corporation. This indicates that the regulatory environment of a corporation works as a strong incentive for corporations to establish environmental management systems and guidelines. It further suggests that there should be close cooperation between governments and business in establishing rules and regulations that best promote corporate EH&S management. Part Three of this report looks into the question of how governments, through regulatory initiatives, can encourage corporations to move further towards sustainable development management.

B. INTERNATIONAL GUIDELINES

In addition to national regulations, corporations are encouraged to observe and adopt a growing number of voluntary standards, codes of conduct, or guidelines developed by international organizations and business associations. Recent years have seen a dramatic growth in the number of such guidelines, and the area has emerged as a highly viable and dynamic policy area.[8] The growth in that policy area has involved industrial associations as well as international organizations.

Industrial associations are developing international environmental guidelines for internal and external reasons. It is important for an industry to keep a level playing-field to avoid detrimental competition among its members as regards environmental standards. Furthermore, the development of

> **Agenda 21:**
>
> "To adopt and report on the implementation of codes of conduct promoting the best environmental practices such as the 'Business Charter on Sustainable Development' of ICC and the chemical industry's Responsible Care initiative" (30.10).

standards and guidelines by industrial associations entails economies of scale for an industry. Instead of each corporation using resources to develop programmes and standards, the group can utilize the industry-wide benchmarks set up by industrial associations. Furthermore, the growing body of industry-initiated guidelines and environmental standards can be seen as ways of communicating environmental experiences among members. Industry guidelines also serve to assure the public that TNCs are taking better care of environmental matters. Thus, voluntary industrial guidelines might be preemptive strikes against binding (international) environmental regulation, which has been vigorously opposed by industry. By establishing environmental guidelines for its members, industrial associations can argue that binding regulation is unwarranted.

Typically, non-binding guidelines from international organizations, like most international regulations, deal with very concrete and tangible sectoral issues such as workers' health and safety, transport of toxic substances or accident prevention, and are inspired by serious accidents such as the ones at Seveso, Bhopal and Basel.

1. Statistical findings

In contrast to the above analysis, which indicates that national regulations directly affect corporate environmental management, the influence of international regulations and guidelines seems to be far less significant. Respondents ranked the utility of 12 sources of voluntary international guidelines as follows: Sectorial trade associations (STA); Chemical Manufacturers Association's *Responsible CARE Program* (CMA); International Chamber of Commerce's *Environmental Guidelines* (ICC-EG); International Standards Organization's *Technical Environmental Standards* (ISO); UNEP's *Environmental Guidelines* (UNEP-EG); ILO's *Code of Practice on Accident Prevention* (ILO-AP); Conseil Européen des Fédérations de l'Industrie Chimique's *Guide to Safe Warehousing for the European Chemical Industry* (CEFIC-SSC); OECD's *Guidelines for Multinational Enterprises* (OECD); ILO's *Tripartite Declaration of Principles Concerning Multinational Enterprises* (ILO-ME); CEFIC's *Principles and Guidelines for the Safe Transfer of Technology* (CEFIC-TOT); FAO's *International Code of Conduct on the Distribution and the Use of Pesticides* (FAO); and UNEP's *Awareness and Preparedness for Emergencies at the Local Level* (UNEP-APELL) (see figure II.2).

As seen in figure II.2, respondents reported only marginal use of existing international guidelines. Although one firm, **Alusuisse-Lonza**, stated that it utilized nine of the guidelines, fewer than half of the respondents reported any use of these whatsoever. In general, less than 10 per cent of the respondents reported that they used guidelines set by inter governmental organizations, such as UNEP, FAO, ILO, and OECD, and only around 20 per cent of the respondents used one or more sectoral trade association guidelines. Those figures, however, might have changed since the survey was conducted in 1990-1991, partly because of the high-profile industrial guidelines received in the UNCED process, and partly because new guidelines, such as the Business Charter for Sustainable Development or the Japanese

Keidanren's Global Environmental Charter, have since been promulgated. In the wake of UNCED, TCMD conducted a survey to determine the level of TNC involvement in the preparations for the Rio conference.[9] It was found that one third of the corporations participating in the Benchmark Survey had signed the Business Charter for Sustainable Development. A recent survey among 500 Japanese corporations found that the Keidanren's Environmental Charter was being utilized by 70 per cent of Japanese corporations (Keidanren, 1992). This indicates that an explosive growth in corporate adoption of EH&S guidelines has taken place in the last one to two years.

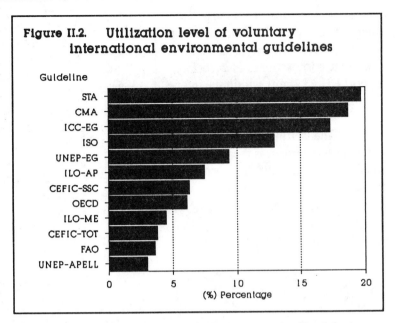

Figure II.2. Utilization level of voluntary international environmental guidelines

Source: TCMD/DESD Benchmark Survey, 1990-91 (see text for abbreviations).

The Benchmark Survey reveals important regional differences. The International Standards Organization (ISO's) technical environmental guidelines and CMA's Responsible CARE Program were adhered to mainly by European and North American firms: 29 per cent and 39 per cent, respectively (see annex table D.3). Over half of the Europe-based corporations stated that they voluntarily followed one or more international guidelines mentioned in the questionnaire, concentrating on the following: International Chamber of Commerce, CEFIC *Guidelines for the Safe Storage of Chemicals* and ISO *Technical Environmental Standards.* Only a few Asian corporations used any of the guidelines. However, the questionnaire's predominant focus on the existing European and United States guidelines may not have done Asian corporations full justice in that regard.

The survey asked the respondents to select the three United Nations activities which, in their view, would best further environmental objectives. The following choices were given: (a) setting international policy guidelines (IPG); (b) setting international technical standards (ITS); (c) assisting in the review of voluntary corporate "performance" standards (VCPS); (d) creating/strengthening national regulatory systems in developing countries (RSDC); (e) creating/strengthening national inspection systems in developing countries (ISDC); (f) reducing differences in environmental rules and regulations of industrialized countries (ERR); (g) reporting on corporate leadership and their achievements (CL); (h) establishing norms and procedures for public disclosure (PD); (i) mediating between corporations and governments on environmental conflicts (M); (j) compiling national environmental laws and regulations (ELR); and (k) other (specify or explain). As shown in figure II.3, 62 per cent of the respondents wanted the United Nations to reduce differences in environmental rules and regulations, and more than half preferred initiatives which would facilitate the development of international policy guidelines. Similarly, the Tufts University study of 1991 found that 76 per cent of 98 United States respondents predicted that the international harmonization of EH&S regulation would lead to improved corporate environmental practices.[10] Clearly the corporate community wants international coordination of EH&S regulations in order to keep a level playing-field. Even if that strong preference for internationally harmonized standards contradicts the present under-utilization of such standards, from a United Nations' perspective it is a positive trend that corporations, *in principle,* support EH&S limits within the international market-place.

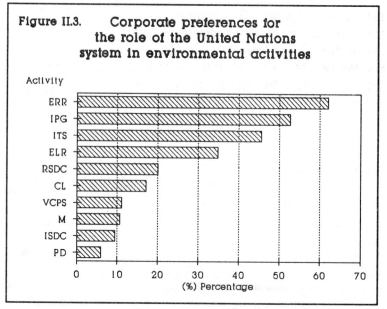

Figure II.3.   Corporate preferences for the role of the United Nations system in environmental activities

Source: TCMD/DESD, Benchmark Survey, 1990-91 (see text for abbreviations).

The setting of international technical standards was the third most noted activity. Establishing norms and procedures for public disclosure was the least cited, along with creating or strengthening national inspection systems in developing countries.

Europe-based firms were the most inclined to request that the United Nations play a role in the setting of international technical standards. That result may have been influenced by the high visibility that this particular subject is receiving at present within the European Community. The North America-based firms were the most likely to ask for the reporting of corporate leadership achievements (see annex table D.4).

With regard to the sole questionnaire received from a corporation based in a developing country, an analysis of its response to the question on the United Nations' role revealed a different priority: the importance of the creation and strengthening of regulatory and inspection systems in developing countries, citing the RSDC and the ISDC categories first in the list of 11 different potential United Nations activities.

2. Summary

The Benchmark Survey found that few corporations utilized international environmental guidelines. However, more recent surveys indicate that this trend is rapidly changing. For the United Nations, and particularly for the United Nations' bodies specialized in dealing with industrial matters, the growing body of voluntary environmental guidelines and their adoption by TNCs have profound implications. Evolving are international minimum standards for the environmental conduct of transnational corporations derived from customary law practices of individual corporations, and guidelines developed by industrial associations and international organizations. An important task for the United Nations' work on business and environment in the future will be to encourage these initiatives in order to develop customary law on those issues to supplement and inform national and international regulatory initiatives. That can be done by developing guidelines for responsive corporate conduct based on existing practices and guidelines, and by disseminating information on innovative practices in order to challenge other corporations to meet or exceed those practices. Moreover, it is crucial that an objective entity, such as the United Nations, monitor progress in corporate implementation of voluntary guidelines in order to hold the corporate community accountable on the promises stated in policies and guidelines. Interestingly, a majority of the respondents wanted the United Nations to play a larger role in harmonizing EH&S regulations. That preference seems to contradict the opposition of some business organizations to an expanded role of the United Nations in setting EH&S standards.

Notes

[1] MITI presented its version of future environmental protection as part of a Japanese industrial strategy in its "New Earth 21". The view of this document is reflected in Keidanren's "Global Environment Charter" of April 1991.

[2] This also seems to be the case in developing nations. A recent study of six Indian corporations concludes that it was only after the passage of the Environmental Protection Act in 1986, when, among other things, top management was made liable for non-compliance, that environmental management activities gained impetus (Bowonder et al., 1992).

[3] The strong relationship between the home country of the corporation and its environmental practices is sustained even when taking into account that the European respondents typically are somewhat smaller than the Asian (Japanese) and North American respondents (see the discussion on methodology in Annex B).

[4] Material submitted in support of responses to the BMS questionnaire.

[5] Ibid.

[6] White Consolidated Industries, Inc., "WCI environmental policy: environmental practices", revised 1 September 1989, pp. 1-6

[7] Pennzoil Company, *Corporate Policy Manual*, 1 August 1990, p. 800-1.

[8] Some of the more prominent guidelines are:
- Conseil Européen des Fédérations de l'Industrie Chimique (CEFIC), *A Guide to Safe Warehousing for the European Chemical Industry* (Brussels, 1987).
- CEFIC, *Principles and Guidelines for the Safe Transfer of Technology* (Brussels, 1987).
- Coalition for Environmentally Responsible Economics (CERES), *The Valdez Principles* (Boston, 1989).
- Chemical Manufactures Association (CMA), *Responsible CARE*, 1989.
- Food and Agriculture Organization (FAO), *International Code of Conduct on the Distribution and Use of Pesticides* (Rome, 1986).
- International Chamber of Commerce (ICC), *Business Charter for Sustainable Development* (Paris, 1991).
- ICC, *Final Declaration of the Second World Industry Conference on Environmental Management* (Rotterdam, 1991).
- International Labor Organisation (ILO), *Tripartite Declaration of Principles Concerning Multinational Enterprises and Social Policy* (Geneva, 1977).
- ILO's *Code of Practice on Accident Prevention*.
- International Organization for Standardization (ISO), *ISO Technical Environmental Standards*.
- Keidanren: *Global Environmental Charter* (April 1991).
- Organisation for Economic Co-operation and Development (OECD), *Guidelines for Multinational Enterprises* (Paris, 1976/1985).
- STA, Sectorial trade associations.
- United Nations Centre Transnational Corporations (UNCTC), *Criteria for Sustainable Development Management* (New York, 1991).
- UNCTC, *Transnational corporations in sustainable development: Recommendations of the Executive Director* (EC/10/1992/2) New York, 1991.
- United Nations Environment Programme (UNEP), *APELL Programme*. Paris, 1988.
- UNEP, *Environmental Guidelines*.

[9] Transnational Corporations and Management Division, "Follow up to the United Nations Conference on Environment and Development as related to transnational corporations" (E/C.10/1993/13).

[10] See Flaherty and Rappaport (1991), p. 12. This finding is also supported by McKinsey's survey, where one of the main conclusions is that policy-makers and fellow industrialists should keep the environmental playing-field level (McKinsey & Co., 1991, p. 13).

CHAPTER III.   CORPORATE EH&S ORGANIZATION

For successful implementation of EH&S objectives, policies and programmes, it is imperative that supporting organizational structures be established and that EH&S programmes and policies be institutionalized. Depending on the size and complexity of the business, divisions or subsidiaries may employ full-time environmental personnel to work on environmental issues. The trend in recent years has been towards full-time environmental specialists in all product lines. In addition, environmental consultants are frequently employed to assist in special projects. This chapter will analyse how corporations organize EH&S matters from a functional perspective (section A: Functional EH&S organization), and how the corporations organize their relationships with subsidiaries and affiliates in other countries with regard to EH&S matters (section B: International EH&S organization).

A. FUNCTIONAL EH&S ORGANIZATION

1. Statistical findings

The management level at which environmental issues are initiated is an indication of corporate commitment to EH&S. Involvement by top management is particularly important, since only through such leadership will EH&S objectives become integrated into corporate activity. Thus, a recent gathering of executives at an international business seminar concluded that management support from the CEOs and the president is the single most important factor required for a company to achieve environmental excellence (*Business International*, 1992, p. 31). The Benchmark Survey findings indicated that in over three fourths of the firms surveyed, top management was involved in initiating environmental programmes. (See figure III.1.) Besides top management, both strategic planning and R&D groups were cited as primary initiators of environmental programmes. Those functional areas appear early in the company value chain and thus help to produce proactive solutions. Ideally, all functional areas play a role in initiating and implementing environmental activities. Human resource groups are a key link between policy development

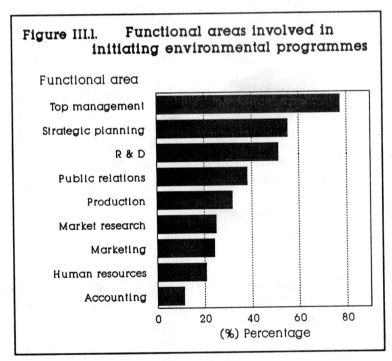

Figure III.1.   Functional areas involved in initiating environmental programmes

Source: TCMD/DESD Benchmark Survey, 1990-91.

47

and employee participation. Accounting groups can tie environmental activities to financial gains. However, the Benchmark Survey shows that the marketing, human resources, and accounting groups were relatively uninvolved in environmental programmes.

In terms of who initiates EH&S policies, top management officials appeared to be significantly more involved in Asia (Japan) than in the other two regions (85 per cent versus 73 and 74 per cent in Europe and North America, respectively.) (See figure III.2.) 85 per cent of the Japanese corporations reported that strategic planning was involved in initiating environmental programmes, but only 46 per cent of the European corporations and 33 per cent of the North American corporations stressed strategic planning. Similarly, 44 per cent of the Japanese corporations reported that market research was involved in initiating environmental programmes, but only 22 per cent of the European corporations and 8 per cent of the North American corporations responded accordingly. Those findings suggest that Japanese corporations seek to integrate environmental programmes in the overall business strategy by involving top management, strategic planning and market research to a higher degree than do corporations from Europe and North America.

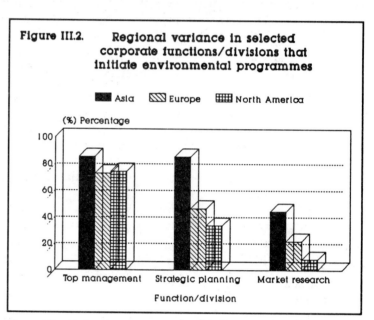

Figure III.2.   Regional variance in selected corporate functions/divisions that initiate environmental programmes

Source: TCMD/DESD Benchmark Survey, 1990-91.

2. Examples of functional EH&S organization

The Benchmark Survey identifies a broad and varied sample of EH&S organization modes. The information it provides about corporate organizational systems varies widely across regions. Consequently, the following discussion of EH&S organization will analyse each region separately.

(a) North America

Only a few North American-based TNCs formally discussed their structures. However, the scattered pieces of information provided by nearly all the TNCs suggest the following five-part hierarchy (from top down):

(i)   Board of directors
(ii)   Corporate policy committees

(iii)	Interdivisional coordinating/steering committees
(iv)	Corporate EH&S
(v)	Divisional EH&S organization
(vi)	Local operational management systems.

Of those, the elements (iv) and (v) are the most common. Only three of the participating corporations in that region indicated having board-of-director-level environment health, and safety committees. Seven additional corporations described less formal avenues for putting EH&S matters on the agenda of the Board of Directors. The EH&S responsibilities of the Board of Directors were described by one of the corporations as follows:

- "A Board of Directors should be required to address the issue of establishing a pollution prevention system. The Board should develop a written environmental policy by which the corporation is to guide its activities.
- Each Director should have responsibility, at a minimum, to ensure that the Board of Directors instructs the officers to set up a system to ensure compliance with environmental laws, ensure the officers report back periodically to the Board on the operation of this system and to ensure that the officers are instructed to report any substantial non-compliance to the Board in a timely manner.
- The Board should ensure that an environmental audit of the corporation's present and future activities is undertaken and that an on-going environmental audit programme is in place.
- The Directors collectively would be responsible for carrying our diligent and thorough reviews of environmental reports provided by the officers of the corporation."

Two corporations (**Amoco** and **Georgia-Gulf**) referred to interdivisional coordinating and steering committees, describing the composition and functioning of those committees in some detail. **Texaco Inc.** reported that a committee of the Board of Directors was in place. Typically, such committees facilitate the application of corporate policies among individual facilities and serve as important feedback mechanisms for environmental health and occupational safety policy-makers.

The most common form of EH&S organization among the participating corporations based in North America consists of a network of corporate-divisional-facility level EH&S specialists. Their responsibilities range from overseeing compliance with company policies and standards to providing assistance to facility managers through access to information and implementation strategies.

In general, the respondents provided little information on the reporting context within the EH&S organization. Based on the information available, facility managers emerged as the persons most directly responsible for implementation of corporate EH&S policies. Their specific duties included performing periodic audits and participating with corporate officials in corporate audits, maintaining general awareness of environmental health and occupational safety through means such as worker training and performance review, and, in cooperation with corporate officers, setting specific goals and rules. As noted by **Air Products & Chemicals Inc.**, "Rules are site-specific ... That means virtually all environmental compliance is at the plant level--from filing a simple report to installing a multi-million dollar treatment process". Moreover, **Company Z** writes: "Each year safety goals are set plant by plant for improvement over the previous year. The plants are responsible for their safety performance, and safety is taken seriously at every level of the corporation's activities".[1]

The examples below illustrate the organizational structure designed by North American-based participants to deal with EH&S issues from a functional perspective.

In 1989, **Cargill Inc.** established a Corporate Environmental Affairs Department to assist the company's operating units in their environmental management efforts. The purpose of Corporate Environmental Affairs was to approach all environmental issues in a proactive manner and to provide direction on environmental policies and procedures; to provide training and education on environmental issues; to keep informed on all relevant environmental legislation; and to stimulate a waste-minimization attitude. Those goals were to be accomplished by working with division, department or subsidiary operations management, the Law Department, and the Public Affairs Department.

The organization of **Cargill's** environmental management efforts reflected the company's decentralized management structure. **Cargill's** philosophy and policy were that environmental protection and compliance with applicable regulations were the responsibilities of every employee. Managers at each of the company's nearly 500 United States and more than 300 non-United States offices and facilities were responsible for keeping pace with changes in environmental regulations and ensuring compliance at their facilities. Local managers were to be supported in the efforts by division operations and environmental specialists.

> **Box III.1. Strategic EH&S Planning in Merck**
>
> In 1990 Merck, a United States-based pharmaceutical company, established a cross-functional team of corporate executives to write a five year environmental strategic plan that will serve as a blueprint for the company's EH&S strategy world-wide to 1995. The task force includes executives from each of Merck's divisions (chemical and pharmaceutical, specialty chemicals and research) as well as representatives from functional areas (environmental resources, public affairs and legal) (*Business International*, 1992, p. 24).

Company X had established an Environmental Marketing Claims Review Committee to ensure that the corporation had a coordinated, consistent and responsible approach to environmental claims against its products among nearly 100 operating units world-wide.[2] The senior officer dealing with environmental matters was the Vice President of Engineering, Quality and Manufacturing, who reported to the company's Board quarterly on environmental matters. When environmental problems arose, the local management could contact the manager of environmental engineering services for information.

Sun Company's organization for environment, health and safety reflected the line management structure of the company and the responsibilities of safety and loss prevention personnel. It also showed those functional relationships that linked every employee to senior management along a route which paralleled the normal line reporting path. The company made its general managers responsible for being aware of all environmental laws, regulations and local conditions that affected their respective areas of responsibility. The managers were expected to ensure that operations were conducted in compliance with such laws, regulations and local conditions. All international exploration and production employees were responsible for performing their individual jobs in accordance with legislation and with company specified environmental procedures and programmes. The Manager of safety & loss prevention was responsible for monitoring the implementation of that policy, for providing advice and counsel to aid in the provision of environmentally satisfactory conditions, and for reporting potential non-compliance to the Managing Director.

The procedure at **Waste Management** was for the Board of Directors to evaluate and address the environmental implications of its decisions. The Executive Environmental Committee of the company reported directly to the Chief Executive Officer and monitored and reported on implementation of that policy and other environmental matters. The company was to prepare and make public an annual report on its environmental activities. The report was to include a self-evaluation of the company's implementation of those principles, including an assessment of the company's performance in complying with all applicable environmental laws and regulations throughout its world-wide operations.

At **Pennzoil**, the Environmental, Safety and Health Department (ESHA) must be informed in a timely manner of pertinent environmental, safety, and health issues and activities; statistics shall be provided to the ESHA director as requested. "The ESHA department is responsible for assessing environmental, safety, and health practices and procedures of **Pennzoil** and its subsidiaries and for providing to operating management and their staff expertise to comply with this policy. To implement this policy, ESHA is responsible for: developing the corporate Environmental, Safety & Health Performance Principles to serve as specific directives for the facilities and the employees who work there; developing, monitoring and maintaining statistics and reports required by senior management to properly assess the company's adherence to these policies and to gauge **Pennzoil's** environmental, safety, and health performance on an ongoing basis; developing and implementing auditing procedures to determine compliance of company facilities with applicable environmental, safety, and health laws; reviewing on a routine basis the ongoing programmes and operating procedures of all divisions and facilities and advising operating management on ways to improve environmental, safety, and health performance."[3]

In 1989, **Texaco** created the Environment, Health and Safety Division, headed by a **Texaco** Vice President. The division was formed to maximize the effectiveness of environmental, health and safety programmes, to confirm the importance ascribed to these activities and to provide strategic guidance within these vitally important areas. **Texaco** had also established the Public Responsibility Committee of the **Texaco** Board of Directors. The committee had oversight responsibility for environmental, health and safety issues throughout the company and reported to the board on the status of corporate policies and procedures that affirm abiding interest in those areas.

The **Tenneco Inc.** Senior Vice President-Group Executive was responsible for the coordination and supervision of the Environmental Compliance Program. That person should:

- "Receive and review the compliance procedures of each of the Company's operating units, and make such recommendations as may be deemed appropriate;
- Consult with the respective chief executive officers of such operating units regarding environmental matters, as requested or required;
- Advise and consult with other senior officers of Tenneco Inc., as appropriate, regarding environmental matters in operating units for which those officers have responsibility;
- Provide the Chief Executive Officer of Tenneco Inc. with an annual report summarizing the organization and operation of the Environmental Compliance Program; and
- Receive and examine final reports of all environmental reviews".[4]

The Director of Environmental Affairs was responsible for providing technical advice and assistance in connection with the implementation and conduct of the Environmental Compliance Program. In **Tenneco Inc.,** owing to the company's diversified nature, it was the responsibility of the management of each operating unit to familiarize itself with the magnitude and gravity of the potential environmental risks associated with respective operations and facilities and with the requirements of all environmental laws and regulations applicable thereto; to adopt appropriate standards and practices reasonably calculated to minimize such risk; and to establish and maintain appropriate procedures designed to ensure compliance with those requirements. Such procedures should, to the extent appropriate, include:

- "Specific assignments of responsibility for environmental matters, including both technical and legal aspects;
- Provision for the collection and dissemination to appropriate personnel, on an up-to-date basis, of current developments in environmental laws, regulations, or standards affecting the operating unit's facilities or operations;
- A system of controls to verify, with reasonable assurance, the adequacy and accuracy of all records maintained and reports rendered in connection with environmental matters;
- A system to measure and record, on a periodic basis, the quantity of waste generated and to effectively recycle or reduce, where practicable, the quantity of waste generated;
- A provision for periodic instruction of operating personnel in applicable legal, technical, and reporting requirements; and
- A program for periodic on-site review of facilities and operations for compliance with legal requirements and internal standards relating to environmental matters".[5]

In **Company U**, the chief executive officer of each Industry Group and direct reporting division, or the CEO's designee, would:

- Develop a program appropriate for the business, which will assure that all current and proposed facilities, equipment, products, and procedures comply with this policy. The programme will include a system for assuring that prompt action is taken with respect to any identified issues and a reporting procedure and timetable for implementing the program.
- Prepare semi-annual reports on the status of the program. The semi-annual reporting may be provided through the Environmental Action System in the form of action plan folios on specific portions of the programme or issues identified for action. These folios will be updated as appropriate.

The Vice President for Health, Environment and Safety, or the Vice President's designee, would:

- Provide guidance and interpretation of the policy requirements as needed.
- Review all programs and semi-annual reports for compliance with this policy and provide comments where appropriate.

(b) Europe

The analysis of the European EH&S organizations will focus on two themes: (i) the way in which corporations have made institutional arrangements for EH&S matters, and (ii) the way in which corporations have designated officers' EH&S responsibilities.

(i) Institutional anchoring of EH&S matters

The institutional anchoring of environmental protection was documented in detail by approximately a third of the responding European corporations. The functional categories of EH&S protection were dispersed over several levels of the corporate hierarchy where different organizational entities are responsible for different aspects of EH&S protection. The pattern represented in figure III.3 illustrates that multilevel structure.

An unequivocal coordination office for environmental questions was found in the case of the chemical concern **Gechem/Recitel N.V.** From its head office in Belgium, it coordinated environmental protection institutions in Germany, France, Switzerland, the Netherlands, Great Britain and Sweden.

Positioning of responsibility in the hierarchy of the Swiss chemical corporation **Ciba-Geigy Ltd.** was similar: the division of Corporate Unit Safety and Environment noted environmental analyses, carried out audits, kept pace with and ensured the implementation of environmental legislation and guidelines, and was responsible for health protection, technical documentation, product policy, technical safeguards against explosion and other special duties.

The world-wide environmental protection activities of **Boehringer Ingelheim** were coordinated by the Environmental Protection Committee. The Central Management appointed a Central Environmental Commission which set up an Environmental Protection Office directly responsible to the Central Management.[6]

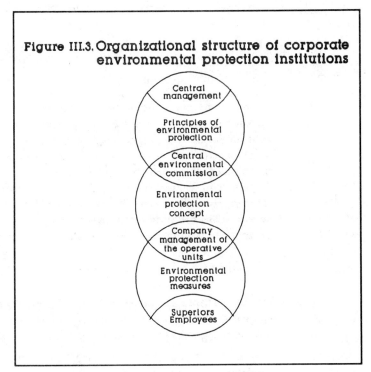

Figure III.3. **Organizational structure of corporate environmental protection institutions**

Source: TCMD/DESD Benchmark Survey, 1990-91.

A Dutch corporation in the electronics sector, **N.V. Philips' Gloeilampenfabrieken**, had arranged responsibility for environmental protection at five corporate levels, with an additional sector for special cases (i.e., emergencies):

- At highest company level
- In the product divisions
- In the national organizations
- In the factories
- In the sales organization
- And for special cases (e.g. crises).

The Board of Management of **N.V. Philips' Gloeilampenfabrieken** was responsible for the policy formulation of **Philips** as a whole, including the provision of the necessary guidelines and resources, and the control of policy implementation. The Product Divisions ensured that in the development of products and processes, as well as in their allocation, due regard was given to all environmental regulations in the different countries. The National Organizations were responsible for compliance with the environmental rules in their own countries. The highest policy board, the Environmental and Energy Council (EEC), presided over by a member of the Board of Management of **N.V. Philips Gloeilampenfabrieken**, determined company policy with respect to environmental affairs. The Council was supported by the Company Environmental and Energy Office (CEEO), and met approximately twice a year. The CEEO functioned as the secretariat of the EEC and also acted as its executive body. All environmental matters were coordinated by that office. The Environmental Inner Circle was a platform for the international environmental affairs of **Philips.** It was chaired by the leaders of the CEEO.[7]

In **Royal Packaging Industries (Van Leer Packaging Worldwide)**, it was the responsibility of the Executive Board, through Subsidiary Business Unit (SBU) and Business Unit (BU) management, to implement all aspects of the environmental policy. An Environmental Steering Committee had been established to assist the Executive Board in that task.[8]

Akzo's Board of Management was in charge of formulating the corporate policy for safety, health and the environment. Within the framework of that policy, the divisions were to have their own responsibility for further elaboration and implementation. Within the Central Staff Departments, the Safety and Environmental Protection Department was charged with the preparation, support and coordination of **Akzo's** policy for safety and the environment. One member of the divisional board was responsible for safety, health and environment within the division. Safety, health and environmental protection were line responsibilities. Every division had a central coordinator for safety and the environment and for health, and the divisions were to have an adequate system for inspection and control.[9]

Alusuisse-Lonza Holdings had established a corporate emergency organization for EH&S at two levels, locally and at the corporate level, with headquarters at **Alusuisse-Lonza**, Basel. The Corporate Staff Ecology and Risk Management was responsible for coordination and provided the necessary infrastructure at Corporate Emergency Headquarters in Basel.[10] From its Risk Management Department, the corporation coordinated the subdivision's product safety, environmental protection, safety and insurance. In addition, there was an emergency organization. The division was placed at the second level of the hierarchy, beside other cross-sectional and central business functions.

The Environmental Affairs Managers in **Degussa AG** were required by law to submit reports to the Plant Managers and the Executive Board. The report's subjects included, but were not limited to, "potentially serious environmental problems". In addition, the Environmental Affairs managers regularly discussed problems with the Environmental Affairs Department at corporate headquarters. In case of potential problems, they would immediately be brought to the attention of the Production Department or the responsible Member of the Executive Board, as well as the R&D Department.

(ii) Officers designated for EH&S responsibility

Among the Europe-based respondents, a large number indicated they had designated special staff to deal with environmental protection. In the information submitted, there were numerous references to the existence of positions with environmental duties and to their integration into corporate organization. The following analysis of the United Kingdom and Scandinavian respondents in that region illustrates the way in which corporations designate EH&S responsibilities to officers at different levels of the corporation.

The most common position was that of the environmental officer; all but two corporations named such an officer. In two thirds of the corporations, the officer reported regularly to top management, and, again, in two thirds of the corporations it was at this highest level that success in meeting environmental targets was assessed. Final responsibility for environmental matters rested with senior officials in the majority of cases. The Chairman or President was the designated authority in seven corporations, the Executive or Executive Vice Presidents in four, and Chief Executive Officer in one. Other officials with responsibility for environmental matters included a Technical Director, a Research Director, a Managing Director and a Director of Engineering. In two cases, the President/Chairman shared responsibility with a Chief Executive Official. Only four corporations in that part of Europe had a senior official who was directly responsible for environmental matters. In one corporation, those designated for responsibility included the Group Director of Corporate Affairs, the Group Legal Adviser, the Head of Group Risk Management, the Group Health, Safety, Environment and Laws Prevention Adviser or the Group Environmental Officer. In only one case did a company fail to report the name of the environmental officer in charge.

Complex and decentralized organizations appeared to leave responsibility to company managers with either a member of the board, the technical director or the chief executive responsible at the group level. The following examples of designated EH&S responsibilities were found among the United Kingdom and Scandinavian respondents. At **BAT Industries plc**, a Main Board Director had specific responsibility for environmental matters, and each business was required to nominate a director responsible for ensuring that appropriate environmental policies and programmes were implemented within that business. The group was confident that strong management control mechanisms were in place to deal with environmental issues.

Electrolux AB stated that it was a strongly decentralized group. "The product line and company managers shall ascertain that their operations are in line with Group policy... The product line managers shall make their organizations aware of the legal responsibility they have in this field... Department facilities within Group Technology have the role on the Group level to support all units with necessary help and guidance."[11]

At **Unilever plc**, while responsibility for implementation remained with the line management, the responsibility for ensuring adherence to policies was central. A specifically nominated **Unilever Main Board Director** had responsibility for environmental standards and practices world-wide. The Director was supported by technical specialists and by committees in which both specialists and line managers might raise the practical issues in the different product groups which were represented.

The responsibility for implementing **Shell Expro's** "Policy on Health and Safety at Work and Protection of the Environment" lay directly and personally with line management, from the Chief Executive through to every employee. Communication throughout the organization was to be regular, open and relevant, with positive leadership from the top. The Managing Director was responsible for providing the resources and developing the organization necessary to implement the policy and for putting the policy into effect. Safety and environmental matters were regularly discussed in Business Unit and Project Management meetings, up to and including the Managing Directors' Committee, which met every two weeks. Every quarter, performance and policy was to be formally reviewed, with the Head of Safety and Environmental Affairs in attendance. The Safety and Environmental Affairs Department was responsible for providing specialist advice and assistance at all stages of **Shell Expro's** activities.

At **ICI plc**, the senior official for environmental matters was designated as the Group Environmental Affairs Manager, who reported to a member of the **ICI** Board. Environmental issues were to be reviewed by the Board of Directors, plus a board subcommittee (called the Group Environmental Affairs Committee) chaired by an Executive Director with overview responsibility for environmental matters. Environmental problems were to be brought to the attention of corporate headquarters through normal line-management channels, via local environmental staff, group environmental staff and formal consultation procedures.

Company M designated the senior environmental official to report to the sector company Managing Director, who in turn reported to the CEO of the Corporate Management Group. The Board did not have an environmental committee as a matter of policy. The entire Board reviewed all environmental issues. Environmental and statutory compliance issues were covered in regular management reporting. Informal communications were also encouraged. For environmental emergencies there was a very open management style. Prompt communication was a requirement. The company stated:

> "Channels should be adequate and open to allow for prompt communication in case of emergencies." Also, "Managers at the decentralized operating level are accountable for performance on these issues, as on other business issues. It is their responsibility to build trust and commitment enabling them, in concert with community groups, to identify the correct priorities for improving the environment...".[12]

(c) Asia

The following practices characterize environmental management organizations in the environmentally-advanced Asian enterprises responding to the Benchmark Survey, which, as noted previously, are based almost exclusively in Japan.

- "Responsibility for carrying out environmental management is put on business line.
- A company environmental management department, headed by an executive, is set up to serve as an organ of central supervision; control is from the top.
- Environmental management organizations, committees, and conferences are established at the center and at all corporate levels for thorough deliberation of management policies and to facilitate relations between management organizations and personnel responsible for implementations.
- At a still more advanced stage, to ensure more comprehensive and organic implementation of environmental management, either service sections for waste, environmental technology research and environmental engineering section are separately set up, or clearly defined organizations are established for the division of their functions."

A cycle of four steps--PLAN, DO, CHECK, AND ACTION--was typically employed in management. The company management section established basic policies, which, after deliberation by the central EH&S committee, were developed on a company-wide scale (PLAN). Those policies were then accepted on the business line for the determination of concrete measures (DO). At the implementation stage, checks were performed on the basis of an inspection system integrated with committees and conferences (CHECK). Discrepancies were then corrected (ACTION).

The tendency to operate a series of subsidiary companies under the same management system is gaining impetus in Japan. In addition, a growing number of corporations indicated that they were expanding the scope of environmental management through safety education systems or systems of study for entire groups of companies.

Among Asia-based participants, it appeared that even when a company did not have a committee on the Board of Directors, there was always a high-level official in charge of environmental matters. In the ten cases where no such committee was indicated, six of the companies

> **Box III.2. Environmental executives in Japan**
>
> A 1992 survey conducted among 500 members of Keidanren found that more than 60 per cent had appointed an executive in charge of environmental issues. (Keidanren, 1992).

had the senior environmental officer reporting directly to the President or a Senior Managing Director. Six companies involved the entire Board of Directors in environmental issues, while one company stated that only important environmental matters were dealt with by its Board.

The following examples illustrate the organizational arrangements for the implementation of environmental policy by the Japan-based firms responding to the Benchmark Survey.

At a major machinery and equipment manufacturer, **Company J**, the Director in charge of environmental assurance reported to the Environmental Assurance Committee. In cases of environmental problems, the Environmental Assurance Organization, the Environmental Assurance Committee, the Central Industrial Safety and Health Committee and the Central Health Care Business Operation Committee were all to be contacted. All divisions initiated and implemented environmental programmes.

At **Company G**, a pulp and paper manufacturer, the General Manager of the Production Engineering Department at the Environmental Control Center was in charge of environmental matters. Only important matters were said to be taken up by the Executive Board of Directors. Every month each mill sent an environmental report to the General Manager. An Environmental Management Committee held meetings at the head office once a year. In cases of environmental emergencies, the Mill Manager or General Manager of the Environmental Control Section was to get in touch with the General Manager of the Engineering Division or the General Manager of the Production Engineering Department.

At **Kawasaki Steel Corporation**, the President and Executive Vice President were the persons to whom the senior official on environmental matters reported. All work on environmental matters was supervised by the Environmental Management Committee. Environmental problems were to be brought up at regular biannual meetings between local management and corporate headquarters. All divisions were to be involved in either initiating or implementing environmental programmes.

At **Nippon Steel Corporation**, the senior environmental official reported to the Representative Director and President. The Environmental Management Committee was to review environmental matters. At regular biannual meetings between local management and corporate headquarters environmental problems were to be reviewed. When necessary, environmental emergencies were to be reported to the environmental department at corporate headquarters.

At **Oji Paper Co., Ltd.**, the Senior Managing Director reporting to the General Board was the senior environmental official. Environmental problems were to be reviewed in a monthly report and in semi-annual summary reports. Regular environmental managers' meetings were scheduled twice a year and an environmental engineers' meeting once a year. Environmental emergencies were to be brought by the mill managers to the attention of the senior Managing Director, and by the Manager of the Environmental Control Department to the Director of the Technical Division at the head office.

At **Sumitomo Chemical Co., Ltd.**, the senior environmental official reports to the President. The Committee of Environment Protection, Plant Safety and Chemical Safety was to review environmental matters. Environmental problems were to be reviewed through the Environment Protection and Safety Audit, the Plant Environment and Safety Committee and at the Plant Operation meeting, held monthly. There was an emergency communication system between each plant site and headquarters in accordance with an intra-company regulations.

Company K, an electronics firm, designated the senior environmental official to report to the President and Chief Executive Officer. A Senior Executive Vice President reviewed environmental matters. Periodic reports on environmental items were to be sent to the business group environmental manager, who reported to headquarters. Alternatively, an environmental inspection report was to be conducted by the business group environmental manager, who reported to headquarters. All operations and affiliates were supposed to report to headquarters on disaster and legal compliance matters.

At **Toyota Motor Co., Ltd.,** an Environmental Protection Committee, a Recycle Committee, a Plant Committee and a CFC Committee oversaw environmental matters. Each had a designated director. Environmental problems and emergencies were communicated directly to headquarters.

3. Summary

The Benchmark Survey results indicate that TNCs have generally responded to public scrutiny and expectations by establishing EH&S organizations. Although a minority among them included Boards of Directors in that organizational structure, it was not uncommon to find corporate officers with EH&S responsibilities in key positions. Clearly TNCs recognized the pivotal role of corporate leadership involvement in achieving EH&S performance. It also appears that EH&S was generally viewed as a line responsibility, with facility managers playing key roles.

Japanese corporations seemed to incorporate functions such as top management, strategic planning and market research more than did firms in other regions. That indicates that Japanese corporations are more inclined to integrate EH&S policies in the overall business objectives and to view EH&S issues as a business opportunity.

Nevertheless, a number of aspects of the corporate EH&S organization remain unclear. For example, are the positions of environmental officers required by law or created voluntarily? Which tasks fall within the realm of the environmental protection institutions? How far does their involvement extend in important decision-making regarding corporate policy (information, consultation, participation, initiation)? Those dimensions of the Benchmark Survey would benefit from further study.

B. INTERNATIONAL EH&S ORGANIZATION

In recent years, the management literature has discussed a trend towards the globalization of corporate management in general, and of EH&S management in particular.[13] Some argue that companies are increasingly setting world-wide standards geared to the toughest laws and are conducting assessments in order to minimize liability and to avoid operating with too many environmental standards. The concept of global environmental management appears to have much in common with the concept of sustainable development. The more TNCs investing in developing countries can apply technologies and practices which are functionally equivalent to their home countries, the less significant the effects of weak environmental regulations and enforcement systems in developing countries will be.

Considering the positive pay-offs from the global application of corporate environmental policies and programmes, it is not surprising that UNCED recommended that world-wide corporate policies on sustainable development be established. That recommendation echoes several recent industrial guidelines.

Agenda 21:

"Be encouraged to establish worldwide corporate policies on sustainable development" (30.22).

"Introduce policies and commitments to adopt equivalent or not less stringent standards of operation as in the country of origin" (19.52 and 20.30).

"Arrange for environmentally sound technologies to be available to affiliates owned substantially by their parent company without extra external charges" (30.22).

"Encourage affiliates to modify procedures in order to reflect local ecological conditions" (30.22).

In the landmark 1991 *Global Environment Charter*, the Japanese industry association, Keidanren, encourages members to "make environmental protection a priority at overseas sites", to "apply Japanese standards concerning the management of harmful substances", and to "actively work to implement effective and rational measures to conserve energy and other resources even when such environmental problems have not been fully elucidated by science". Similarly, the 1991 UNIDO Conference on Ecologically Sustainable Industrial Development adopted a resolution stating that TNCs should implement and apply "general standards of environmental responsibility to their foreign operations which are fully consistent with those used in their home countries". Recently, OECD prepared a series of *Guiding Principles for Accident Prevention* which states that "hazardous installations in non-OECD countries should meet a level of safety equivalent to that of similar installations in OECD countries". Finally, ICC's *Business Charter on Sustainable Development* encourages corporations to apply the same business principles internationally and to encourage suppliers to observe them as well.

1. Statistical findings

One way of examining the structure of international management and organization in a corporation is to analyse the relationship between headquarters and subsidiaries and affiliates. Thus, the respondents to the Benchmark Survey were asked whether they had formal arrangements between headquarters and overseas affiliates and subsidiaries for coordinating EH&S efforts. Less than half of the firms had such arrangements with their fully-controlled affiliates. Even fewer firms (15 per cent) had such arrangements with partially controlled joint-venture affiliates. (See figure III.4.)

Considering that 75 per cent of the respondents had company-wide environmental policies and programmes of some sort in place, the relatively weak formalization of relations with foreign subsidiaries was striking.

Whereas 57 per cent of the North American corporations had formal arrangements for allocation of environmental management responsibilities between corporate headquarters and controlled foreign affiliates, only 32 per cent of the Asian (Japanese) respondents had such programmes. Also, North American companies were significantly more likely to have arrangements with non-controlled affiliates (19 per cent compared to 8 per cent in Asia) (see annex table D.6). That finding was consistent with other findings of the survey, suggesting that North American companies are relatively more sensitive to or aware of the international aspects of their activities than corporations from other regions. For example,

North American respondents were more inclined to have international policy statements and to cite changes in legislation in a host country as the impetus prompting company-wide environmental policies and programmes (18 North American companies quoted changes in host-country legislation as influential, but only five Asian and nine European companies did so; see annex table D.2). Two thirds of the companies having EH&S arrangements with non-controlled affiliates were in the extractive-based sector (see annex table D.6). That finding is probably related to the lengthy experiences which many chemical corporations have had with EH&S management in general, and accidents among affiliates and subsidiaries in particular. Given this history, most firms prefer to control the environmental aspects of foreign ventures.

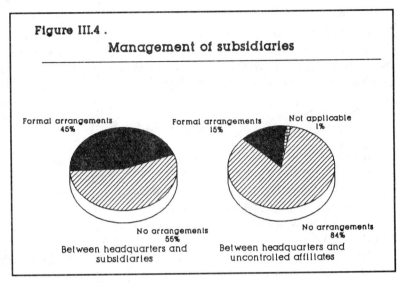

Figure III.4.

Management of subsidiaries

Formal arrangements 45%

No arrangements 55%

Between headquarters and subsidiaries

Formal arrangements 15%

Not applicable 1%

No arrangements 84%

Between headquarters and uncontrolled affiliates

Source: TCMD/DESD Benchmark Survey, 1990-91.

2. Examples of international EH&S organization

Another way of examining the structure of a corporation's international organization involves analysis of the content of corporate policy statements for explicit recognition of responsibilities in international operations. In general, explicit international references were found in only a few statements.

(a) North America

Of several more or less explicit references to the international application of EH&S standards by North America-based respondents, only one corporation, **Amoco Corporation**, discussed directly the international application of its environmental and occupational standards. A column entitled "The environment knows no borders" in its employee journal stated that **Amoco's** past environmental and safety standards, "based on United States laws and modified to accommodate operations in other countries", were being replaced by "new international environmental and safety standards that Amoco can apply throughout the world". The article did not elaborate on its new company policies other than to state that they would "meet the legal requirements of all nations in which Amoco operates, including the United States". In the same article, **Amoco** stated its belief that "U.S. business also should become more active in helping formulate the global environmental philosophy that almost certainly will be reflected in future international agreements". The company was also "encouraging a trend towards constant regulations from one country to another".[14]

A handful of corporations made limited references to international EH&S activities: **Company Z** reported that it conducted workshops for safety professionals in the United States and abroad. **Amoco Corporation's** introduction of its anaerobic wastewater treatment technology at a Taiwan plant referred only to the growth of its pilot compliance review programme into a "major international effort", and its desire to help nature conservation groups by expanding their activities overseas to countries where **Amoco** operated. **Borden Inc.** reported that it had recently introduced an expanded safety, quality and productivity programme to all divisions and some international sites. The health safety and environmental policy of **BFGoodrich** "applies to all activities conducted by **B.F. Goodrich Company** and its subsidiaries, both domestic and foreign". **Caterpillar Inc.'s** water treatment centres at its facilities outside the United States were required to "meet United States' standards, even though in many countries there are no laws requiring them" to do so.[15] **Oryx Energy Co.** stated that the company would manage its operations to make them compatible with the global environment, with the land, air and water, and the human and other life forms found there.

> **Box III.3. IBM's hazardous waste disposal in Argentina**
>
> IBM's subsidiary in Argentina engineered its own waste disposal and recycling program when the staff could not find disposal sites that met headquarters standards. Consequently, facilities now store waste on site or find new uses for it. Today the Argentinian plant recycles 75 percent of all the wastes it generates (*Business International*, 1992, p. 57).

A few companies in that region made specific references to the responsibilities of suppliers, joint ventures and other affiliated companies. For example, **Union Carbide**, based in the United States, had a specific policy for affiliates which, among other things, stated that "affiliate companies will design their facilities and conduct their operations to meet or exceed the corporations standards for the protection of health, safety and the environment". That policy reflects the recommendations of the ICC's *Charter for Sustainable Development* which encourages subscribers "to promote the adoption of these principles by contractors acting on behalf of the enterprise, encouraging and where appropriate, requiring improvements in their practices to make them consistent with those of the enterprise; and to encourage wider adoption of these principles by suppliers".

(b) Europe

The analysis of European corporations shows that EH&S policies have only limited validity internationally in that region. Among the corporations referring to specially drawn-up programmes of environmental policy, only a small number referred explicitly to the international relevance of such programmes. Each company in the **BAT Group** was required to pursue positive environmental policies aimed at achieving "best international practice" in addition to complying with existing legislation and regulations. Few German-based participants cited German environmental legislation as the standard for affiliates in their environmental policies.

Six other European corporations made specific reference to the international application of their EH&S policies. **Glaxo Holdings plc's** international environmental programme was reported to include the organization of international seminars on health, safety and environmental issues where company delegates from across the globe may meet and discuss matters particularly relevant to the company such as new policies, standards, procedures, and areas of special concern. Other important functions of the programme were to act as a central clearing-house and database on environmental matters and to disseminate information throughout the group.

ICI's policy was to promote the interchange of environmental information and technology among ICI and its subsidiary and related companies and to provide information for ICI's processes used under license so that they might be employed without unacceptable effects on the environment. **Company Q** set forth the general policy that all the operations and activities of the group should exemplify the best contemporary practices in respect to the environment, health and safety. Also included were guidelines on the principles to be incorporated into each company's policy and information on best contemporary practices, environmental-impact work, mine closures, monitoring of policy implementation, the company's Head Office responsibilities and personnel resources. For **Company R**, business activities in the electrical engineering and electronics industry, concentrated in Germany, were greatly influenced by German standards, which were applied, as appropriate, to plants abroad. The company stated that it observed the legal stipulations in the countries concerned. **Sandoz's** activities in those areas were also to become more supra-national under the new structure as the company pursued a policy of strict compliance with national and international regulations and of contributing its expertise to the debate with the authorities both at home and abroad. **Boehringer Ingelheim** reported that it applied the same principles at home and abroad; in view of the large number of production centres, the company decided at a very early stage to apply standard principles throughout **Boehringer Ingelheim**. **Ciba-Geigy** stated that its environmental policy principles were valid world-wide in **Ciba-Geigy** group companies. Finally, **Akzo N.V.** undertook programmes to encourage wider use of its principles by its contractors and suppliers. It did so by requiring improvements in their practices to make them consistent with those of the enterprise.

There were, in addition, examples of guidelines which help local management to apply policies and a range of technical and scientific support services available on a world-wide basis. Thus, **Unilever** had mandatory policies which were implemented world-wide, for product safety and for health and safety at work. Implementation of those policies was a major responsibility of the chairman of each of its operating companies throughout the world and was facilitated by a series of **Unilever** guidelines and technical policies, including guidelines for environmental protection.

Only six among the participating European corporations reported formal allocation of responsibilities on environmental matters to non-controlled affiliates. One company stated that this was on a case-by-case basis. In half of the group no formal arrangement for allocation of responsibilities between corporate headquarters and affiliates was said to exist. Among those which had made arrangements for allocation of responsibilities in environmental matters between headquarters and controlled affiliates, very few provided further information.

A few patterns emerged from the analysis, however. In one, the environmental policy was approved at group level, and the Group Risk Management had the responsibility to audit the companies against the Group Policy Statement and to provide guidance on company policies and practices. Another corporate approach utilized a decentralized style of management in its operations. Major sectors were responsible for developing their own policies and programmes on the environment under the basic guidelines. **Gechem/Recitel N.V.** was an example of a corporation where direct links between head office and affiliates were said to exist in the area of environmental protection. In **Royal Packaging Industries**, the group's "Packaging and Environment" constituted the link between the various affiliates, whereas the Group Environmental Affairs Steering Committee, further up in the corporate hierarchy, had only indirect links with foreign affiliates.

(c) Asia

According to the responses from Asian (Japanese) corporations, there were a few instances where efforts were being undertaken to protect the environment of the host country even more extensively than local environmental standards required. Examples of such policies were:

- Striving to transcend host-country standards in working for environmental conservation.
- When host-country standards were lax, applying standards used in Japan.
- Attaching importance to international standards and guidelines.
- Providing and dispatching to overseas operations technology, information and specialists.
- Harmonizing with local society.
- Enthusiastically providing information.

Several of the Asia-based corporations indicated that they performed thorough surveys before they initiated overseas operations, to familiarize themselves with local regulations for instance. The surveys included:

- Thorough prior investigations before initiating operations in other countries and then feedback from the evaluations performed after such investigation.
- Thorough familiarization with regulations, environmental conditions, and local characteristics.
- Assessment of the environment.
- Accumulation of data from observations after initiation of corporate activities to ensure readiness to take all appropriate measures.

Many corporations displayed eagerness to demonstrate a positive attitude towards environmental protection to local communities by:

- Always responding with the latest knowledge and the finest technology.
- Assuming a positive attitude toward coping with problematic situations.
- Demonstrating willingness to cope with issues.
- Stimulating understanding for investments in environmental conservation.

In some cases, the respondents reported that they had established an environment management system tailored to local conditions. That involved:

- Setting up an environmental department, posting personnel to be in charge of it, and clarifying responsibilities.
- Providing personnel training.

- Stimulating home offices to understand and support environmental programmes.
- Developing management know-how for technological and organizational aspects.

Finally, some corporations gave priority to the training and public relations aspects of their international activities. That included:

- Providing and dispatching of technology, information, and specialists.
- Cooperating with all activities contributing to scientific and rational environmental measures.
- Promoting corporate advertising related to environmental concerns.
- Facilitating transfer of environment-related technology and know-how to overseas facilities.
- Cooperating in the acquisition of fundamental environment-related information.

3. Summary

The participating companies were all large transnational corporations. Thus they could be expected to have extended procedures and policies for overseas subsidiaries and affiliates. However, both the statistical analysis and an evaluation of the material submitted by individual corporations indicated surprisingly little consideration for the international aspects of corporate activities. Regulatory discrepancies and the decentralized organization favoured by many TNCs may account for that finding.

Approximately half of the respondents had allocated EH&S responsibilities to their controlled affiliates; only 15 per cent had arrangements with their non-controlled affiliates. Other companies stated that they intended to observe local regulations. Some companies gave explicit accounts of their international responsibilities in their policy statements. Other corporations stated that they were prepared to establish their own standards if local ones were inadequate or absent. The more positive finding was that a handful of corporations had pledged to employ the same standards world-wide, thus meeting the recommendations of UNCED. That group included **BFGoodrich**, **Amoco**, **AB Volvo**, **Union Carbide**, **Boehringer Ingelheim**, and **Ciba-Geigy**.

Notes

[1] Materials submitted by the firm to support responses to the BMS questionnaire.

[2] Progress report from the firm submitted to support responses to the BMS questionnaire.

[3] Pennzoil Company, "Corporate Policy Manual", 1 August 1990, p. 800-4.

[4] Tenneco Inc., "Corporate Policy Manual", 1 April 1990, p.1.

[5] Ibid.

[6] Boehringer Ingelheim, *Annual Report 1989*, p. 19; see also material sent in support of responses to the BMS questionnaire.

[7] N.V. Philips' Gloeilampenfabrieken, "Environmental care within the Philips concern", May 1987, pp. 6-7.

[8] Royal Packaging, "Group policy on environmental affairs", August 1990, p. 2.

[9] Akzo N.V., "Corporation rules of conduct concerning safety, health and the environment", October 1987, p. 5.

[10] Alusuisse-Lonza, "Ecology and risk management fundamentals", March 1991, p. 4.

[11] Electrolux AB, "Electrolux and the environment", 16 May 1990.

[12] *Report on the Environment; Annual Report 1990*, p. 5.

[13] See for example, Peter Dickens, *Global Shift: The Internationalization of Economic Activity*. (New York, Guilford Press, 1992) or Reis and Betton, "The environment and its effect on today's management", *International Management*, February 1992; "Environmental concerns gaining importance in industry operations", *Oil and Gas Journal*, 6 July 1992; Nazli Choucri, "The global multinational", *Technology Review*, April 1991; C.K. Prahalad and Yves Doz. *The Multinational Mission: Balancing Local Demands and Global Vision* (New York, The Free Press, 1987) or Halina Brown, Jeff Himmelberger and Alan White, "Development - environment interactions in the export of hazardous technologies: A comparative study of three multinational affiliates in developing countries", in *Technological Forecasting and Social Change* (forthcoming); Barry Castleman, "Workplace health in developing countries". In Charles Pearson, ed..*Multinational Corporations, Environment, and the Third World: Business Matters* (Durham, Duke University, 1987.); ESCAP/UNCTC Joint Unit on Transnational Corporations, *Environmental Aspects of Transnational Corporation Activities in Pollution-Intensive Industries in Selected Asian and Pacific Developing Countries*, (Bangkok: ESCAP/UNCTC Publication Series B, No.15, 1990).

[14] Amoco Corporation, *Span: For the Future of Our Planet*, Number 3, 1990, p. 30.

[15] A study by Tufts University of 98 United States corporations found that less than 20 per cent of the respondents had made an explicit commitment "to meet or exceed United States laws overseas when foreign law is less stringent" (M. Flaherty and A. Rappaport, 1991).

CHAPTER IV.   MANAGEMENT PRACTICES AND TOOLS

In this chapter the focus will shift from the rules and the organization that provide the framework for corporate EH&S management to specific management practices. The chapter will examine the way corporations control EH&S management on operational levels, and how they communicate environmental issues internally as well as externally. It will thus deal with:

    (a)   Management control and data collection;

    (b)   Public relations: communication and education *vis-à-vis* the public at large and the community and cooperative projects with other industries, government, academia and the public; and

    (c)   Human resource management.

A. MANAGEMENT CONTROL AND DATA COLLECTION

The collection and dissemination of environmental data throughout the corporation is a crucial first step in improving the firm's impact upon the environment. Information-gathering practices, such as EH&S audits or environmental accounting, are important means by which executives become aware of the firm's processes and liabilities, and they ensure that corporate policies and principles are observed at all operational levels.

1. Statistical findings

Almost two thirds of the firms surveyed by the Benchmark Survey had enacted standardized procedures and programmes for EH&S audits (see table IV.1). In addition to auditing, table IV.1 lists several other EH&S data-collecting procedures such as assessments, monitoring and accounting. Where hazards were involved, most respondents had data-collection procedures in place. Fifty-seven per cent had procedures for hazard assessment, and half of the corporations with activities in developing countries were monitoring the disposal of hazardous wastes there. Thirty per cent of the respondents reported that they conducted environmental accounting, a notable improvement from a study conducted by UNCTC/TCMD only two years earlier, which found that less than 10 per cent had established environmental accounting procedures.[1] Other data-collecting procedures, such as environmental impact assessments or surveys in developing countries, were utilized less frequently by corporations.

There were slight variations between the North American-based and Asian-based firms (see annex table D.7). The Asian (Japanese) corporations were more involved with safety audits (82 per cent versus 69 per cent), whereas the North American-based corporations emphasized environment audits (75 per cent versus 62 per cent). Both North American-based and Asian-based (Japanese) corporations were considerably more inclined to utilize environmental data-collection procedures than are European corpora-

Agenda 21:

"Industry should establish environmental management systems including environmental auditing of its production and distribution sites" (20.13).

"Develop, improve and apply environmental impact assessments to foster sustainable industrial development" (9.18).

"Develop procedures for monitoring the application of a "cradle to grave" approach, including environmental audits [for hazardous waste]" (20.19).

"Conduct environmental audits of existing industries to improve in-plant regimes for the management of hazardous wastes" (20.31).

"Give high priority to the hazard assessment of chemicals" (19.15).

"Work towards the development and implementation of concepts and methodologies for the internationalization of environmental costs into accounting and pricing mechanisms" (30.9).

tions. For example, only 31 per cent of the European corporations had environmental audits, and 42 per cent had safety audits.

In terms of sectoral variations, the Benchmark Survey findings revealed that the extractive-based sector (oil and chemicals TNCs) was approximately 10 to 15 per cent more inclined to utilize EH&S data-collecting procedures than the average corporation.[2] That finding probably reflects the high environmental liabilities which characterize this sector. The service sector was as likely to have audit procedures as any other sector; in fact, 77 per cent of the service companies had safety audit procedures, but only 65 per cent of all respondents did. That response suggests a strong corporate desire to keep track of environmental issues, even though the adverse environmental impacts of corporations in this sector presumably are limited.

While there are significant regional and sectorial differences, the central factor in explaining the scope and content of EH&S data-collecting procedures is corporate size. Those in the top-third sales group were generally twice as likely to have such data-collecting procedures in place as were those in the bottom-third group. It is probable that the larger corporations require formal procedures to manage environmental performance effectively, whereas the smaller corporations can rely on more informal ways of collecting environmental data.

2. Examples of EH&S data collection

Many of the corporations provided comprehensive information on specific procedures for collecting, assessing and storing EH&S data. In particular, they provided information on the use of risk analysis and environmental auditing as a means to filter out, at the earliest possible stages, future environmental risks resulting from corporate activities. The following specific examples of means and instruments for achieving information on the state of the environment in the corporation emphasize promising and innovative initiatives. The analysis will focus on: (a) general procedures for collection of EH&S data; (b) auditing procedures; and (c) EH&S data collection in Japan.

```
┌─────────────────────────────────────────────────────────────────────────┐
```

Table IV.1. Environmental data collection

Higher-priority programmes/procedures	Percentage of respondents
Standardized company-wide safety audit procedures	64.7
International safety and environmental audits	64.7
Standardized environmental audit procedures	57.8
Standardized hazard assessment procedures	56.9
Monitoring of hazard waste disposal procedures in LDCs	47.8
Environmental bulletin for company managers	44.4

Lower-priority programmes/procedures	Percentage of respondents
Standardized pollution monitoring techniques	39.9
Standardized environmental impact assessment procedures	39.6
Separate annual environmental statement for the corporate board	37.8
Company-wide environmental impact assessment	37.2
Monitoring of stacks for air emission components in LDCs	36.6
International environmental accounting	29.7
Survey on biological species on undeveloped lands in LDCs	8.7

Source: TCMD/DESD Benchmark Survey, 1990-91.

```
└─────────────────────────────────────────────────────────────────────────┘
```

(a) General procedures for collection of EH&S data

Many corporations have elaborate programmes for EH&S assessments, reviews and evaluations. In the case of the **Kellogg Company**, each operating facility was to develop specific programmes that ensured the intent of corporate policy. Those programmes were to consist of: (a) environmental assessment of each operating facility; (b) development and execution of action plans to address issues identified in the assessments; and (c) continuing reviews of programmes to maintain effectiveness. Issues addressed in the company's environmental assessments included but were not limited to:

- "Compliance with regulations.
- Utilization of recycled materials.
- Recycling of materials used in plants.
- Promotion of community recycling, including packaged materials.
- Waste reduction programmes.
- Air and water resource conservation.
- Disposal of waste by safe and responsible methods.
- Cooperation with governmental agencies and other official organizations engaged in improving the environment."[3]

Broken Hill Proprietary Co., Ltd. (BHP), conducted an Environmental Review the purpose of which is to provide senior management with information on the status of BHP's environment performance and related management systems. The scope of that review included:

- "All operations world-wide focus on Australia.
- Management systems, including policies and procedures.
- Air, dust and noise emissions as well as liquid effluents, monitoring and performance *vis-à-vis* regulations.
- Solid wastes.
- Chemical management.
- Recycling and waste minimization.
- Energy conservation.
- Effects on flora and fauna.
- Community/government interactions.
- Site rehabilitation.
- Potential contaminated sites.
- Environmental emergency response procedures.
- Environmental training for staff and managers."

At **Shell**, environmental impact assessment was integrated with health, safety and environment procedures and had been routinely applied since 1981. A Health, Safety and Environment (HSE) Planning Cycle within the service companies had been established for the chemical function to ensure the systematic generation of relevant data on both new and existing products, including raw materials, intermediates and process chemicals. The Cycle involved an annual discussion between the HSE Division and the business sectors to identify requirements for hazard assessment. The data obtained were presented in HSE data sheets. Environmental audits were said to be routinely carried out (since 1981 by Shell Oil, since 1984 by Shell Canada, since 1984 by E P Function, and since 1985 by Chemical Functions).

At **Union Carbide**, any departure or suspected departure from its environmental policy must be reported to the Corporate Vice President of Health Safety and Environmental Protection (HS&EP). Health, safety and environmental management systems must be designed, implemented and maintained at all management levels to provide reasonable assurance that the corporation complies with governmental and internal requirements. Capital projects must be reviewed to identify health, safety and environmental hazards and to evaluate potential risks. Acquisitions must be reviewed to identify health, safety or environmental hazards and to evaluate potential risks and liabilities. Divestitures must be reviewed for health, safety and environmental liabilities prior to the execution of a definitive sale agreement. Variances from internal health, safety and environmental requirements must be approved by authorized persons and documented prior to implementation.

(b) Auditing

Apart from more general procedures for gathering and assessing EH&S information, some corporations had developed quite elaborate procedures for EH&S auditing. For example, **Noranda, Inc.** reported that it used elaborate environmental audits as the means of enforcement, indoctrination, communication, corporate culture development, and consciousness-raising training. In a presentation at the Conference on British Industry and the Environment, Meeting the Strategic Challenge of Stricter Pollution Controls, the Vice President of Environmental Services for **Noranda** delivered a paper entitled "Environmental auditing -- A key element of a modern environmental management system" in which environmental auditing was described as a "systematic and objective method of verifying that environmental health industrial hygiene, safety and emergency preparedness standards, regulations, procedures and corporate guidelines are being met".[4] Objectives of environmental auditing programmes were "to assure compliance with

regulatory requirements and corporate guidelines; assure application of best management practices; and minimization of environmental liabilities and risks"; and minimize potential risks and corporate and personal liabilities. Auditing goals included timely correction of all deficiencies and findings; liability reduction through improved practices, engineering design, process modifications and chemicals subsitution; heightened awareness and understanding among operational staff; technology transfer and increased awareness of good environmental management systems; improving efficiency and cost-effectiveness; and auditing at least once every four years.

Noranda's environmental auditing was comprised of three phases: pre-audit, activities at site, and post-audit. Most critical were post-audit activities: preparation of an audit report, action plans and follow-up activities. Audit teams (internal and external) and the training of auditing staff are essential to health, industrial hygiene, emergency response, safety, acquisition, divestiture, and plant closure.

The **NEC Corporation** used comprehensive inspection mechanism-auditing indices. The company provided TCMD/DESD with flow-diagrams illustrating its EH&S auditing procedures. Figure IV.1 shows how different auditing systems inside the corporation relate to each other.

Texaco, Inc. stated that it used a comprehensive corporate environmental auditing programme to ensure that its facilities met government and company environmental standards. In 1989, the United States Environmental Protection Agency (EPA) gave its highest award for compliance with industrial waste management regulations to the Convent, Louisiana, refinery of Star Enterprise. In presenting the award, the EPA noted that the plant's hazardous-waste practices "exemplify the federal goals of protecting human health and the environment".

Some corporations stressed the use of auditing and assessments before acquisitions. Thus, at **Cargill Inc.**, an environmental evaluation must be completed by the appropriate division or department for every purchase, sale or lease of a business or of real estate. The Corporate Environmental Affairs Office must review the evaluation prior to the closure of such transactions. An initial internal environmental audit was to be conducted at every location. Subsequent audits were to be determined by

Figure IV.1.

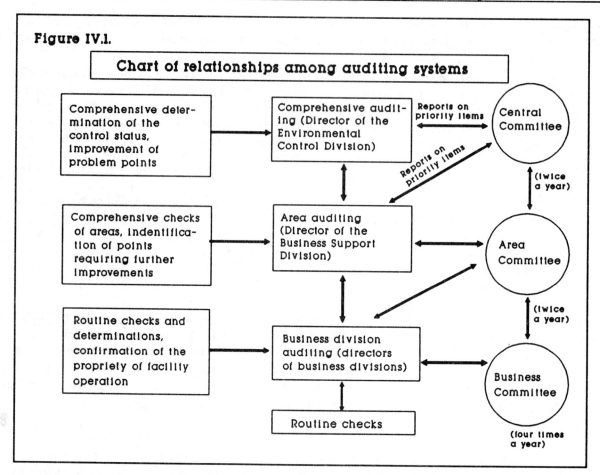

Chart of relationships among auditing systems

Source: NEC Corporation, "Environmental control based on preventing & self-reliant approach report"

the Corporate Environmental Affairs Office on a case-by-case basis. A report on the status of the required environmental permits and a Waste Management Plan must be included in the commitment request for new projects. Each location must review the generation of waste from all activities and submit a Waste Management Plan to its division management. All locations are to evaluate their facilities to determine if asbestos is present and, if so, in what form and conditions.

Any requests for information, inquires, or notices of involvement or potential involvement regarding any hazardous-waste sites received by any **Cargill** facility must be referred immediately to the **Cargill** Corporate Environmental Affairs Office. Each **Cargill** facility is to maintain appropriate environmental files indefinitely in a central location at the plant. To ensure privilege and confidentiality, the files created solely for internal purposes, i.e., environmental activity reports in conjunction with an environmental legal matter, must be segregated from the general files. Detailed examination must be made of past and present environmental problems affecting soil, water, waste, compliance with government regulations and citizen lawsuits.

Degussa AG strictly followed the *Vorsorgeprinzip* (principle of prevention) such as soil sampling and site investigation programmes to be conducted before any real estate transaction, even though it was currently not required by law. Furthermore, every plant site had an emergency hotline. The members of the Executive Board would be informed immediately in case of emergencies.

In **Royal Packaging**, other companies or assets cannot be acquired unless thorough investigations of potential environmental liabilities have been made and any risks, if present, have been quantified.

Another auditing approach, used by **Company L**, creates a Conference on Enviornmental Information (see figure IV.2).

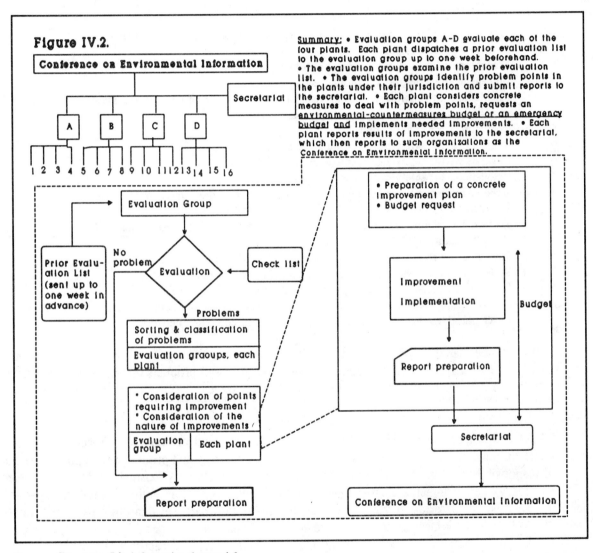

Figure IV.2.

Summary: • Evaluation groups A–D evaluate each of the four plants. Each plant dispatches a prior evaluation list to the evaluation group up to one week beforehand. • The evaluation groups examine the prior evaluation list. • The evaluation groups identify problem points in the plants under their jurisdiction and submit reports to the secretariat. • Each plant considers concrete measures to deal with problem points, requests an environmental-countermeasures budget or an emergency budget and implements needed improvements. • Each plant reports results of improvements to the secretariat, which then reports to such organizations as the Conference on Emvironmental Information.

Source: **Company L's** informational material.

(c) EH&S data collection in Japan

In Japan, TNCs expend a great deal of effort on managerial data collection systems. Diverse standards and manuals were being prepared to facilitate proper functioning of the prior-evaluation system. The range of standards and manuals under preparation varied with the business category. Some major examples are:

- "Environmental management guidelines/regulations for environmental management evaluation systems.
- Management systems for chemical substances.
- Management guidelines for product safety.
- Regulations for equipment management (regulations for equipment management/safety/regulations for inspection management).
- Regulations for quality control.
- Regulations for safety/preservation management.
- Regulations for safety management in affiliated companies.
- Regulations for safety and sanitation management.
- Disaster-prevention guidelines for avoiding effluence of dangerous and harmful substances.
- Technical guidelines for evaluating safety in the event of fire or explosion in a chemical plant.
- Standards for reporting information in the event of accident or disaster.
- System for group-wide safety education/regulations for commendations
- Regional disaster-prevention agreements, pollution-prevention agreements.
- Computerized observation system for water quality and use of a safety database for chemical matters accessible through a personal computer network."

Environmental management is concerned with production activities. In addition, it must devote attention to all environmental influences, including the disposal of end products that have become waste. The basic approach is to deal with both at the prior-evaluation stage.

TNCs are beginning to realize that compliance with laws and ordinances, efforts to minimize environmental influences, and integration of environmental technology and product development are not only social responsibilities, but also reinforce the basis of a company's very existence. Many companies ensure the efficacy of environmental management by introducing a system of environmental-management inspections. Because an exterior driving force--an objective third-party evaluation--effectively raises managerial levels, company inspection systems frequently concentrate on (a) acquiring a comprehensive grasp of supervisory practices and (b) employing indications and advice to rectify failings.

3. Summary

In general, most corporations had activities directed towards measuring the state of the environment in the corporation. Not surprisingly, corporations with the highest safety risks and the most hazardous production processes that had the most elaborate procedures for keeping management informed on EH&S issues. Companies like **Noranda, Inc.**, **Cargill**, **Ciba-Geigy**, and **NEC** seemed to have given a great deal of thought to ways of collecting EH&S data and making them available both within and outside their companies. In particular, audits are important for keeping managers informed on EH&S issues. Audits were first developed in the United States in the wake of the Superfund legislation as a way of identifying liabilities and checking that the corporation complied with regulation. Several respondents seemed to view that procedure as absolutely essential, especially before new acquisitions. In that sense, TNCs have moved a long way towards the recommendations of Agenda 21.

One of the cutting-edge areas of environmental management is EH&S accounting. About one third of the corporations reported having green accounting procedures. However, no examples of concrete methodologies were submitted, and only a small proportion of the respondents could actually estimate their environmental expenditures. That indicates that environmental accounting is still quite embryonic. TCMD has sought to develop methodologies for corporate environmental accounting through the Intergovernmental Working Group on International Standards of Accounting and Reporting (ISAR), in order to establish international standards for measuring the depletion of natural resources. It is crucial that those efforts be upgraded in the future.

B. PUBLIC RELATIONS ACTIVITIES

1. Statistical findings

Many of the recommendations in Agenda 21 deal with information dissemination and collaboration with communities. Corporations must make information on their EH&S impacts widely accessible in order to allow the public to assess corporate environmental responsibility. Such access also helps corporations to learn from one another's EH&S experiences. Collaboration with community groups can help build trust within the community and can provide corporations with ideas about how to solve EH&S problems.

Table IV.2 lists 15 public relations activities that corporations have undertaken, grouped as higher- and lower-priority activities. Between 40 and 50 per cent of the respondents published reports and brochures on their environmental performance. Nearly two thirds of the firms published material safety data sheets (MSDS) for their products to help users of products and company employees to understand the risks associated with them. Half of the firms reported that they engaged in product and safety information labelling. The relatively frequent utilization of those measures reflects recent mandatory requirements such as right-to-know legislation which are becoming common in many countries. Despite

Agenda 21:

"Adopt, on a voluntary basis, community right-to-know programmes based on international guidelines" (19.50).

"Report annually on their environmental record as well as on their use of energy and natural resources" (30.10).

"Share their environmental management experiences with local authorities, national governments and international organizations" (30.22).

"Be transparent in their operations and provide relevant information to the communities that might be affected by the generation, management and disposal of hazardous wastes" (20.14).

the pressure from environmental groups for corporate use of "green" labelling, it was much less widespread (12 per cent) than legislation-induced labelling practices.[5]

Both in the questionnaires and in the supplementary information submitted, corporations proved rather reticent on their information policy regarding environmental risks resulting from their products and processes. Only about 30 per cent of the respondents had company-wide policies and programmes for the disclosure of product and process risks. Through its work, in collaboration with ISAR, TCMD/DESD has noted that a high level of awareness of environmental issues in TNCs. In a survey, the Working Group on ISAR found that 89 per cent of the responding corporations provided some information regarding their impact on the environment. Despite the high degree of awareness, it also noted that much of that information was qualitative and descriptive and that there was no consistent pattern of disclosure.[6] The general impression of an unwillingness to disclose concrete, comparable information on environmental risks was reinforced by a recent survey conducted by "The Company Reporting" in Europe. That survey found that only 11 per cent of corporations disclosed concrete information such as environmental policies or achievements. An additional 12 per cent disclosed information, but it was "general to the point of being virtually meaningless".[7]

With regard to community-related activities such as community participation in emergency planning or financing of environmental groups, TNCs seemed to be quite aware of the importance of good community relations for the operation of the corporation. As shown in table IV.2, more than half of the corporations responded that representatives from headquarters met annually with local environmental officials, and that communities participated in the corporations' emergency planning. Impressively, more than half the corporations contributed financially to environmental organizations, although they seldom specified the kind of environmental organizations to which they contributed.

Specific examples of community-related activities identified in the attachments to the questionnaire included maintaining nature sanctuaries, sponsoring science and environmental fairs, sponsoring ecological campaigns, underwriting environmentally-oriented educational programmes, and supporting non-governmental organizations in developing countries.

Public relations awareness and activities were most extensive among corporations which had experienced environmental disasters, and, more generally, among chemical corporations, which apparently had engaged in a collective learning and improvement process in the wake of Bhopal (see annex table D.8). Thus, more than half the corporations in the extractive-based sector, which consists of oil and chemical industries, disclosed product and process risks. Several corporations in that sector also published information on previous environmental incidents or problems of product and process risks not

Table IV.2. Public relations activities

Higher-priority activities	Percentage of respondents
Contents of material and data safety sheets	63.7
Contents of product labels and safety instructions	52.3
Community participation in emergency planning	51.4
Voluntary financing of environmental organizations	51.0
Annual meeting between headquarters and local environmental officials	50.3
Separate environmental report/environmental section in annual report	47.2
Contributions to local environmental and nature societies	46.1
Formal published international policy/programmes	43.1
Toxic education programs for workforce or the surrounding communities in developing countries	40.5

Lower-priority activities	Percentage of respondents
Special public briefing/brochure on environmental performance	38.5
Disclosure of product-risk information	32.7
Disclosure of process-risk information	28.5
Public access to environmental R&D results	27.2
Public access to corporate lands for nature walks	25.2
Green labelling	12.3

Source: TCMD/DESD Benchmark Survey, 1990-91.

yet resolved by the corporation. For example, **Sandoz International Ltd.** had published a special bulletin on the 1986 incident at its Basel plant.

In general, North American-based TNCs employed more of the public relations procedures and practices displayed in table IV.2 than their Asian (Japanese) and European counterparts. North American-based TNCs led in terms of disclosure procedures and relations with communities. For example, almost half the North American-based corporations--twice that of European and Japanese corporations--disclosed product risk. Furthermore, North American-based companies were almost twice as likely to report formally and inform on environmental performance as the Asian (Japanese) corporations (60 to 70 per cent in North America vs. 30 to 40 per cent in Japan), with the European corporations falling in between. Those findings are consistent with the tendency of North American-based corporations to publish EH&S policy statements and the relatively large proportion of North American corporations that want the United Nations to report on corporate leadership achievements.

The strong North American involvement in public relations activities can be explained in part by the fact that United States corporations have a longer history of public relations, and in part by the fact that legislation, such as the Superfund laws, requires disclosure. There are notable exceptions to that trend: Japanese corporations are somewhat more likely to have green-labelling programmes. And European corporations are more likely than North American-based TNCs to arrange annual meetings with local environmental officials (57 per cent vs. 44 per cent). The latter difference probably reflects the relatively more *corporatistic* regulatory approach found in many European countries.[8]

2. Examples of corporate public relations activities

The subsequent analysis of corporate relations with the general public and environmental groups distinguishes between (a) policies addressing the corporation's relationship to the community and the general public and (b) examples of specific collaborative initiatives with communities and environmental groups.

┌─────────────────────────────────────┐

Box IV.2. International disclosure

In a recent survey among 43 chemical corporations conducted by Friends of the Earth it was concluded that although a number of multinational corporations are displaying a willingness to provide the public with toxic release information about their facilities outside the United States, the majority are not. The result is, the survey concludes, a double standard in which United States citizens are able to receive far more information than citizens of other countries (Friends of the Earth, 1992, p. 5).

└─────────────────────────────────────┘

(a) Corporate community orientation

Across all regions, TNCs reported a commitment to corporate citizenship. That was typified by the **Kimberly-Clark Corporation's** fundamental policy. The firm stated that the very basis of its existence, was its corporate citizenship, and that the public interest was to be considered at all times when construing the policy on environmental protection and concern. The intent was to foster a proper environmental ethic throughout the company and all of the people serving it which would be a permanent part of the company's culture.

A similar corporate citizenship approach was apparent in **Borden's** "Social Responsibility" subsection of its annual report. The section began, "**Borden Inc.**, strives to be a responsible citizen, contributing to the well-being of society in general and to the benefit of the communities in which our people work and live". The subsection then described **Borden's** community responsibilities under four headings: (a) equal employment opportunity; (b) minority purchasing; (c) charitable contributions; and (d) environmental protection.

More specifically, TNCs employed an array of outreach activities to demonstrate corporate citizenship with regard to environmental issues. In Japan, when communicating with the public at large and the local community in particular, some corporations promote harmonization with their local settings. For the sake of long-term coexistence and co-prosperity with the local society, the typical Japanese corporate response was that it was essential to eliminate feelings of insecurity, distrust, and unpleasantness and to strive to satisfy local expectations. The following are some concrete ways in which that was achieved.

- "Active participation by company staff in local groups and events.
- Invitations to local people to attend company events.
- Opening company facilities to the public.

- Improving the appearance of factories and planting ample trees and shrubbery to contribute to local greening programmes.
- Sponsoring lectures on the environment for the local citizens.
- Providing access to the public to observe operations, including environmental management efforts."

In North America, the legal requirements of disclosure have led corporations to adopt policies for communication with the public. **Air Products & Chemical Inc.** reported that it complied in both letter and spirit with the Superfund Legislation SARA Title III provisions effective for the year 1987, gathering toxic emissions data for every facility it owned and reporting annually to the public. Each plant had environmental experts who worked with the local community under the provisions of voluntary and mandatory environmental programmes. Each plant maintained an open-door policy with the public that it served, including a mix of public outreach programmes.

Amoco Corporation stated that it had instituted mutual-aid pacts with other industrial facilities, local police and fire departments. It conducted drills and training sessions with community emergency-response departments. Pipelines and refineries had outreach programmes aimed at informing local officials about **Amoco** lines and products as well as establishing emergency procedures. The company stressed that participation in a combinations of public outreach programmes went beyond compliance with the legal requirements for disclosing such potential dangers. Management wanted employees to call its attention to any threatening situations. If such situations were significant, **Amoco** reported them to the proper government authorities. "Notice will be published in **Amoco's** quarterly (10-Q) and annual (10-K) reports to the federal Securities and Exchange Commission if there is reasonable belief that any **Amoco** company could be ordered to pay fines and/or penalties in excess of $100,000 because a government authority has made an administrative or judicial change under a local, state or federal pollution-control law."[9] In line with SARA Title III, **Amoco** maintained that proper cooperation between its facilities and the public agencies or close communities would help everyone respond more effectively if an emergency did occur.

Waste Management Inc. reported that it provided information to assist the public in understanding the environmental impacts of its activities. It sought to conduct public tours of facilities, consistent with safety requirements, and worked with communities near facilities to encourage dialogue and exchange of information on facility activities. The company stated that it supported and participated in the development of public policy and in educational initiatives that would protect human health and improve the environment. It sought cooperation in that work with government, environmental groups, schools, universities, and other public organizations.

At **Oryx Energy Co.**, the company pledged to disclose promptly to its employees, and the communities in which it did business, whenever its operations posed any significant health, safety, or environmental risk to them. That included working with communities, where appropriate, in developing contingency plans.

(b) Collaboration

Cooperation within industry and with government and other groups such as academia and the general public was more evident in the supplementary material received from North American companies than that from the other regions.

According to the policy of **Noranda Inc.**, for example, communication of environmental principles must be based on open, honest and factual dialogue with internal audiences (employees and shareholders) and external audiences (local publics, environmental groups, scientific communities, govern-

Box IV.3. MacDonalds' cooperation with EDF

McDonalds' cooperation with the Washington-based Environmental Defense Fund (EDF) in doing away with its styrofoam packaging and replacing it with coated paper containers has received wide publicity. It also led to the development of a solid waste reduction strategy in the corporation that goes well beyond the replacement of foam with paper. (*Business International*, 1992, p. 101.)

ment agencies, the media, and industrial associations). Targeting local communities particularly, public meetings and open houses should be held on a regular basis for the purpose of exchanging information. **Noranda** reported that it funded 20 environmental groups whose priorities included education of the public on environment, conservation and environment and economy linkages, as well as major national issues such as toxins, acid rain and the greenhouse effect, and the enhancement and conservation of environmental resources. Communications with media should include simple, factual messages.

Oryx Energy Co. intended to participate in the legislative and judicial process to achieve a proper balance between the use of natural resources and the protection of health, safety and the environment. The company worked hand in hand with the Audubon Society to create nesting areas for birds in its production fields in South Texas and Louisiana. One recent effort involved providing new, improved nests for nearly 1,000 baby wood ducks in a Louisiana wildlife migration project initiated by **Oryx** and the United States Fish and Wildlife Service. In addition, the company stated that it had been among the first to cooperate with harvesters of bay mussels from productions platforms along the Santa Barbara Channel.

Oryx recently had helped to fund the Texas Conservation Corps, a summer employment programme for Texas youth. Supervised by the Texas Parks and Wildlife Department, the programme involved hiring 60 teenagers to build trails, clear trees, improve parks and help preserve natural resources. **Oryx** also reported that it had been the first company to participate in a Texas Parks and Wildlife Commission special conservation fund. The donation of more than 300 acres of critical flyway property near Galveston Bay, worth nearly $200,000, provided a resting spot for birds migrating across the Gulf of Mexico. In Montana, **Oryx** helped the United States Department of Agriculture Forest Service in a research study of grizzly bears. Using funds provided by **Oryx**, forest rangers were able to monitor the bears' wanderings in relation to oil drilling and seismic equipment.

Some corporations reported projects in which a firm joined with government or an environmental organization on special projects. A case in point involved the **Amoco Corporation** and the United States EPA which were working on a joint project at the company's Yorktown, Virginia, refinery to study ways of preventing pollution.[10] The project had technology and policy components. It was reportedly the first industry-government effort to evaluate environmental management at a refinery. The project was divided into two phases. The first, undertaken in 1990, concentrated on gathering information. The **Amoco/EPA** team attempted to link refinery releases of all media (air, water, and soil) with their sources as a basis for either eliminating the sources or proposing changes in the process to reduce emissions. The second phase, completed in 1991, weighed alternative pollution-control plans, stimulated their effect on refinery operation and the surrounding area, ranked the alternatives according to technical feasibility, cost and other considerations, and identified problems that could prevent the carrying out of a pollution reduction plan. **Amoco** welcomed the joint project in the hope that it would promote better working relations between industry and government. Both sides had an interest in how to apply most effectively limited time, people, and money, as well as to allow the permitting process to achieve pollution-prevention goals. The approaches selected as best by the project team were receiving further review by outside organizations. The "peer" review was designed to help ensure sound, scientific analysis. The results may be applied to the Yorktown refinery and other **Amoco** facilities, as well as to those operated by other companies.

> **Box IV.4. Cooperative schemes in Canada**
>
> Senior executives from several Canadian companies, including Dow Chemicals Canada, Nova Corporation and Dofasco, have joined with environmental groups such as Friends of the Earth and Pollution Probe to form a coalition called New Directions. Their purpose is to gather data on toxic-waste emissions in Canada and eliminate the worst problems by 1994 (*Business International*, 1992, p. 3).

Company P focused its public relations activities on wildlife preservation in its vast forests. One project described in the employee journal submitted to the survey had reportedly been implemented jointly with the local communities, government and one university.

"Nestled amidst 6 million acres of [company-name]'s timberland resource base is an abundance of wildlife. ...Ironically, harvesting trees ends up helping many wildlife species by allowing sunlight to filter through and stimulate browse that grows under the forest canopy. ...And we make sure to leave just the right trees for the various species in order to maintain the forest ecosystem. ...But we do more than just share the forest with these creatures; we help in the research and management of wildlife and their habitats. ...The company has initiated a major elk management programme which addresses habitat issues and hunting opportunities. ... [company-name] is working with the Oregon Department of Fish and Wildlife and University of Idaho researcher to determine what might be necessary to develop long-range management guidelines for elk that inhabit our timberlands. ...[company-name] is currently involved in fish habitat improvement projects on [company name] Canadian operations have participated in a joint research project to establish and maintain a spawning site for walleye near Fort Frances, Ontario. The company, a local sporting club, and the Ministry of Natural Resources (MNR) combined resources for a stream stabilization project. ...Since 1988, [company-name], the Northwest Steelheaders Association, and the Oregon Department of Fish and Wildlife have teamed up for the Salmon and Trout Enhancement Program (STEP), backed by a $50,000 contribution from [company-name]. For example, along a stretch of the Siletz River, which meanders through [company-name] Timberlands, a backhoe moves boulders and logs along the river to be anchored in place. This forms pools of water and cover and proved to be very inviting to the fish. ...Since 1981 [company-name] has been working with the Peregrine Fund president, Dr. Bill Burnham, who believes that this type of cooperative arrangement is the key to protection of wildlife. Protection of ecologically unique, undisturbed areas is important, but managed lands and management of wildlife are equally significant. Our purpose is to help wildlife adapt to an existence in modified environments, because locking up extensive areas alone will not result in preserving many species which require large amounts of land to exist. ...[company-name] now co-sponsors a peregrine release programme with the State of Washington as well. By 1990, our monetary contribution to the restoration of the peregrine falcon amounted to more than a quarter of a million dollars. ...In Louisiana, for instance, we've contracted nearly 100,000 areas of our timberland to the state for co-op wildlife management areas. And in Maine, the company manages a wetlands preservation zone on its timberlands to protect riparian wildlife."

White Consolidated Industries indicated that it targeted the protection of public health and the environment by working constructively with government agencies, trade associations and others to develop balanced, cost-effective and realistic laws, regulations and standards.

Waste Management Inc. reported that it encouraged its employees to participate in and to support the work of environmental organizations. It also collaborated directly with environmental organizations by providing support for the advancement of their programmes in environmental protection.

Texaco Inc. stated that it had played a major role in the American Petroleum Institute's oil industry task force, which resulted in the 1989 formation of the Petroleum Industry Response Organization--a body of trained experts in the field of oil-spill response. That collaboration grew out of **Texaco's** own oil-spill plan, which included multilevel response teams which could call on each other for support when necessary. In the United States, some 70 individuals were assigned as members and alternates to Texaco's umbrella organization, the National Oil Spill Response team, and to three regional teams based on the East, Gulf and West Coasts. In addition, each operating group in producing, refining and transportation had appropriate emergency plans and a trained response team. Each year, the company held national and local oil spill response drills. Following scenarios developed by an outside consultant, the drills tested equipment, plans and staff under realistic conditions.

In a further example of community outreach and collaboration in Europe, the United Kingdom-based corporation **Shell** coordinated a 20-year (1970-1990) Shell Better Britain Campaign and produced literature for voluntary groups to obtain financial help from **Shell** to undertake projects to improve their local environment. The company reported that in 1990 the total amount of the fund was £12,000, with a maximum grant available of £500.

Some of the Japanese respondents offered descriptions of cooperation with other companies:

Company O had explained its recycling policy "to some 140 manufacturers, including suppliers of steel, aluminum, plastics and other materials as well as part suppliers...The purpose was to enlist the support of these firms in building a cooperative organizational structure for promoting recycling activities... In cooperation with these companies, [company name] plans to work out specific recycling goals and guidelines".[11]

Or, alternatively, specific technical assistance may be offered, as is the case with **Ebara Corporation** which stated that it supplied other companies with engineering for environmental protection, including water purification, emissions treatment and heat recovery.

3. Summary

Sharing environmental experiences with stakeholders and reporting on EH&S issues will play a central role in the implementation of Agenda 21's recommendations. Information on individual corporations' experiences can inspire other corporations not as yet engaged in EH&S management, and can influence the shaping of new policies on sustainable development. The high Benchmark Survey response rate and the numerous initiatives by individual corporations and industrial associations which submitted examples of progressive practices to UNCED, point towards a willingness within the business community to share EH&S experiences.

Many of the company publications collected through the Benchmark Survey stressed the importance of being good corporate citizens and neighbours, and of supporting various public charities and undertakings. Although the public outlook has a long history in corporations, the strong emphasis on the public-relations aspects of EH&S issues is a noteworthy trend. Several factors might have forced corporations to address those aspects. More and more consumers are becoming environmentally conscious and considering not only the price and quality of the product, but also the way in which the product has been produced.[12] Also, the NIMBY ("Not in my back yard") factor makes it increasingly important for corporations to have good community relations in siting situations. Finally, good relations with regulators and environmental groups can help to offset the adverse consequences of regulations. Thus, it is probable that corporations stress public relations because public goodwill is a solid business asset.

North American corporations were significantly more engaged in public relations activities than European, and especially Asian (Japanese), corporations. That is partly a reflection of a more stringent United States regulatory environment and disclosure requirements in United States' environmental laws, but it might also indicate that North American corporations have realized that openness and positive public relations are crucial for a successful business. Corporations in the extractive-based sector were significantly more engaged in activities such as disclosure than those in other sectors.

In spite of the positive findings, less than one third of the respondents had procedures for disclosing product or process risks. Furthermore, the material collected through the Benchmark Survey showed that each corporation had its own reporting methods, format and media. That makes it difficult for stakeholders to evaluate and compare the information. In the future, standardized ways of reporting should be developed and adopted by corporations in collaboration with governments and international organizations.

C. HUMAN RESOURCE MANAGEMENT

Employee awareness of environmental problems and pollution control measures is crucial for the successful implementation of environmental objectives. Training is required to build up awareness and expertise and to improve knowledge as technology changes.

1. Statistical findings

Survey questions in the area of worker-related issues are listed in table IV.3. More than 60 per cent of the respondents had worker-related activities, such as training programmes and workers' participation in developing EH&S procedures. Moreover, more than 80 per cent indicated that EH&S responsibilities were a part of the job description, and nearly 70 per cent included environmental performance in employees' performance records. To motivate staff effectively, EH&S objectives may need to be integrated into compensation systems so that EH&S criteria, along with cost, quality, and profit, influence salaries and promotions. Approximately half the corporations reported that they had incentive schemes to induce staff to contribute to company environmental objectives. That result was much higher than previous industry estimates of only 10 per cent.[13]

Agenda 21:

"Industry and business associations should cooperate with workers and trade unions to continuously improve the knowledge and skills for implementing sustainable development operations" (30.13).

"Integrate cleaner production principles and case examples into training programmes and organize environmental training programs for the private sector and other groups in developing countries" (20.18).

Despite the importance that corporations seemed to give to labour aspects of EH&S management, only 16 corporations reported worker-related events as influential in formulating their company-wide EH&S policies (see figure II.1). Interestingly, one of the European companies which responded that worker-related events were influential, reported that it viewed environmental training of its 50,000 employees and their attentiveness in the workplace as its biggest environmental problems.

Looking at regional variations, the general trend was for Japanese corporations to have more EH&S-related activities for workers (see annex table D.9). For example, nine of ten Japanese TNCs had worker-safety training programmes. Moreover, Japanese corporations were considerably more inclined to integrate environmental concerns in personnel policies than their European and North American counterparts. Interestingly, though, European firms, which in most other EH&S activities ranked third behind the North American and Japanese, were second to Japanese corporations in the case of labour aspects of EH&S management, with North American corporations trailing behind. Regarding the involvement of workers in setting EH&S standards, European firms were leading, a fact that probably

```
┌──────────────────────────────────────────────────────────────────────────┐
│                                                                            │
│            Table IV.3.  Human resource management activities               │
│                                                                            │
│   Higher-priority activities                       Percentage of respondents│
│                                                                            │
│   Environmental protection or health and safety responsibilities    82.3   │
│     a part of an employee's job description                                │
│   Educating staff on the environmental impact of the firm's operations  68.6│
│   Environmental performance and safety records part of staff's      68.6   │
│     performance evaluations                                                │
│   Workers' participation in setting EH&S standards                  67.8   │
│   Workers' health and safety as a company-wide policy               67.5   │
│   Standardized company-wide worker safety training programmes       67.3   │
│   Standardized contents of material and data safety sheets          63.7   │
│   Standardized management safety training programmes                58.2   │
│   Incentive schemes at the plant level to induce staff to contribute 47.4  │
│     to the company's environmental objectives                              │
│                                                                            │
│   Lower-priority activities                        Percentage of respondents│
│                                                                            │
│   ILO Code of Practice on Accident Prevention                        7.5   │
│   ILO Tripartite Agreement on Multinational Enterprises              4.5   │
│                                                                            │
│   ──────────────────                                                       │
│   Source: TCMD/DESD Benchmark Survey, 1990-91.                             │
│                                                                            │
└──────────────────────────────────────────────────────────────────────────┘
```

reflects the relatively high level of unionization in Europe and the historically high degree of institutionalization of labour relations in most European countries.

2. Examples of human resource management EH&S activities

Worker training in environmental, health and safety was fairly standard for TNCs across the regions surveyed. In addition, many corporations utilized performance reviews for employees. There were also a significant number of corporations which engaged workers in problem-solving activities. The analysis of employee-oriented corporate activities identified in the material attached to the Benchmark Survey questionnaire will distinguish between (a) training-activities, (b) performance evaluations, and (c) employee involvement in problem-solving.

(a) Training

Typical of employee training practices was the Japanese **NEC Corporation**, where the entire corporation staff was to be made aware of the corporation's environmental objectives and policy goals in order for environmental management to proceed smoothly. To achieve that end, various devices were used by **NEC** which reappeared in other TNCs:

- "Education graded by stratum within the organization (new employee, mainstay employee, administrative or supervisory personnel) or training of personnel to engage in actual environmental management).
- Encouragement of personnel to become qualified in environmental matters.
- Hypothetical accident training.
- Holding special events such as Environmental Improvement Week.
- Publishing informational and educational bulletins on environmental matters".

Box IV.5. Training is crucial for compliance

" In the worst case scenario a manager chooses to violate the law rather than spend money to control waste. His bottom line may look good for a while, but the corporation is on the line. The right decision in a plant comes from good people, good policy and a culture of compliance, not from a corporate staff 1,000 miles away" (Lynn Johnson, Corporate Director of Safety Health and Environmental Affairs at Rohm and Haas) (*Business International*, 1992, p. 78).

To ensure the application of worker training programmes, most corporations had instituted management structures that placed additional responsibility on supervisors and senior officials. Thus, the **Amoco Corporation** indicated that it had trained intensively more than 100 engineering and technical staff members to head teams charged with identifying potential processes to address safety problems in various operations. One example cited was the coordination of industrial fire-training schools.

Similarly, **Company W** stated that it required each employee who handled or stored hazardous waste to undergo safety training and responsibility training consisting of:

- "Record-keeping practices.
- Labeling practices.
- Use of appropriate containers.
- Furnishing of information on the general composition of the hazardous waste.
- Use of the manifest system.
- Reporting as to quantities of hazardous waste generated and disposition of those wastes.
- Emergency procedures".[14]

Safety meetings were to be held periodically to address the handling of hazardous wastes and emergency procedures. Incentives were to be provided for ideas about improved compliance. Under development was an internal displinary programme to penalize careless or reckless conduct with respect to hazardous wastes.

Box IV.6. Training of employees from LDCs

A pioneer programme in providing training for LDC employees has been developed by the United States-based World Environment Center's International Environment and Development Service (IEDS) in conjunction with TNCs and the United States Agency for International Development (AID). Examples of IEDS activities include an Indonesian chemical engineer who worked three months at a United States pulp and paper plant to learn about safety, quality control and environmental management and a mining engineer from Zaire who spent two months in Canada and the United States studying exploration techniques (*Business International*, 1992, p. 57).

In Europe, **Akzo N.V.** offered a similar set of priorities. It informed its employees about the potential risks they were exposed to during their activities and about the measures that had been taken to minimize those risks. Employees were obligated to participate in safety, health and environmental education.

(b) EH&S Performance evaluation

At **Pennzoil,** all employees were expected to conduct themselves in an environmentally responsible and healthful manner at the job in accordance with policy. Any violation of that policy or of environmental, safety, or health laws or regulations might be grounds for disciplinary action, including, in extreme cases, termination of employment. All plant, field and facility supervisors and certain employees were to be evaluated each year on their environmental, safety, and health work performance under the company's employee appraisal programme. Managers within the division headquarters were responsible for operating facilities and for assuring compliance with that policy, and with all laws and regulations. All employees were expected to have read or received instructions regarding the policy. The company reported that it provided frequent, high-quality training programmes to instill in employees the ability and desire to achieve high levels of environmental, safety, and health performance on the job.

At **Company P,** performance planning and review forms were reportedly filled out by supervisors with the consent and cooperation of each employee. EH&S goals and expectations were agreed upon by the employee and the supervisor or manager and were stated in such a way that the employee's performance could be compared against them. The stated object was to determine how effectively the company's safety guidelines manual served to evaluate performance in terms of each goal in the performance plan. It also guided the determination of salary-range placement based upon sustained performance. Violation of **Company P's** environmental compliance policy by an employee was sufficient grounds for disciplinary action, including demotion, reduction in pay, or dismissal for disciplinary reasons.

Company U emphasized the importance of monitoring environmental quality. It ceased to manufacture any product or continue any operation if the environmental impact or cost became unacceptable. It gave line managers individual responsibility for the environmental performance of their activity. It also charged the corporate environmental protection staff with the responsibility to provide leadership for the implementation of that policy throughout the corporation. As a demonstration of its environmental concern, the company trained employees in identification of issues, individual responsibilities, and actions to be taken to protect the environment. It was also implementing programmes for self-monitoring, reporting through multiple organizational channels, and environmental assessments to ensure compliance. Every employee was expected to observe the spirit of that policy as well as the letter.

Oryx sought to harmonize environmental and financial concerns by stressing that health, safety and environmental goals need not conflict with the company's economic goals. Both were said to be woven into the company's decision-making fabric and used prominently in measuring the performance of all employees, especially management. **Oryx** reported that management committed the funding and manpower necessary to accomplish the objectives of the company's health, safety and environmental programmes--including the use of modern technologies, employee training, and periodic health, safety and environmental audits. Performance on those areas was reported to the Board of Directors at least annually.

(c) Participation

Company Z was characteristic of the corporate approach which coupled worker education with incentives for the active participation of employees in environmental problem-solving. As in the examples cited above, the firm reported that it conducted specific safety-training courses for management, professional staff, and supervisors to teach them how to instruct their workers in safe working procedures. It then highlighted safety themes at management meetings and implemented programmes through plant safety meetings of employees in small groups to permit individual employee participation in problem-solving and in executing safety procedures. Also, a "theme-of-the- month" employee awareness programme had been established.

Ciba-Geigy reported that it had introduced an "eco-factor" for calculating the premium paid for suggestions which improved the environmental performance of the corporation. A "zero error" programme had been in operation since 1973 which allowed employees to report environmental problems without necessarily proposing a solution. That had been supplemented by "Oekogenda", an environmental management-by-objectives scheme introduced in 1990, and the "be smart" programme for disseminating environmental success stories started in 1989.

Similarly, **Arvin Industries'** North American Automotive Division had instituted an employee-involvement programme. "Employee-involvement teams are encouraged to consider waste minimization projects in the same manner as other process improvement ideas."[15]

Union Carbide Corporation indicated that it sought to simplify and streamline the organization at every level. Employees must adhere to corporate standards for health, safety and environment, and thereby re-establish the corporate reputation for excellence in those areas. It delegated to the individual businesses the functional activities that would help them to be self-sufficient and independent, reserving only those that must be retained at the corporate level. Communications were to be timely, forthright, and credible for people both in and outside the corporation. The company also sought to promote an atmosphere of cooperation among the businesses that took advantage of skills, knowledge and experience across organizational lines.

3. Summary

Labour communications and training are crucial for effective EH&S management in that they alert employees to management expectations and give them the necessary technical skills and procedures to achieve those expectations. Most respondents reported a high degree of involvement of workers in EH&S activities, and most corporations had elaborate procedures for ensuring that employees complied with management directives. Furthermore, most corporations had integrated health and safety responsibilities into employees' performance evaluation. Evaluation of performance based on an employee's health and safety record is an effective way of ensuring compliance with internal and external rules and guidelines.

The emphasis on labour-related activities was clearly in emergency and safety matters. Accidents, which can be extremely expensive for a corporation, often derive from human error at operating levels. Training and close supervision can minimize that liability. The health and safety procedures elaborated in the Benchmark Survey outline the direction for extended training on environmental issues.

One of the aims of Agenda 21 is to improve training and the raise awareness among employees in developing nations. The Benchmark Survey findings show that only a few corporations referred specifically to training of employees in overseas facilities, particularly to those in developing countries. As discussed in chapter III, some corporations had safety workshops and seminars for employees at home as well as abroad. Others reported that they dispatched specialists and consultants to developing nations in order to ensure compliance with health and safety regulations.

Utilizing information technology to improve awareness in overseas plants could contribute significantly to the level of EH&S management in developing nations, with relatively small costs for the corporation. Unfortunately, only a few corporations reported that they had international databases and clearing-houses with easily accessible information on EH&S matters.

Notes

[1] In response to a request by the Intergovernmental Working Group of Experts on International Standards of Accounting and Reporting (ISAR), UNCTC undertook two environmental accounting surveys in 1989 and 1990. The results suggested that "the accounting for environmental expenses was feasible". The study also noted that (a) despite the heightened awareness, the consideration of environmental issues in annual reports was not widespread, and (b) the absence of accounting standards allowed enterprises wide discretion in what they reported and led to a lack of consistency even within the same corporation. See "Accounting for environmental protection measures" (E/C.10/AC.3/1991/5) and "Information disclosure relating to environmental measures" (E/C.10/AC.3/1990/5).

[2] A 1982 survey conducted by the United States' Chemical Manufactures Association found that 93 per cent of the responding companies conducted environmental audits (CMA, 1983).

[3] Kellogg Company, "Corporate quality statement".

[4] Noranda Inc., "Environmental auditing: A key element of modern environmental management system", statement by Dr. Frank Frantisak, Vice President, Environmental Services, October 1989 pp. 6-7.

[5] A recent study of United States TNCs by Deloitte-Touche reported only a 20 per cent usage of "green" labelling (Deloitte & Touche, 1991).

[6] UNDESD/TCMD, "Report of the Intergovernmental Working Group of Experts on International Standards of Accounting and Reporting on its tenth session" (E/C.10/1992/12).

[7] *Financial Times*, 16 September 1992.

[8] "Corporatism" is a term often used in the political science literature to describe political systems where the major organized interests such as business and labour are directly incorporated in policy-making and policy implementation. This decision-making style is, according to the literature, common in several European countries, particularly the Scandinavian countries and Germany. In contrast, interest groups in the United States are often described as "pressure groups" far less integrated in political decision-making and policy implementation. Valid explanations for the differences in decision-making and

policy implementation styles in European and United States environmental politics can be found in Lundquist, 1982, and Vogel, 1986.

⁹ Amoco Corporation, *Span: For the future of our planet.* Number 3, p. 19, 1990.

¹⁰ The Virginia refinery was chosen for the complexity of its process (typical of many other refineries), its manageable size for study purposes, its location in an environmentally sensitive area near Chesapeake Bay, and its proximity to Washington, D.C.

¹¹ Materials submitted by the firm in support of responses to the Benchmark Survey questionnaire.

¹² For example, a recent public opinion poll found that over three fourths of United States consumers expressed concern about the environmental impact of the products they purchased, and that they were influenced by the environmental image of the producer. Sixty-eight per cent responded that they would pay five to ten per cent more for environmentally acceptable products, (Michael Peters Group, 1990).

¹³ Pilko & Associates estimate, cited in Cahan and Smith, 1990.

¹⁴ Company's corporate policy, December 1987.

¹⁵ Arvin Industries, Inc., attachment 10 to question 23(a) on innovative environmental management practices.

The general impression from the analysis in Part One is that transnational corporations are responding to public and governmental pressures for improved corporate environmental performance. In all probability, some changes are largely superficial, initiated only for public relations purposes. But there are indications that in many corporations some level of environmental, and especially health and safety considerations, are being incorporated within corporate identities. Similarly, the linkages between EH&S and business objectives are beginning to be recognized. Overall, the analysis suggests that most corporations engage in a kind of environmental management in which short-term costs and liabilities are sought, anticipated, and prevented through environmental-management procedures. Thus, activities such as audits, safety procedures, waste and recycling policies, and energy-saving programmes are well established among the responding corporations. Apparently, the majority of the respondents subscribe to 3M's slogan, "Pollution Prevention Pays". However, more diffuse pollution conditions, such as air, noise, land or water pollution, are less frequently addressed than issues that affect health and safety, and/or involve immediate savings. Perhaps pollution prevention pays less in those areas.

> **Box V.1. 3M's 3Ps**
>
> 3M's "pollution prevention pays" (3P), dates back to 1975, and since then more than 3000 projects to prevent pollution at the source have been undertaken. 3M estimates that it has saved $537 million as a result of 3P, and cut pollution in half per unit (*Business International*, 1992 p. 145).

Some corporations still had not established the most basic procedures for managing their environmental impacts. One quarter of the respondents had no environmental policies and programmes, and often the respondents reported that they did not have information about their EH&S activities or impacts. International guidelines were rarely observed, even though most corporations found international harmonization of environmental standards important. Moreover, less than one third of the respondents utilized relatively inexpensive means of confidence-building, such as disclosure of hazards and risks.

There was little indication that the responding corporations had undertaken genuine sustainable development activities. In relation to developing countries, only a handful had specific accounts of their responsibilities in developing nations, such as policies pledging to employ the same EH&S standards globally or special training programmes for employees in developing nations. The corporate community seemed to be slightly more engaged in activities related to the global commons such as oceans, the rainforest, or biodiversity. Although, in general, few corporations had policies and programmes in those areas, close to one third of the respondents had activities aimed at greenhouse gas reduction and afforestation.

The relatively low level of sustainable development activities suggests that the corporate community has only just started considering its role in sustainable development and that a huge gap exists between the international community's expectations, as expressed in Agenda 21, and the actual state of corporate environmental management in that regard.

One of the most striking findings of Part One is that management practices vary significantly among corporations. Which management path a particular corporation chooses seems to depend on a variety of factors.

Dynamic leadership and direct involvement from the board of directors is no doubt important. Strong leaders in the field of EH&S management, such as Shell, DuPont, or Apple Computer, have a history of hands-on involvement from their boards of directors, and environmentally engaged top executives such as Edgar Woolard of DuPont, Bob Kennedy of Union Carbide or Allen Jacobsen of 3M are well known outside business circles. But

> ### Box V.2. Green CEOs
>
> "We in the industry have to develop a stronger awareness of our selves as environmentalists. I am personally aware that as Du Pont's chief executive, I am also Du Pont's chief environmentalist." (Edgar Woolard, CEO of DuPont).

often factors other than management leadership determine the level of corporate EH&S management. The Benchmark Survey points towards at least three such factors.

First, the corporation's line of business is an important factor. The extractive-based sector, which consists of the chemical and oil industries, is inclined to be ahead in its environmental policies and programmes, probably due to the extremely costly accidents in terms of money and loss of public confidence that occurred in the eighties. That sector appears to have engaged in a collective learning process in the wake of those accidents.

Apart from the chemical and oil industries, corporations in the computer industry and the pharmaceutical industry seem to be significantly more innovative than those in other industries. The explanation probably is that new and more dynamic industries often will have the resources to invest in long-term environmental programmes. It might be more cost-effective to do so because environmental concerns can be taken into consideration at an early stage in the planning of production. Consequently, newer and more dynamic industries are more likely to have total quality, cradle-to-grave programmes than older ones, which tend to concentrate on end-of-pipe solutions and compliance. On the other hand, companies in sunset, crises-ridden industries have few resources to invest in long-term environmental programmes. Also, the costs of incorporating environmental concerns into older industries with already established infrastructures might be much higher than those in newer industries.

Second, the Survey results indicate that larger corporations (roughly defined by annual sales) are ahead of smaller corporations in terms of EH&S management. Economies of scale make it easier for the large corporation to develop comprehensive environmental programmes and policies and to allocate resources for R&D in EH&S improvements. It is more likely that larger corporations can afford to have a separate environment office and/or an officer of the board designated to work with EH&S issues. Moreover, the larger the corporation, the larger the stakes if environmental disasters should occur. The large corporation simply can not afford to rely on informal methods to keep management informed on EH&S issues. On the other hand, EH&S responsibilities in smaller corporations tend to be less formalized, more decentralized, and smaller corporations tend to concentrate on compliance, the minimal requirement, and on preventive management, to the extent that it pays in the short run, because they cannot afford to allocate considerable amounts of resources to those tasks. The clear positive relationship between the size of the corporation and the scope and content of environmental activities suggests that environmental management is even less developed in small and medium-sized corporations which did not take part in the survey.

Finally, the Benchmark Survey clearly shows that there is a close relationship between EH&S management and the home country of the corporation. Thus the scope and content of environmental practices in corporations varies significantly among regions and countries. It was found that EH&S practices in developing nations depend on the home region of the corporation. Regional variances could indicate that particular cultural factors affect the way in which corporations organize EH&S management. Japanese corporate culture, particularly, is often described as significantly different from United States and European corporate cultures. More probably the nature of the regulatory environment in the home country of the corporation explains variations between regions in the nature of EH&S management practices. The tendency of Asian corporations to view EH&S activities as a business opportunity could be related to the fact that Japanese EH&S policy is formulated to a large extent by the Ministry for International Trade and Industry and not the Environmental Agency. The relatively low utilization of EH&S policies and practices in Europe is probably related to the fact that European environmental regulation tends to rest on administrative enforcement and cooperation between industries. On the other hand, United States environmental regulation has traditionally been described as adversarial and aggressive and that, in turn, seems to have encouraged TNCs to establish EH&S procedures to minimize liabilities.

The finding of a close relationship between the regulatory environment of a corporation and its EH&S practices will provide the basis for the analysis in Part Three of ways in which corporations, encouraged by governments and international organizations, can integrate sustainable development objectives to decision-making.

PART TWO

PART TWO: CORPORATE MANAGEMENT IN SPECIFIC AREAS OF ENVIRONMENTAL PROTECTION

Apart from generic management issues, the Benchmark Survey has provided considerable insight into many of the specific pollution procedures addressed at UNCED. The major pollution problems discussed at the conference cover more than twenty different issues, and can be grouped under three essential themes, as set forth below.

One theme discussed at UNCED was the responsible and fair management of the global commons, that is, the atmosphere, the oceans, the coastal areas and the living marine resources. There TNCs play a particularly vital role because of the transnational nature of their activities. Often TNCs are in the best situation to exploit those resources, as well as to provide the means of minimizing and managing adverse impacts on the global commons.

A second wide-ranging theme discussed at UNCED was the efficient use of resources. The discussion focused on the urgent need to reverse the destruction of renewable resources and to implement strategies for the sustainable use of land, freshwater, biological and genetic resources, biotechnology and energy. A substantial part of those resources is in the province of TNCs. The way TNCs choose to exploit them in the future will significantly alter the environment as well as the development process in many developing countries.

A third theme addressed at UNCED was the question of how to manage toxic chemicals and hazardous waste. The fact that TNCs, especially corporations in the chemical and manufacturing sectors, generated some of the most dangerous wastes, made it that much more important for the Benchmark Survey to focus on this area. TNC engagement in waste-generation, recycling of wastes, and safe disposal practices is crucial not only to short-term EH&S considerations but to the achievement of sustainable development goals.

The Benchmark Survey chose to focus on seven issues representative of each of those three themes, issues considered to be of particular relevance to TNCs. They are protection of the atmosphere; environmentally sound management of toxic chemicals and hazardous waste; protection of freshwater resources; protection and management of land resources; protection of the ocean; environmentally sound management of biotechnology; and conservation of biodiversity.

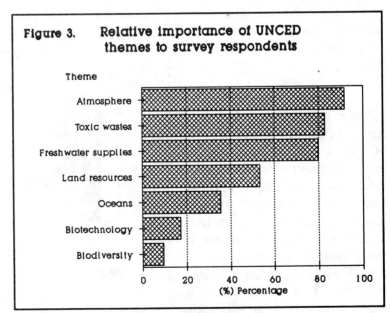

Figure 3. Relative importance of UNCED themes to survey respondents

Source: TCMD/DESD Benchmark Survey, 1990-91.

The Benchmark Survey asked TNCs to rank those seven different UNCED issues in order of importance. As figure 3 shows, 92 per cent of the respondents found the discussion of atmospheric problems important, closely followed by toxic waste issues and freshwater issues. Slightly half the respondents considered land resources an important issue, one third considered issues related to oceans and coastal areas important, and less than one fifth of the respondents found issues such as biotechnology, and biodiversity important.

The corporate ranking of the UNCED themes probably reflects the primary concerns of corporations with regard to their own operations. Air pollution has become one of the most contentious and costly issues for corporations in recent years. Toxic waste issues have also been prominent on the corporate agenda for decades, due to the considerable damage in the form of compensation and insurance costs that a company can incur if it fails to meet social expectations in that area. In many parts of the world, supplies of freshwater are becoming scarce, and, increasingly, fees are being introduced to limit water consumption and wastewater emissions. Thus, there will often be a positive pay-off for the corporation in conserving water resources.

On the other hand, few corporations engage in biotechnology projects, and the relationship between biodiversity and corporate activities may seem minor, except in a few cases where a corporation controls vast natural resources like forests or agricultural land. The same can be said about oceans, where only a few corporations have a direct impact. Therefore it is not surprising that those issues are low on the corporate agenda.

Corporations in the agricultural products processing sector, which include pharmaceutical corporations, attached significantly more importance to conservation of biodiversity and management of biotechnology than do other sectors. Corporations in the heavily polluting extractive and finished-goods sector attached relatively more importance to the issue of environmentally sound management of toxic wastes (see annex table D.10).

Different regions reveal different priorities (see figure 4). Asian (Japanese) respondents gave priority to atmosphere-related issues, European respondents to toxic waste issues, and North American corporations to freshwater issues. It also seems that land issues have considerably more importance in North America than in Europe and Asia. The regional differences probably reflect different historical experiences as well as differences in current business conditions.

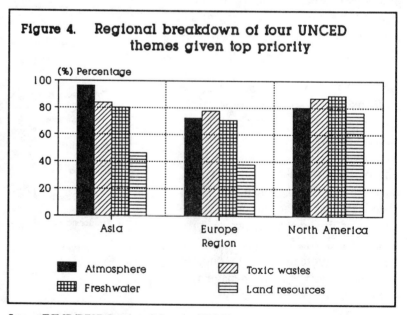

Figure 4. Regional breakdown of four UNCED themes given top priority

Source: TCMD/DESD Benchmark Survey, 1990-91.

The subsequent chapters will analyse corporate activities in relation to the seven selected UNCED issue areas and provide some explanation as to why corporations in different regions have different priorities.

Atmospheric issues are of pivotal importance to the responding corporations. Reasons why corporations appear more concerned about atmospheric protection than any other UNCED issue are: (a) Air quality and atmospheric protection are areas highly regulated by most governments. The United States Clean Air Act is one of the most comprehensive and costly environmental regulations in the world, and international discussions on ozone depletion and climate change have signaled to the corporate community that the future will see further initiatives in that field; (b) The quality of the air is a tangible issue for most people, and public awareness is high in that area; (c) Historically, air-pollution legislation has been given priority attention by governments; and (d) Ozone protection ranks high on the international agenda.

Agenda 21:

"Formulating...appropriate objectives or policies relating to energy production and consumption in order to improve energy efficiency..." (9.9h).

"Establish or enhance...labelling programmes for products to provide decision-makers and consumers with information on opportunities for energy efficiency" (9.49k).

"Increase and strengthen...capacity to develop products and processes that are more energy efficient, safe and environmentally sound" (9.15a).

"...contribute...towards ongoing efforts under the Montreal Protocol and its implementing mechanisms, including making available substitutes for CFCs and other ozone depleting substances and facilitating the transfer of the corresponding technologies to developing countries..." (9.21a).

Air-pollution issues have regained attention in recent years as scientific evidence has indicated potentially disruptive developments in the global climate. Anthropogenic activities, which result in the release of carbon dioxide, chlorofluorocarbons and other chemicals into the atmosphere, threaten to change the earth's climate and damage the protective stratospheric ozone shield.[1] Industrial activities are closely associated with the chemicals involved in ozone depletion and greenhouse gas emissions. Hence, the Benchmark Survey examines atmospheric concerns.

By sheer volume, carbon dioxide, produced principally by the combustion of fossil fuels, is the most important of greenhouse gases. It is responsible for about 50 per cent of the global warming problem. CFCs, however, also contribute to at least 15 per cent of the global warming. This is because the greenhouse effect of these compounds per molecule, relative to carbon dioxide, equals several hundred to 20,000, depending on the compound. That effect is compounded by the fact that their lifetime is 100 years or more.[2] Moreover, CFCs and halons deplete the earth's ozone layer. Other greenhouse gases such as nitrous oxides (NO_x), sulphur dioxides (SO_2), methane (CH_4) and tropospheric ozone (O_3), the cause of acid rain and of smog in the cities, also result from the production and use of fossil fuels.

Approximately 50 per cent of all greenhouse gas emissions can be traced directly or indirectly to transnational corporations. That amount includes about half of the oil-production business, virtually all the production of road vehicles in the industrialized world, most CFC production, and significant portions of electricity generation and use.[3]

In addition to the impact on the global climate, a number of chemical substances such as asbestos, dioxins, polychlorinated biphenyls (PCBs) and volatile organic compounds (VOCs) produced and used by TNCs, when emitted into the atmosphere, can pose serious health problems because of their toxicity. Those substances can also contaminate land or water.

At UNCED, climate change may have received the most attention. The international community adopted a convention on climate change inspired by the Montreal Protocol in order to tackle the problem in a comprehensive and equitable manner. The convention made commitments on issues such as greenhouse-gas reductions and maintaining carbon sinks, but the issue of financing the required transition in developing countries was not resolved. In addition to the convention, Agenda 21 addresses climate change problems in a separate chapter (9), which deals with, among other things, sustainable transport and industrial strategies, sustainable energy development, sustainable land use, ozone depletion, and securing the scientific basis for decision-making on those issues.

A. STATISTICAL FINDINGS

1. Ozone-depleting activities

As seen in figure VI.1, a large number of respondents to the Benchmark Survey participated in activities which involve products or processes generating greenhouse gases, ozone-depleting gases and high-hazard pollutants principally in the automotive, chemical, metal, oil and gas, and paper industries.

Three quarters of the firms in the finished-goods sector, which included the automotive, electrical, electronics, machinery and metal products industries, used CFCs and related compounds in their manufacturing processes. Forty per cent stated that they manufactured products containing CFCs. (See annex table D.11.) A similar trend appeared

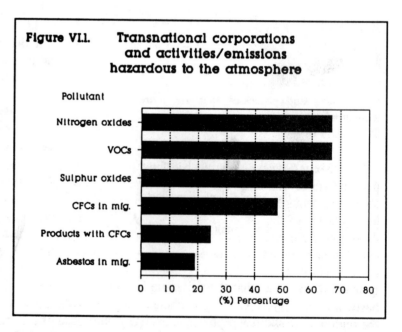

Figure VI.1.   Transnational corporations and activities/emissions hazardous to the atmosphere

Source: TCMD/DESD Benchmark Survey, 1990-91.

among all respondents. Twice as many firms reported using CFCs in manufacturing processes as those firms selling products containing such chemicals. That may imply that perhaps it is easier to substitute the CFCs used in certain products, but not in the manufacturing process. It should be pointed out that the electronics sector, particularly, had made impressive progress in eliminating CFC use in the cleaning of components.

The extent of CFCs usage nonetheless raises the following question: will the production and use of CFCs be phased out internationally by the year 2000, the target date of the Montreal Protocol? CFCs remain for a long time in the stratosphere, so that even after the chemical is phased out, ozone damage will occur for most of the next century.

The Asia-based (Japan) respondents were more likely to use CFCs in their manufacturing process than either the Europe-based or the North America-based firms. Eighty-seven percent of the Japanese firms that did so were in the finished-goods sector.

2. Transboundary pollution

Sulphur dioxide and nitrogen oxide emissions from industrial and mining activities cause acid rain. The combustion of fossil fuel in urban areas, mainly from transportation and industrial activities, is also responsible for the formation of those and other pollutants such as ground-level ozone. The environmental damage caused by transboundary air pollution is abundantly documented in Europe and North America. The European and North American regions are the only areas for which reliable time-series data and computer calculations on the transfrontier dispersion of air pollutants exist.[4]

Europe and North America are also the only two regions where formal regional agreements for air pollution control and reduction exist. The 1979 Economic Commission for Europe (ECE) Convention on Long-Range Transboundary Air Pollution (in force since 1983) has been ratified by 31 states and the European Community. The Convention has been supplemented by a 1985 protocol on the reduction of sulphur emissions or their transboundary fluxes by at least 30 per cent (ratified by 30 parties and in force since 1987); and a 1988 protocol concerning the control of emissions of nitrogen oxides or their transboundary fluxes (ratified by 18 parties and in force since 1991). A further protocol on the control of volatile organic compounds and their transboundary fluxes was signed in November 1991.[5]

Sixty per cent of the respondents to the Benchmark Survey stated that they emitted SO_2, and 67 per cent stated that they emitted NO_x. Those numbers are quite high considering the level of awareness about the damage already suffered due to acid rain and urban smog in the regions where the corporate headquarters of the respondents are located. Alternatively, the results may indicate the degree to which those gases are endemic to modern manufacturing processes. Volatile organic compounds (VOC) were also found to be emitted by 67 per cent of the respondents. The Asia-based (Japan) respondents were more likely to emit SO_2 and NO_x than the Europe- and North America-based firms. In both cases, three quarters of the Japan-based respondents reported emitting those gases. Roughly 50 per cent of Europe-based and North America-based firms emitted SO_2 and 60 per cent emitted NO_x. In the case of VOCs, the regional breakdown was equally divided. (See annex table D.11.) A likely explanation for the regional difference in industrial emissions could be the existence of the Convention and its attendant Protocols.[6] By becoming a party to an international protocol, a state commits itself to adhere to the protocol's terms which, in those cases, may have resulted in lower emissions by both Europe- and North America-based respondents.

3. High hazard pollutants

Asbestos has been considered a carcinogen since the early 1970s. It becomes a health hazard when its fibers become airborne and are inhaled. Inhaling asbestos fibers can result in asbestosis, a crippling lung disease, as well as in various forms of cancer. Asbestos has been used extensively for insulation, noise reduction and fire retardation.

Despite the common knowledge of asbestos' carcinogenic nature, 19 per cent of the respondents to the Benchmark Survey indicated that they used asbestos in manufacturing. The regional breakdown showed the Europe-based respondents as less likely to use asbestos than their North American and Japanese counterparts. A likely explanation for the smaller number of European firms using asbestos could be the existence of European Community Directives laying down provisions on asbestos removal and worker protection in industrial plants.[7] In the United States on the other hand, the 1986 Asbestos Hazard Emergency Response Act mandated asbestos removal or management only in public schools. Among industrial sectors, as expected, the finished-goods and extractive-based sectors were the most likely to use asbestos, and firms in the top third were twice as likely as those in the bottom third to use asbestos in manufacturing (see annex table D.11).

4. Policies and programmes

Atmospheric protection was cited more frequently as a top corporate concern than any other environmental issue. That concern was demonstrated, in varying degrees, by having in place policies and programmes on air pollution, on reduction of generating greenhouse gases and energy efficiency.

Forty-seven per cent of the respondents stated that they had corporate-wide policies on air quality or pollution beyond those required by national legislation. The Asia-based firms were more likely to have such policies, 66 per cent, compared to 47 per cent and 29 per cent, respectively, for the North America- and Europe-based firms. The extractive-based and finished-goods sectors led the other sectors with 60 and 56 per cent of positive responses, respectively (see annex table D.12). Concern with air quality policies was associated with the emissions resulting from industrial operations in those sectors.

Policies reducing greenhouse-gas generation which go beyond national legislation, however, do not appear to be have received the same corporate attention. This may be due to the fact that greenhouse-gas generation reduction policies were more specific and had not been as formalized as those for air quality. In general, 30 per cent of the respondents had greenhouse-gas reduction policies, another quarter found them to be inapplicable to the firm's operations. Again the Asia-based respondents led having these policies, 42 per cent compared to 27 and 22 per cent for the North America- and Europe-based firms respectively. As with policies on air quality and pollution, the extractive-based and finished-goods sectors led with 41 and 37 per cent, respectively.

that it had implemented numerous changes to replace the use of chlorinated hydrocarbons from its manufacturing processes. In the few remaining processes where chlorinated hydrocarbons were still used, the company had lowered emissions by using special recovery measures, such as absorption on activated charcoal.

Company Y intended to notify all suppliers that the company expected compliance with the Montreal Protocol in order to end the use of CFCs in manufacturing and packaging, and was supporting efforts to strengthen the protocol. This last caveat in the company's policy on CFCs, aimed at influencing other, presumably smaller, companies to comply with the protocol, followed those of other leading environmental firms, demonstrating their commitment to their own goals.

Company T reported that its goals included to phasing out, then eliminating the use of CFCs and related chemicals in its manufacturing, repair and facilities operations. Among the stated reasons for the phase-out were: (a) the anticipation of restrictive regulatory tax measures that could adversely affect the company's operations; and (b) concern about stockholder perception of the company as an environmentally responsible business.[8] In its policy manual, the company defined as ozone-depleting chemicals (ODCs) any substance specified in the Montreal Protocol Agreement or designated as an ODC by a country, state, provincial, or local government, or otherwise regulated as an ODC. To ensure the implementation of that policy, the company asks its business units not to purchase, procure, or otherwise obtain equipment that uses or depends upon ODCs for its operation unless they can demonstrate clearly that there are no alternative technologies available. This is yet another example of a corporation trying to influence the environmental practices of other business concerns through its own policies. Each local business unit that uses any ODC will designate a "local program owner" to be responsible for establishing phase-out goals consistent with corporate goals, as well as for developing strategic plans, and to ensure the timely implementation of such plans.

As the examples from the above policy statements demonstrate, the phasing out and elimination of CFCs and related ozone-depleting chemicals are progressing in a number of leading firms. All but one of the sample policies from CFCs users indicate that the effort by the responding firms in phasing out CFCs goes towards the process rather than the product. That supports the statistical finding that more firms are still more likely to use CFCs in their processes than in their products and are therefore more apt to concentrate their efforts in the former direction rather than in the latter.

2. Emissions related to fossil fuels

Unlike the examples regarding CFCs, the reduction of CO_2 emissions is not among the stated policies for greenhouse-gas reduction or protection of the atmosphere in general noted by the respondents to the Benchmark Survey. General protection of the atmosphere, reduction of NO_x and SO_2 emissions, and the increase in energy efficiency are more likely to be stated explicitly. One possibility for the lack of explicit policies on CO_2 emissions may be the lack of government regulation on CO_2 emissions such as those on air pollution or on pollutants contributing to the creation of acid rain. Moreover, there is not as yet an international agreement to reduce or stabilize CO_2 emissions such as the Montreal Protocol on CFCs or the protocols on the reduction of NO_x and SO_2.

It is encouraging, however, that a larger number of respondents, 39 per cent, undertook environmentally-oriented research and development programmes for the reduction of greenhouse-gas generation. The Europe-based firms led (43 per cent) in such programmes implying that action in this area was ahead of policy formulation.

Programmes for the conservation of energy supplies were given importance by the majority of the respondents; 54 per cent of the respondents stated that they had such programmes. Economic considerations may be the driving force for having such programmes. The regional distribution of having such programmes, however, appeared quite

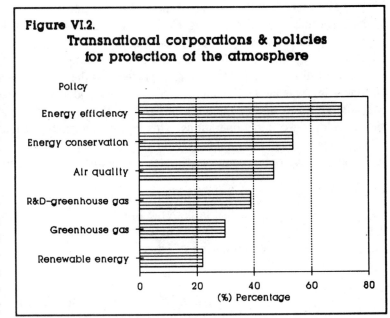

Figure VI.2.

Transnational corporations & policies for protection of the atmosphere

Source: TCMD/DESD Benchmark Survey, 1990-91.

uneven. Over three quarters of the North America-based firms had such programmes compared to slightly more than half of the Asia- (Japan) and Europe-based firms.

As a rule, the top third firms with regard to sales were more likely to have policies and programmes in place for air quality, greenhouse-gas reduction and energy conservation. Similarly, the smaller firms, (size being relative, since all the respondents reported annual sales over $1 billion) were found to be either less likely to have such policies and programmes or to have found them inapplicable to their operations.

5. Sustainable development programmes

Renewable energy sources such as solar, photovoltaic and wind energy were being utilized by over one fifth of the respondents. That usage demonstrated that some firms were already taking a long-term view with regard to energy use. The finished-goods and extractive-based sectors, possibly because of their usually high energy requirements, led in the use of such renewable resources. Firms in the top third by sales were more likely to use renewable energy resources.

Almost three quarters of the respondents had undertaken research and development for energy efficiency production methods. All three regions appeared to be attentive to the matter, with the Europe-based firms slightly behind the Japan-based and North America-based respondents. As with the programmes for renewable energy sources, research and development for energy efficiency were undertaken mainly by the extractive-based and finished-goods sectors. Again, firms in the top third by sales were more likely to undertake such research and development (see annex table D.13).

The picture with regard to practices in developing countries was rather mixed. Twenty per cent of the respondents reported using CFCs or related products in developing countries. (See annex table D.14.) As with previous questions regarding the use of CFCs, the finished-goods sector was ahead of the other sectors in such use. When it came to monitoring air emissions in developing countries, however, only about a third of the respondents reported that they monitored, and an equal number did not. More disconcerting was the fact that a quarter of the respondents indicated that they did not have sufficient data at headquarters to answer the question, and another 13 per cent did not know whether CFCs are used in their developing-country operations. This lack of information could be related to the decentralized nature of the respondents' operations. Given the heightened sensitivity with regard to ozone depletion or accidents in developing-country affiliates, those answers gave cause for concern.

The firms in the top third by sales led in reducing both CFC use and air-emission practices. That may be related to the fact that in both the finished-goods and extractive-based sectors more of the larger firms answered in the affirmative. These sectors were more likely to use CFCs and to have operations which required closer monitoring of emissions.

B. EXAMPLES OF CORPORATE RESPONSES TO PROTECTION OF THE ATMOSPHERE

Protection of the atmosphere encompasses activities aimed at controlling emissions of greenhouse gases, ozone-depleting chemicals and transboundary pollutants. For some of the respondents to the Benchmark Survey, commitment to such activities could be inferred from general environmental policy statements. For others, explicit reference was made to one or more of those issues, sometimes accompanied by descriptions of specific processes, products, or operational initiatives which had a direct impact on climate change.

1. CFCs and related chemicals

With regard to policies for the reduction of greenhouse-gas emissions, in most cases the respondents referred to general corporate environmental policy as a demonstration of concern with the climate change problem. There were are more explicit policies, however, for the phase out and elimination of CFCs and other ozone-depleting chemicals and for dealing with transboundary pollutants.

The signing and implementation of the Montreal Protocol has had a catalytic effect on the efforts by industry to phase out and eventually eliminate ozone-depleting CFCs and related chemicals. Efforts have been undertaken both by CFC producers and CFC users, although, with one exception, the examples of policies on phasing out CFCs provided by CFC users. Box VI.1 contains some samples of corporate goals for phasing out CFCs in manufacturing processes.

Imperial Chemical Industries (ICI) plc was one of the leading CFC manufacturers which responded to the Benchmark Survey with specific information on the phasing out of CFC and the corporation's replacement programme. ICI indicated that it was in the forefront in developing alternatives to CFCs and had committed £100 million to identifying and commercializing suitable compounds. **ICI**

Box VI.1. Corporations and ozone-depleting chemicals

Company Y has as a major corporate target:
- Elimination of CFC usage from cleaning electronic assemblies by 1992.
- End use of CFC in manufacturing and packaging by 1993.

Deere & Company has set three goals in its CFC reduction policy:
- Reduce chlorinated solvents by 90 per cent by the end of 1991 using 1985 as a base
- Eliminate CFC use except for closed systems by November 1990.
- Capture and recycle CFC in production and maintenance by January 1991.

Company T has established a Corporate ODC Working Group with the following prog
- Phase out the use of ODC in printed circuit board manufacturing by the end of 1993
- Phase out the use of ODC in all manufacturing by the end of 1995.
- Phase out the use of ODC in CSD operations by the end of 1993.
- Eliminate the use of CFC foam packaging by the end of 1992 and the use of HCFC fo the end of 1994.

Company X will eliminate the use of ODC from all products and manufacturing process follows:
- CFCs by the end of 1990.
- Carbon tetrachloride by the end of 1991.
- Methyl chloroform by the end of 1992.

Toyota Motor Corporation has set the following goal for new vehicles:
- Place air conditioners containing HFC-134a refrigerant by 1994.
- Start conversion process for refrigerant in 1992.
- Provide service centers world-wide with recovery/recharge equipment to prevent CF atmosphere by 1991.

Westinghouse Electric Corporation intends to:
- Phase out CFCs by the year 2000.
- Phase out methyl chloroform by the year 2002.
- Phase out HCFCs by the year 2030. Ban their use in aerosols and insulating materials
- Require certification of technicians to capture and reuse CFCs in servicing by 1 Janu

Source: TCMD/DESD Benchmark Survey 1990-91; see annex D for corporate profiles.

---

had developed KLEA 134a, a refrigerant to substitute for CFC 12 in refriger automobile air-conditioners and was considering other chemicals for replacement manufacture of insulating foams. ICI indicated that KLEA 134a would be at least five as CFC 12 and warned that such costs might well be reflected in higher prices for t

Amoco indicated that Amoco Foam Products Company had recently becom insulation manufacturer to completely eliminate CFCs from its products. **Boehringe**

Among the Asia-based (Japan) respondents, none stated that it had plans aimed directly at the reduction of its CO_2 emissions into the atmosphere. Some, however reported plans to decrease emissions by decreasing fuel use; others were developing technologies for the recovery and fixation of carbon dioxide.

For example, **Company E** reported plans for a 20 per cent cut in the use of electricity and oil by March of 1994. **Toyota Motor Corporation's** "...efforts to prevent air pollution thus center around the use of top quality fuel, improving combustion methods, and measures directed at special equipment for processes and facilities".[9] With regard to CO_2 emissions, **Toyota** indicated that it had initiated a stringent energy conservation programme to complement the fuel policy and combustion improvement programme. **Toyota** also reported reducing CO_2 emission by "piggybacking processes: electricity is generated through the production process, waste heat is recovered and stored, and control system efficiency is continually improved". More specifically, in order to reduce emissions of SO_2 **Toyota** has promoted the use of low-sulfur fuel since 1971 and had lessened the average sulfur content of heavy oil from 2.5 per cent in the early 1970s to 0.5 per cent in 1978. In order to counter pollution from NO_x, **Toyota** stated it had improved combustion at the boilers where a relatively large volume of NO_x was generated. With respect to VOCs, **Toyota** stated: "In efforts to prevent air pollution, VOC has become a special emphasis. Painting work is the principal source of VOC, and we have developed water-based paints at Toyota to address this issue...Also, we are using a minibell system and other high efficiency techniques to minimize waste in paining..."[10] In addition, **Toyota** reported it was investing time and capital in developing vehicles that would run on new energy sources such as electric power and methanol.[11]

Company O indicated that it saw energy conservation as a way to avoid an increase in global warming, and was proceeding with research and development in two areas: improved automotive fuel economy and alternative energy sources. Furthermore, the company reported that it was continuing its efforts to reduce car emissions contributing to urban smog and to remove SO_2 from factory emissions where, over a period of 15 years, a reduction of more than 80 per cent had been achieved.

DAF N.V. and **Boehringer Ingelheim** demonstrated their concern with transboundary pollution, a cause of great concern in Europe, by developing systems to reduce emissions of NO_x, SO_2, CO_2 and particulates such as soot.

Broken Hill Proprietary (BHP) had prepared a submission to an inquiry by the Australian Senate Standing Committee on Industry, Science and Technology on reducing the impact of the greenhouse effect. Box VI.2 highlights excerpts from that submission, summarizing some of the actions **BHP** took. In that particular instance, the corporation was actively involved in the legislative process for two reasons: (a) to demonstrate its concern for a problem to which the company, as a major producer of fossil fuels and consumer of energy was contributing, and (b) to safeguard its competitive position against inefficient and low-quality producers.

Box VI.2. BHP and the greenhouse effect

BHP has already made significant progress in reducing greenhouse emissions mainly through its desire to reduce energy costs. There are in progress a significant number of programmes that will ensure further improvements both in terms of energy conservation and substitution of lowest impact fuels and reducing agents...

- ...BHP has commercialized a system for intrinsically safe detection of methane in mines which can be used in other applications...
- BHP operations have banned CFC based aerosols and have embarked on a programme of eliminating CFCs from existing and future operation...
- Many operations have energy conservation and waste minimisation programmes in hand...
- ...BHP has undertaken research work in support of a major programme at CSIRO on fuel cells, potentially the most efficient means known for conversion of fossil fuels into electricity...
- Major energy savings are made by casting steel as close as possible to the final shape in which it is to be used...
- Most BHP centers have major [tree planting/revegetation] programmes for site improvements, usually far exceeding statutory requirements.

Source: BHP, "Reducing the impact of greenhouse effect", submission to the inquiry by the Senate Standing Committee on Industry, Science and Technology, 26 June 1990, pp. 1, 5-6.

C. SUMMARY

In general, the respondents were responding actively to traditional transboundary air pollution issues such as SO_x and CO_2. The positive achievements of transboundary air pollution abatement might to a large extent be attributed to the advanced state of regional cooperation and the existence of regional agreements covering emissions that contribute to transboundary pollution.

Greenhouse-gas reduction policies did not have very high priority on the corporate agenda. More respondents indicated that they had general air quality policies than specific policies for greenhouse-gas generation reduction. That might be due to the fact that greenhouse-gas reduction policies had not been formalized as much as those concerning air quality. It could relate to the fact that climate change as such had not been addressed specifically by national legislation in most countries.

The phasing out and elimination of CFCs and ODCs, though, was an area where corporations had made progress. It seems that the corporate world, in the wake of the Montreal Protocol, had positioned itself in the forefront to phase out the production of ODCs. Similarly, it seems that the respondents were actively engaged in energy-related activities. Both issues have been and still are salient on the political agenda, and numerous national, regional and international programmes exist to address them. Clearly, public attention, political salience and regulatory action have been catalysts for corporate action.

In almost all programmes and policies on atmospheric protection, the smaller corporations, even those with a cut-off sales point of $1 billion, were found to be lagging behind. Surprisingly, that was the case even for programmes such as energy conservation which should be more economically appealing to smaller firms. That leads one to believe that this attitude must have been even more prevalent among small and medium-sized firms which were not represented in the Survey.

Notes

[1] UNCTC, *Climate Change and Transnational Corporations: Analysis and Trends*, (United Nations publication, Sales No. E.92.II.A.7), p. 1.

[2] Ibid., p. 39.

[3] Ibid., pp. 2-3.

[4] Preparatory Committee for the United Nations Conference on Environment and Development, "Protection of the atmosphere: transboundary air pollution" (A/Conf.151/PC/59, 28 June 1991), p. 2.

[5] Ibid., p. 6.

[6] It should be pointed out that SO_2 and No_x are emitted largely by public utilities and transport and only to a lesser degree by industry.

[7] Council Directives 83/477/EEC of 24 September 1983, 84/360/EEC of 16 July 1984 and 87/217/EEC of 19 March 1987.

[8] Material submitted in support of responses to the BMS questionnaire.

[9] Toyota Motor Corporation, "Toyota plant environmental measures, manufacturing facilities and environment department", 1990, p. 5.

[10] Toyota Motor Corporation, "Overview of environmental measures at Toyota, Preventing air pollution: voc countermeasures", Slide A-8.

[11] Ibid., slide A-14.

CHAPTER VII.   ENVIRONMENTALLY SOUND MANAGEMENT OF TOXIC CHEMICALS AND HAZARDOUS WASTE

Since the beginning of the present century, about 10 million chemical compounds have been synthesized in laboratories world-wide. Some chemicals, such as pesticides and fertilizers, are used directly. Most chemicals, however, are "base" or "intermediate" chemicals used for the manufacture of millions of end-products for human use.[1]

All chemicals are toxic to some degree. The health risk from any particular chemical is a function of toxicity and exposure. A health hazard can be created either after brief exposure to few parts per billion of a potentially toxic chemical or by extended exposure to high doses of another, less toxic compound. An important development of the past two decades has been the shift from a focus on the acute health effects of chemicals alone to a focus on the chronic health effects.

The carcinogenicity of many substances is hard to establish in the strict sense of the word. One reason is that many substances are not carcinogenic in themselves but can be transformed into carcinogens by living organisms. Other substances act as cancer promoters, meaning that they promote the growth of tumours. A problem with establishing the carcinogenicity of certain substances is the latency period between exposure and the appearance of clinical symptoms. Another problem is that a carcinogen may cause clinical symptoms of cancer only in the offspring of those exposed.

The highly polluted environment in which we live makes it difficult to establish epidemiologically which substances have caused a cancer, since the average person is exposed daily to a large number of known or suspected carcinogens. Another difficulty is that many carcinogens are harmful at levels so low that they are difficult to measure, or, as in the case of dioxin, can be measured only at a prohibitive cost.

Because toxic chemicals are released into the environment directly as a result of human application such as the use of pesticides, fertilizers and different solvents, and indirectly in waste streams from various human activities, such as mining, industrial processes, incineration, fuel combustion and other activities, that was another significant category for the Benchmark Survey to study.

Chemicals can be released in solid, liquid or gaseous form into the air, water and land. Wastes having metallic compounds, halogenated organic solvents, organo-halogen compounds, acids, asbestos, organo-phosphorus compounds, organic cyanide, phenols, or ethers as constituents, are considered hazardous. Most hazardous wastes are produced by industry, although a small quantity is generated by other means. In 1987, United States industry alone generated 275 million tons of hazardous waste.[2] In the United States, 79 per cent of hazardous wastes consists of chemicals such as plastics, paints and solvents. In the developed countries of Europe, the main wastes include solvents, waste paint, heavy metals, acids and oily wastes.[3]

The international community has made progress in recent years towards controlling the international movement of toxic chemicals and hazardous wastes. The FAO Code of Conduct on the Distribution and Use of Pesticides, and the London Guidelines for the Exchange of Information on Chemicals in International Trade, which govern the joint responsibility in the use of pesticides and the

> **Agenda 21:**
>
> "apply a "responsible care" approach to chemical products, taking into account the total life cycle of such products" (19.51b and 20.18d);
>
> "phase out, where appropriate, and dispose of any banned chemicals that are still in stock or in use in an environmentally sound manner" (19.53j);
>
> "be transparent in their operations and provide relevant information to the community that might be affected by the generation and management of hazardous waste" (20.14f);
>
> "make available to Governments the information necessary to maintain inventories of hazardous wastes, treatment/disposal sites, contaminated sites that require rehabilitation, and related information on exposure and risks" (20.23a);
>
> "conduct environmental audits of existing industries to improve in-plant regimes for the management of hazardous wastes" (20.23g and 20.32h);
>
> "develop an internationally agreed upon code of principles for the management of trade in chemicals" (19.51a).

comprehensive exchange of information on all chemicals, have recently been strengthened with provisions for prior informed consent.

The trend extends to developing countries. The 1991 Bamako Convention on the Ban of the Import into Africa and the Control of Transboundary Movement and Management of Hazardous Wastes within Africa was adopted in an effort to stop the export of hazardous waste to Africa. The Bamako Convention is a response to the Basel Convention on the Control of Transboundary Movement of Hazardous Wastes, which, while it includes a procedure for prior informed consent by the importing party, is seen by many developing countries as failing to address the problem of the export of hazardous wastes to developing countries. In addition, the Basel Convention does not address the problem of export of radioactive waste. The Lomé IV Convention between the European Economic Community (EEC) and the African, Pacific and Caribbean (APC) countries bans export of toxic and radioactive wastes from the EEC to the APC countries.

At UNCED issues related to hazardous and toxic products and process received widespread attention. In two chapters of Agenda 21, one on toxic chemicals and one on hazardous wastes, UNCED addressed two of the most publicized environmental problems in the post-Bhopal era. UNCED concluded that international activities needed to be strengthened to adequately support programmes for risk management of toxic chemicals in member states through out the world. This implies improved programmes for chemical risk assessments, cooperation to harmonize chemical classification and labelling, and improved information exchange between countries. Furthermore, the conference made a series of recommendations to prevent and minimize hazardous waste, to improve international waste management, and to promote cooperation in the management of transboundary movements of hazardous wastes.

A. STATISTICAL FINDINGS

Forty-four per cent of the respondents to the Benchmark Survey stated that they used known carcinogens (other than asbestos) in their manufacturing processes. Among the North America-based respondents, 60 per cent did so, while the Asia- and Europe-based were less likely to use such substances

(36 per cent of the responding firms in each of the latter regions). Two thirds of the firms in the extractive-based sector, where chemical firms have been classified, use carcinogens in manufacturing, followed by firms in the finished-goods sector. (See annex table D.15.) Polychlorinated biphenyls (PCBs), mainly found in electrical transformers, are highly toxic and are especially dangerous in a fire, when they may disperse into the environment and produce highly poisonous combustion products such as dioxin and furans.[4] According to the United States Senate Subcommittee on Superfund and Environmental Oversight, "...only thermal destruction at extremely high temperatures and exposure to ozone appear to be viable methods of PCB destruction".[5] When incinerated, PCBs enter the atmosphere. In 1976, the EEC and the United States enacted legislation banning PCBs manufacture and use.

Dioxin is an industrial by-product, particularly of paper-pulp mills, hazardous waste incinerators and municipal incinerators. Dioxin is never manufactured deliberately but occurs as the inevitable by-product of a number of products and processes involving chlorinated phenols. Dioxin is considered carcinogenic, and its release to the air, soil or water has been associated with increased rates of cancer and birth defects. Workers can be exposed to dioxin during chemical operations, particularly during the manufacture of herbicides, and especially in the absence of suitable emission controls, or as a result of explosions. Studies have shown that exposure to dioxin at the workplace can cause some specific forms of cancer.[6]

About one third of the respondents to the Benchmark Survey stated that its processes involved PCBs, and a much lower percentage (14 per cent) stated that it emitted dioxin. North America-based firms were more likely to emit PCBs (52 per cent) than Europe-based (25 per cent) and Asia-based firms (13 per cent), although all three regions had stringent regulations regarding PCBs emissions. The regional distribution with regard to the emissions of dioxin shows all three regions with much lower emission levels. (See annex table D.15.)

Disposing of radioactive waste is the biggest problem facing the civilian nuclear power industry. After 50 years of costly research, a permanent and safe way to dispose of radioactive waste has yet to be found.[7] Although nuclear facilities produce the largest amount of radioactive waste, industry also produces some.

Twenty-one per cent of the responding firms stated that they emitted radioactive wastes, with North America-based firms three times as likely to do so as the Europe-based firms. One third of the firms in the extractive-based sector stated that they produced radioactive waste.

Disposal of waste outside the country of origin was not a widespread occurrence among the Survey participants. Only 14 per cent of the respondents reported such disposal. North America-based firms, however, were more likely to dispose of waste outside the country of origin. In fact, the trend in the United States towards exporting waste has been heading upwards. Notifications of intent to export hazardous waste filed with the EPA increased from 12 in 1980 to 626 in 1989.[8]

According to the same report, efforts to introduce strengthened legislation regarding export of wastes in the United States have not been very successful. A system of prior informed consent that has been in place since 1984 was found by an internal EPA audit to be wanting. Numerous bills introduced in the United States Congress aimed at tightening the law by banning exports except under stipulated circumstances have not been passed. On the other hand, the EEC, by signing the Lomé IV Convention with the APC countries, has taken an active role in banning the export of hazardous waste to developing countries. In Eastern Europe, where political liberalization is slowly revealing the past extent of the toxic trade, new restrictions are being implemented.[9]

1. Policies and programmes

For the respondents, this theme ranked third among the nine UNCED themes targeted by the Benchmark Survey. Eighty-three per cent of the responding firms rated this subject important.

Industry plays an important role in the waste cycle from the product design, to manufacture (which influences their consumption), to ultimate disposal. Since waste minimization is a multidisciplinary issue, each corporate function plays a key role in the decisions regarding the subject. Although product design, production management, marketing, environmental impact, and finance play important roles in waste minimization, the initial impetus often comes from research and development, where new technologies for waste reduction are developed.

Figure VII.1.   Polices and programmes pertaining to toxic wastes & chemicals and going beyond national legislation

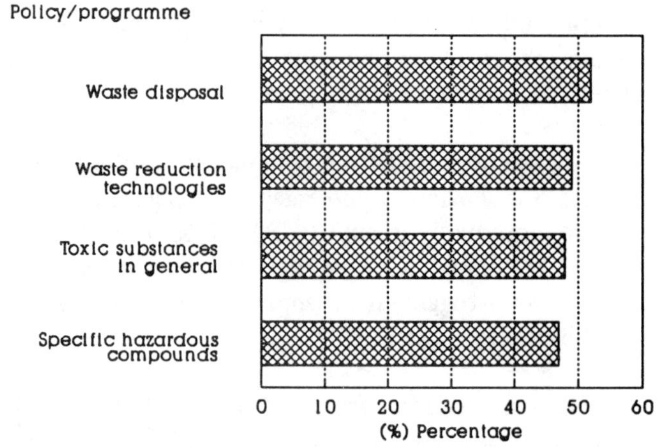

Source: TCMD/DESD Benchmark Survey, 1990-91.

The Survey results show that policies going beyond those required by national legislation for toxic substances in general; policies for specific hazardous compounds; policies for the development of waste reduction technologies; and polices on waste disposal, had been developed by 48, 47, 49, and 52 per cent of the responding firms, respectively. (See figure VII.1.) In all four areas, the North America-based firms were more likely to have such policies than their Asian and European counterparts. That is probably because the United States has required that all companies make public the amount of certain substances emitted from all their locations since 1986. In addition, federal law requires that companies pay the EPA each time they dispose of hazardous waste. Similarly, the extractive-based sector was ahead of the others in having those policies, followed by the finished-goods sector (see annex table D.16).

Among the three suggested responses--(a) the development of internal company standardized programmes and procedures for waste handling; (b) the contents of material safety data sheets (MSDS); and (b) training for workers safety--a striking 56, 64 and 67 per cent of the responding firms stated that they had so acted. In those activities, the Asia-based firms demonstrated an impressive performance, followed by their North America-based counterparts, while the finished-goods and extractive-based sectors were ahead of the other sectors.

In terms of firm size, more than 60 per cent of the top-third firms stated that they had developed company-wide policies going beyond national legislation on the above areas. When it came to the development of standardized company version of waste handling, MSDSs and training for worker safety, those same size firms showed more impressive percentages for having such procedures. (See annex table D.16.)

Fifty-eight per cent of the responding firms stated that they voluntarily financed waste technologies, with an almost equal distribution among the three regions. Where the Europe-based respondents were concerned, there appeared to be a discrepancy in the regional breakdown between having policies beyond those required by national legislation for waste disposal and waste-reduction technologies and the voluntary financing of such technologies. Significantly more Europe-based respondents appeared to be financing the development of such technologies rather than having policies beyond those required by national legislation. (See annex table D.16.)

A possible explanation for that discrepancy could be that in most European countries the national laws on waste disposal are sufficiently strict and the corporations do not feel that they need to go beyond them. At the same time, those corporations may feel that it pays to make extra effort in developing more efficient waste-disposal technologies. The sectoral and firm-size breakdowns on this question followed the same pattern as previous questions on waste disposal.

2. Sustainable development programmes

With regard to international operations in developing countries, 40 per cent of the responding firms reported having toxic education programmes for their workers in developing countries, while 48 per cent reported monitoring the disposal of hazardous waste in those countries. Although with both issues it appeared that the majority of the respondents gave a positive answer, one quarter stated that it did not have sufficient data at headquarters that would enable it to respond. Even in the decentralized business environment of today, it would appear unusual and possibly dangerous for the leading firms which participated in the Benchmark Survey to state that such important issues were not being monitored closely by their headquarters.

B. EXAMPLES OF ENVIRONMENTALLY SOUND CORPORATE RESPONSES TO MANAGEMENT OF TOXIC CHEMICALS AND HAZARDOUS WASTES

Although an average 40 per cent of the responding companies reported having policies and programmes for toxic substances and hazardous wastes, only about 20 per cent overall forwarded attachments to support those statements. A number of the same companies sent numerous attachments on developments in the two areas. Many of the corporate respondents included in their corporate environmental policies or other general environmental reports or publications, statements indicating that the elimination or reduction of toxic chemicals and wastes formed part of the objectives or standards to be met.

1. Sample programmes

On the environmentally sound management of toxic chemicals, **Amoco Corporation** cited five articles in its SPAN publication.[10] One concerned emergency preparedness with respect to oil spills. It discussed **Amoco's** leadership in the Petroleum Industry Response Organization, a $500 million force to deal quickly and effectively with catastrophic oil spills. A second discussed **Amoco's** efforts, as a founding member of the Council for Solid Waste Solutions, in developing new disposal technologies for trash and garbage, particularly plastics. To that end, **Amoco** reported that it had established the world's first polystyrene recycling facility. A third article discussed the company's concern for product stewardship and risk management, including its systems for comprehensive product-hazard evaluation, toxicity testing, hazard communications, and increasing assistance to customers around the world through education and training. A fourth discussed employee-protection efforts as reflected in asbestos identification programmes, PCB programmes, and in another toxic control programme for chromium. A fifth article reiterated the company's general environmental policy, based on responsible care. In the management of hazardous waste, an article in the same publication focused on pollution prevention and waste management. It contained a subsection which described activities of the corporation's Waste Management Committee which included inventory, preparation, auditing, evaluating and establishing guidelines.

Company Y cited three attachments drawn from the company's EH&S manual. The first was the company's Hazardous Waste Management Policy to ensure compliance with federal, state, local and EH&S requirements when handing, storing, and disposing of hazardous waste. It included information on waste minimization, waste identification, training of employees, and responsibilities for implementation. The second was the Hazardous Materials Management System, a computer-based tracking system which emphasized the use of MSDSs, chemical inventories, labelling and worker training. The third was the company's New Facility Assessment Policy which stressed the importance of collecting information about hazardous materials use, storage and waste disposal practices and the possible impacts of hazardous materials and wastes on the buildings, soil and groundwater.[11]

Company N cited three attachments on the topic. One was the index to its manufacturing standards manual, which included sections on personnel and training for safety: laboratory safety, chlorine safety, caustic safety, materials handling, processing safety, electrical safety, fire protection, and equipment safety and inspection. That was accompanied by a detailed and technical 40-page section on chlorine safety. A second item was the index to the laboratory-safety subsection of the manufacturing standards manual. The third document of corporate programming was the syllabus to a three-day course covering hazardous materials training for managers.[12]

Deere & Company offered several attachments on toxic chemicals and hazardous wastes. On the management of toxic chemicals, the company quoted its "Corporate hazardous material policy-material safety data sheets", stating that as of 1 January 1989 no product which required MSDS would be ordered or received at any John Deere facility until a properly executed MSDS had been received and approved. A second attachment contained corporate guidelines for toxic-chemical reduction which, in addition to citing reduction goals, called for the creation of a chemical management system to evaluate new chemicals in comparison to those which were being replaced, and to monitor progress in chemical reduction and usage. The third was "Facilities application guidelines for asbestos control procedures".

Deere & Company's "General Strategy and Guidelines on Waste Management" document states that the ultimate goal of each unit's waste management programme is the development of a strategy plan that (a) eliminates the need to dispose of or treat hazardous waste outside of a **Deere & Company** owned facility; (b) avoids future liabilities; and (c) assures regulatory compliance. The document also provided general guidelines that should be considered by each unit in achieving that goal. The final attachment represented **Deere's** PCB management guidelines. That 19-page document was very detailed, covering intent, definitions, prohibitions (including effective deadlines), documentation, inspection, evaluation, engineering and maintenance, reporting of spills, spill cleanup, disposal, and emergency procedures.[13]

> **Box VII.1. Broken Hill Proprietary - Chemwise**
>
> "The **Chemwise** chemical control system is a computerized method of maintaining up-to-date information of consistent quality about all chemicals in the workplace. At the centre of **Chemwise** is a database containing information on several thousand chemicals...**Chemwise** was designed to be available to all employees not only supervisory staff, occupational health professionals and the computer literate....The system is already operating...at about two thirds of the total workforce within BHP...The most exciting opportunity lies in the area of environmental management where an expanded control and information system has the potential for assisting in the management of emissions and waste disposal..." (Broken Hill Proprietary Co., Ltd. *Chemwise-A chemical management system for occupational health and the environment*).

Chevron Corporation's commitment to reduce pollution was embodied in its programme "Save Money and Reduce Toxics" (SMART). In SMART's first three years, facilities reduced hazardous waste by 60 per cent and saved more than $10 million in disposal costs. A representative of the United States Congressional Office of Technology Assessment is on record as designating this effort "one of the top 10 waste-reduction programmes in the country"'.[14]

The **Imperial Chemical Industries (ICI)** stated that it planned to reduce waste from its operations by 50 per cent by 1995, paying special attention to that which was hazardous. Waste would be disposed of under strict, monitored conditions, preferably within **ICI** sites. The company had as a further objective the setting up of waste recycling programmes, not only in-house by also in collaboration with customers. These programmes were to include the recovery of CFCs from commercial and domestic appliances, the recycling of waste solvents used in making paints, and the reprocessing of plastic bottles to make fillings for duvets and sleeping bags.[15]

The **James River Corporation** stated that prior to 1990, it had reduced by 60 per cent the amount of dioxin generated in its mills as an unwanted by-product of the paper-making process. Over the next several years, process changes were expected to reduce dioxin to background levels in the environment.[16]

Alusuisse-Lonza indicated that it had continuously assessed company risk management policies, systematic hazard identification, and risk assessment. All existing activities were subject to periodic safety and environmental controls. The corporation also reported that it prepared annual registers of emissions (air, water, wastes, noise) in which the quantities and qualities were recorded, together with measures to reduce those emissions. There were programmes on employee responsibility and training for safety and environmental protection; alarm and information systems; information to the public and response to public concern; information exchange and collaboration with the authorities; and information to customers on the safe handling, use and disposal of products. Measures exist to prevent accidental releases and catastrophic events damaging to people, property and the environment. Those consist of organizational measures, such as safety data sheets, control, inspections, audit, staff rules, and technical measures, such as warehousing type, alarm system, waste-gas treatment, waste water treatment, construction type, and accessibility.

Orkla Borregaard A.S. stated that it was working to eliminate completely the use of chlorine for bleaching wood pulp. The company also stated that it was currently supplying pulp bleached with chlorine dioxide, which resulted in far fewer chlorinated organic compounds. In addition, it had begun delivering the first supplies of pulp using peroxide as a bleaching agent, which produces no chlorinated compounds at all.[17]

Company X has gained international recognition for its pollution programme. It has an approach that prevents pollution at the source rather than removing it after it has been created. The basis of the programme is:

- Product reformation
- Process modification
- Equipment redesign
- Recycling/reuse of waste.

The criteria for the programme recognition are:

- Eliminate/reduce pollutant
- Benefit the environment through reduced energy use or more efficient use of materials/resources
- Demonstrate technical innovation
- Save money.

The company further stated that in its first 15 years, 1975-1989, the programme had prevented the accumulation of more than 500,000 tons of pollutants and saved the company more than $500 million. It also intends to cut by 90 per cent all hazardous and non-hazardous releases to air, water and land and to reduce by 50 per cent the generation of waste by the year 2000, using 1987 as a base year. That is to be achieved through an updated and expanded version of the programme. The new programme focuses on long-term scientific research and stepped-up efforts to reduce sources of pollution in the manufacturing process.[18]

2. Organizational restructuring

In order to deal more effectively with the management of hazardous waste, corporations are forming new partnerships with other corporations or are creating their own specialized companies. The **Westinghouse Electric Corporation** had reportedly developed technologies to destroy contamination and was perfecting processes to reduce the amount of waste that would be generated in the future. **Westinghouse** had coupled that new technology development with corporate expansion by acquiring companies that specialize in laboratory analysis, field engineering, transportation and storage. Westinghouse Environmental and Geotechnical Services, Inc. provides environmental and geotechnical services to governments and industry. Its "Aptus" technology is used to destroy PCBs and other hazardous wastes. The company has also acquired Scientific Ecology Group,, which performs low-level nuclear waste reduction and operates the nation's first licensed nuclear-waste incinerator.[19]

Euroc Cementa reported that **Cementa AB**, its cement producer in Sweden, had a company called Environmental Techniques which collects and processes hazardous waste. **Sandoz Ltd.** created MTB Environmental Engineering Ltd. on 1 January 1989 to provide services in environmental protection, to analyse environmental hazards and to design studies for cleanup or recycling projects and process technology.[20] **Company H** stated that it had created a joint programme with **Browning-Ferris Industries, Inc. (BFI)** to promote plastic recycling in BFI's curbside recycling programmes.[21]

Innovative thinking allows corporations to see new solutions, as well as new markets, to help solve some of their problems. **Elkem Corporation** indicated that it was helping Laclede Steel solve its problem with heavy metals hazardous waste, while recovering some valuable by-products such as zinc that offset most, if not all, of the projects' costs. **Elkem's** new Multi-Purpose Furnace incorporates proven, leading-edge technology able to transform electric arc furnace emissions into synthetic by-products that could be returned to nature safely. In the process, Laclede could recover top-quality zinc and lead to help to finance the entire system.[22]

C. SUMMARY

The way TNCs handle toxic and hazardous substances is one of the most salient environmental issues, and rightly so. Catastrophic events in recent years urge an unrelenting focus on those issues. Several chapters in Agenda 21 address these issues, and concern over trade in hazardous wastes especially was expressed at UNCED. Judging from the findings of the Benchmark Survey, it seems that corporations have learned to give top priority to management of toxics and hazards. Most corporations are engaged in policies to control toxics and hazards, even in developing countries.

The establishment of programmes on those issues has given corporations experience in how to organize EH&S management and how to cope with a highly critical public. Such experiences can be useful when corporations extend their environmental management programmes to include other EH&S areas. The chemical industry, which has pioneered EH&S management of toxics and hazards, is today also home to the corporations that have activities in other EH&S areas. Thus, there seems to be a spillover effect from risk-management to management in general. As some of the examples of advanced corporate policies in that area show, corporations have a considerable vested interest in financing the development of new technologies.

Unfortunately, emissions of high-hazard pollutants such as PCBs and dioxin are often treated as local pollution problems to be covered by national legislation. Also awareness at corporate headquarters of the handling of toxic chemicals and hazardous waste in developing countries is often absent. It is crucial that corporations upgrade the transfer of their technology and management expertise in those areas to developing nations. It is equally important for them to minimize local exposure to these substances. Export of toxic wastes to developing nations should not take place under any circumstances.

Notes

1   United Nations Environment Programme, *Saving our planet-challenges and hopes* (United Nations, Nairobi, 1992), p. 75.

2   B.M. Thompson, "Good riddance - solving America's hazardous waste problem", *Vital Speeches*, vol. 55 (22), 1 September 1989, p. 683.

3   Ibid., p. 78.

4   Robert Derks, "Be safe - eliminate PCBs from transformers", *Chemical Engineering*, January 1991, p. 133.

5   Cheryl Lomo, "Caution: contains PCBs (polychlorinated biphenyls)", *Public Utilities Fortnightly*, 4 August 1988, p. 34.

6   "Cancer deaths at chemical plant are linked to dioxin", *Environmental Impact*, vol. VI, No.1, January 1992.

7   N. Lenssen, "Facing up to nuclear waste", *Worldwatch*, vol. 5, No. 2, March-April 1992, p.10.

8   H. French, "A most deadly trade" *Worldwatch*, vol. 3, No. 4, July-August 1990, p.12.

9   Ibid., pp. 13-14.

10   Amoco Corporation, *SPAN: For the future of our planet*, No. 3, 1990.

11   Material submitted in support of responses to the BMS questionnaire.

12   Internal company material sent in support to responses to the BMS questionnaire.

13   Deere and Company, internal company material sent in support to responses to the BMS questionnaire.

14   Chevron Corporation, "1990 Report on the environment: A commitment to excellence", p.4.

15   Imperial Chemical Industries Plc, *Annual Report 1990*, p. 4.

16   James River Corporation, *Working to protect the environment we share*, August 1990, p. 11.

17   Orkla Borregaard A.S., *Annual Report 1988*, p.24.

18   Material submitted in support to the BMS questionnaire.

19   Westinghouse Electric Corporation, *Annual Report 1989*, p. 12-13.

20   Sandoz Ltd., Corporate Affairs Department, "Refrain, recover, reduce", p. 41.

21   Material submitted in support of responses to the BMS questionnaire.

22   Elkem Corporation, *Annual Report 1989*, p. 45.

CHAPTER VIII.   PROTECTION OF FRESHWATER RESOURCES

During the past three centuries, global freshwater withdrawals are believed to have increased more than 35 times and are projected to increase by 30 to 35 per cent by the year 2000. Many countries are already suffering serious water shortages, and if, as projected, human population reaches 10 billion by 2050, current patterns of freshwater use cannot be sustained.[1]

This is of basic importance to TNCs, and thus a topic of study for the Benchmark Survey. In most countries, the main consumer of water is irrigated agriculture, accounting for about 70 per cent of the world freshwater withdrawal. In industrial countries, however, it is expected that water consumption by industry will double between 1967 and 2000, while agricultural consumption is projected to decrease by 28 per cent.[2]

Industry uses substantial amounts of water for cooling, processing, cleaning and removing industrial wastes. With industrial use, most of the water is returned to the water cycle; however, it is often heavily polluted with chemicals and heavy metals. Wastewater now comprises 87 per cent of total water withdrawals by industrial sectors.[3]

> **Agenda 21:**
>
> "Introduction of precautionary approach in water quality management...with a focus on pollution minimization and prevention through the use of new technologies, product and process change, pollution reduction at source and effluent reuse, recycling and recovery, treatment and environmentally safe disposal" (18.40).
>
> "Mandatory environmental impact assessment of all major water resource development projects" (18.40c).

Among the major industrial sectors which contribute to freshwater pollution are pulp and paper, chemicals, petrochemicals and refining, metalworking, food processing, and textiles. The wastes, which are broadly categorized as heavy metals or synthetic organic compounds, reach bodies of water either through direct discharge from the atmosphere or by leaching from waste sites.[4]

In the developed regions of the world, many industrial discharges are strictly controlled. Yet pollution of freshwater bodies from the accumulated wastes discharged over the past 100 years continues. In developing countries, industrial discharges are largely uncontrolled, and water quality is directly affected. In those regions, pollution is a significant and growing problem in areas where industry is concentrated.[5] The contamination of the Rhine after the **Sandoz** fire in Basel, Switzerland, of the Rio Grande by the *maquiladora* industry in Mexico (the border zone housing United States-based companies), and of freshwater throughout Eastern Europe, only now being revealed, are reminders that industrial activity can result in very serious freshwater contamination irrespective of the location.

In order to secure the availability and quality of water resources for human development activities, and with due consideration to its supply and the functioning of aquatic ecosystems, UNCED included in Agenda 21 a separate chapter on the protection of freshwater resources. That chapter considers issues such as integrated water resources assessment and management, protection of water quality and aquatic ecosystems, drinking-water supply and sanitation, and water for sustainable food production and rural development. In relation to industry, the chapter urges international cooperation in establishing water-quality and management programmes and in establishing enforceable standards for major point-source discharges and high-risk non-point sources.

A. STATISTICAL FINDINGS

1. Sources of freshwater contamination

Pesticides, one of the main threats to freshwater quality, did not appear to be a central issue with the participants to the Benchmark Survey. The majority of the respondents stated that they did not manufacture pesticides.

Over half of the respondents, however, indicated that they did emit heavy metals, and among the North America-based respondents, that practice appeared to be more prevalent (three quarters of the responding firms). Firms belonging in the extractive-based and finished-goods sectors, where the chemical, metal processing and manufacturing firms are classified, were more likely to emit heavy metals than firms in the agricultural and service sectors. (See annex table D.18.)

Wastes containing heavy metals are dangerous in that they can find their way to underground water tables or into rivers, where they can contaminate not only the water itself but most organisms living in it. The Minamata Bay incident in Japan is one of the most famous cases of poisoning by mercury, emitted by a factory, which found its way up the marine food chain into the fish which was eaten by the local people, who suffered severe consequences. Some heavy metals can be recycled, but since they often appear in complex mixtures, recycling can be difficult. A number of governments have started to restrict the use of certain heavy metals to prevent their appearing as wastes and subsequently causing pollution.

Contamination to soil and to freshwater tables and aquifers can also be caused by leaking underground tanks. Although the use of underground tanks is not necessarily hazardous to the environment, the nature of the materials usually stored in underground tanks, (toxic liquids, gasoline or other volatile organic compounds etc.) can make leaks by such tanks extremely dangerous to the soil and freshwater water-tables located nearby. Close to 40 per cent of the responding firms stated that they used large below-ground tanks, with over half of the responding firms in the service sector replying in the affirmative. (See annex table D.18.)

Only 16 per cent (19) of the responding firms stated that they had plants near drinking-water supplies in developing countries; the majority of those firms were based in North America (11). One third of all respondents reported that they did not have sufficient data at headquarters to answer the question. Forty-one per cent of the firms in the finished-goods sector were among those firms. Given the grave pollution problems already extant with regard to freshwater supplies in developing countries, that type of omission is significant. (See annex table D.20.)

Only three per cent (4) of the responding firms stated that they had products hazardous to drinking water supplies in developing countries, with an impressive 86 per cent declaring that they did not have any such products. All four companies that responded affirmatively were in the extractive-based or agricultural sectors (three and one firms, respectively), with three in the top-third sales group. Asia-based firms exhibited more sensitivity on the issue, with an impressive 91 per cent stating that they had no products hazardous to drinking water supplies.

2. Policies and programmes

Eighty per cent of the respondents to the Benchmark Survey rated protection of freshwater resources among the top five most important issues for their corporations. Freshwater protection appeared to be an equally important subject for respondents in all three regions. The firms in the extractive-based and finished-goods sectors appeared more concerned with the issue, possibly due to the extremely polluting nature of some of their activities. There was not much variance among the three sales groups on the subject. (See figure VIII.1.)

Nearly half of the respondents to the Benchmark Survey (48 per cent) stated that they had company-wide polices on water quality going beyond national regulation. Although the majority of both the Asia-based and the North America-based firms appeared to have such policies, that was not the case with the Europe-based respondents, only 24 per cent of which had policies

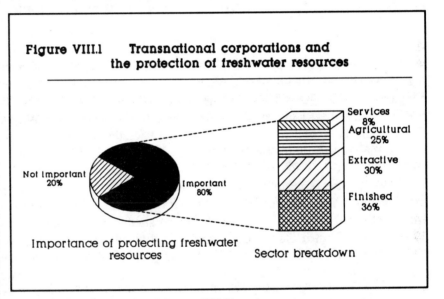

Figure VIII.1   Transnational corporations and the protection of freshwater resources

Not Important 20%
Important 80%

Importance of protecting freshwater resources

Services 8%
Agricultural 25%
Extractive 30%
Finished 36%

Sector breakdown

Source: TCMD/DESD Benchmark Survey, 1990-91.

for water quality that exceeded national requirements. Both Japan and the United States, where the majority of the Asia-based and North America-based respondents were located, have strict freshwater protection legislation.

Eleven firms (6.9 per cent) found water-quality policies to be inapplicable to them; considering that all companies utilize water in some part of their operations, that was a somewhat unusual response. The fact that half of the firms belonged to the agricultural and extractive-based sectors, which include industries that are heavy water users, makes that response all the more interesting (see annex table D.20). More Asia- and North America-based companies than Europe-based companies had company-wide policies for storage tanks that went beyond national legislation. Forty per cent of all respondents stated that they had such company-wide policies. It is interesting to note that none of the North America-based companies found storage tank policies inapplicable to them. Liabilities arising from soil or water contamination as a result of tank leaks may have sensitized United States' corporations on the subject.

Approximately the same number of respondents which stated that they used large below-ground storage tanks are also found to have corporate-wide policies for storage tanks. That is an encouraging indication of the importance attached to storage facilities by corporations.

Sixty-eight per cent of all responding firms stated that they had undertaken programmes to conserve water resources. Among the North America-based respondents, the issue received more attention than among Asia- or Europe-based firms (82 vs. 60 vs. 62 per cent). The sectoral breakdown showed that firms in the extractive-based and finished-goods sectors were more likely to have such programmes, and the top-third firms in terms of sales were almost twice as likely to have water conservation programmes as those in the bottom third (see annex table D.21).

B. EXAMPLES OF CORPORATE RESPONSES TO WATER QUALITY AND FRESHWATER PROTECTION

Many of the responding firms had plants, especially chemical plants, near major rivers, or canals, e.g., **Hoechst** off the Rhine-Main conurbation, **Bayer AG** off the Rhône, **ICI** off the Tees in the United Kingdom, the Ganges in India and the Seine in France, **Astra** off the Södertälje Canal, **Ciba-Geigy** off the Rhine and the Rhône, and **Sandoz** off the Rhine, to mention only a few. Therefore most of those firms would be expected to have some kind of wastewater treatment system in place and/or policy or programme guidelines for the treatment of wastewater.

A number of respondents to the Benchmark Survey reported impressive results in water protection programmes. **Ciba-Geigy** dated the construction of mechanical and biological wastewater treatment plants back to the mid-1960s; all five manufacturing sites in Switzerland have been equipped with them since 1982.[6] In the United States, **Company V's** alloy plant in Alabama was recognized by the Alabama Governor's Award competition for outstanding achievement in wastewater management. The company's wastewater treatment facility in Washington, created to meet rigorous new federal water-discharge guidelines, is considered the most modern in the industry.[7]

Company Y reported having developed extensive guidelines governing the use of storage tanks and groundwater protection.[8] The guidelines for storage tanks were detailed on the design, construction and installation and operating procedures. The groundwater protection programme encompassed all of that company's potential water-pollution sources, and focused on prevention of releases as a means of protecting the groundwater. The company placed on its managers the responsibility for selecting equipment and designing processes that helped reduce the probability of a contaminant release and for the on-site environmental health and safety of staff. The responsibility for using state-of-the-art equipment for monitoring and detecting releases for each potential groundwater contamination source fell to the managers as well. Where monitoring and detection systems were not employed, it was the responsibility of the corporation managers to report all releases of hazardous materials or wastes to the on-site EH&S specialist.

The company guidelines recommend the continuing use of enclosed decreasing units for PC-board cleaning, the use of secondary containment for storage of hazardous materials, the maintenance of stringent controls on hazardous wastes, and the operation of monitoring, detection and release control systems for both above-ground and underground storage tanks. Finally, in the event of release of contaminants to soil or groundwater, the company location should be prepared to take the necessary remedial action to clean up the release.

Bayer AG indicated that extensive guidelines were in place for water protection in case of fire in a chemical warehouse. **Xerox Corporation** had a monitoring programme for water effluents that applied to Xerox and its subsidiaries. **Union Carbide's** Environmental Protection Procedures called for "programmes to provide reasonable assurance that **Union Carbide** locations do not have an adverse effect on groundwater or surface water as a result of their operations".[9]

A combination of new production processes and wastewater facilities and systems appeared to work well in reducing water pollution. Many of the

---

Box VIII.1. Better technology for wastewater that also conserves energy and land

Amoco Chemical Company has introduced a major new technology for anaerobic wastewater treatment at the Taiwan plant of the China American Petrochemical Company Ltd.

Because air is kept out of the wastewater treatment process, waste-eating bacteria are forced to produce methane instead of oxygen. The methane then is piped directly from water-treatment tanks to gas boilers, where it is burned to generate steam for other plant operations.

Anaerobic wastewater treatment also saves electricity. Giant mixers no longer are needed to force air into the wastewater, so electricity to power the mixers is not needed.

Additionally, the new technology conserves land, requiring far less real estate than does the older, aerobic system...

Source: Amoco Corporation, _Span: For the future of our planet_ (Special environmental issue) Number 3, 1990.

---

respondents stated that they utilized that combination as an integrated environmental protection procedure. The prevalent protection standard among the responding companies appeared to be preventive rather than curative. The companies were more likely to have wastewater systems to prevent pollutants from entering natural water reservoirs than systems to treat contaminated reservoirs. It thus appears that a large portion of the capital expenditure for water protection goes into preventive measures.

Corporations themselves or their research institutes have developed a number of new technologies to treat wastewater. Treating water with ultraviolet radiation is a technology reportedly being developed by Ultrox International. This is a "treatment technology that uses ultraviolet light combined with ozone and hydrogen peroxide to destroy a range of organic compounds in groundwater and industrial wastewater".[10] The emphasis is on permanent treatment remedies. Another treatment technology being researched was the anaerobic packed-bed reactor process. Researchers at the Georgia Institute of Technology were working on microbes that degrade wastes into combustible gases. Shredded used tires could be substitute inputs in the process. The technology may be commercially available in about two years.[11]

For many respondents, water protection means conservation of water resources and water recycling. Water can be stored and used to irrigate the landscape around a facility. Recycling water, especially in cooling systems, enables major savings to be realized in water consumption. Many companies are recycling their wastewater rather than discharging it.

Chevron Corporation had reduced freshwater usage by 30 per cent since 1986 by recycling and reducing the use of cooling water at its Richmond refinery. Additional cutbacks had been realized through the purchase of "used" treated water from a local water district.

Toyota Motor Corporation employed a number of water saving measures, including recycling cooling water, multi-stage use of rinsing water in the painting process, and a low-pressure water supply. At least 98 per cent of the water used at **Toyota** was reclaimed. (See figure VIII.2.) According to the company, water used for industrial purposes at **Toyota** plants was all recycled. Wastewater to be released was processed until it was cleaner than that of rivers and public-sewer processing facilities in the area.[12] In addition, although **Toyota** indicated that it had two separate drainage systems for rainwater and other wastewater, it treated any rainwater that might fall into roads within the plants and other areas where it might be contaminated by oil or other pollutants as contaminated wastewater, directing it to the general wastewater-treatment plants.[13]

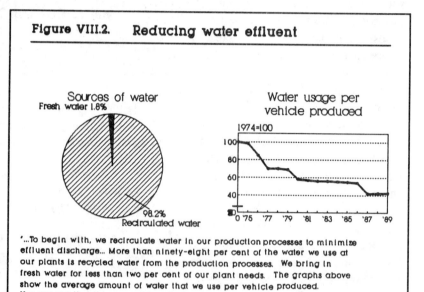

Figure VIII.2.   **Reducing water effluent**

'...To begin with, we recirculate water in our production processes to minimize effluent discharge... More than ninety-eight per cent of the water we use at our plants is recycled water from the production processes. We bring in fresh water for less than two per cent of our plant needs. The graphs above show the average amount of water that we use per vehicle produced. You can see that this amount has declined sixty per cent since nineteen seventy-five...'

Source: Toyota Motor Corporation, *Overview of Environmental Measures at Toyota.*

Boehringer Ingelheim also reported that it had two separate sewage systems for wastewater and rainwater. Rainwater was also treated as wastewater "should hazardous substances enter this accidentally". **Boehringer** utilized a mechanical-biological wastewater treatment plant, keeping "...fish in the last flow tank which the purified wastewater flows directly into the tiny river. The fish serve as biological monitors; their condition is an indicator of the high degradation efficiency of the treatment tanks and hence the safety of the water".[14] **Sandoz** has constructed catch basins for contaminated firefighting water in two of its plants whereby wastewater, which has reached the set maximum value for pollution concentration, is diverted for treatment rather than discharged into the Rhine.[15]

Norsk Hydro reported that "during the last decade nitrogen emissions to water have been reduced by 90%...By continuous efforts over the last 20 years phosphate discharges to the sea have been reduced by 98%...".[16] **Degussa AG** used zeolites as a substitute for phosphate in washing detergents, and hydrogen peroxide as an environmentally acceptable disinfectant to contribute to reducing water pollution.[17] **Alusuisse-Lonza** reported that "mercury emissions have been reduced to levels which are several times lower than natural levels in the Rhône river".[18]

Imperial Chemical Industries (ICI) reported building a £66 million plant for recycling sulphuric acid to avoid discharging it into the River Tees and the North Sea. The company indicated that it had reduced by 75 per cent, the oxygen-reducing waste entering the Tees. The company had also invested in a process that would "completely eliminate the need for disposing in the Tees and at the sea the acidic ammonium sulphate waste arising from its manufacture of methyl methacrylate". **ICI France** stated that, when it acquired control of Francolor company, whose industrial discharges in the river Seine had effectively killed all life in the river, it substantially improved its liquid waste disposal methods after it opened a new biological treatment plant that reduced by more than two thirds the oxygen-destroying waste materials being discharged. A new black dye for leather had been developed to replace a process which used hazardous materials. **ICI** claimed to have played an important part in saving the Seine and bringing the freshwater fish back to its waters.[19]

Astra stated that "no wastewater--not even in purified condition--is released into the Södertälje canal...". All contaminated water is pretreated in the company's entirely-closed purification plant; only then is it released into the municipal network of sewers.[20]

C. Summary

The Benchmark Survey identifies a broad array of innovative practices to protect and save freshwater resources. Several corporations reported a reduction of 90 per cent or more in water consumption as a result of water conservation programmes. This indicates both an enormous waste currently takes place and that corporate commitment to preserving water can achieve significant results.

Saving freshwater resources and reducing emissions to ground and surface waters is probably one of the most crucial sustainable development activities that can be undertaken by transnational corporations. The importance of clean surface water for health, especially in developing countries where it is likely to constitute most to the drinking water supply, cannot be overemphasized. Disappointingly, only a minority of the corporations operating in developing countries had policies for freshwater protection. That is another crucial area where corporations could establish monitoring and preventive programmes with relatively small costs and high pay-offs, utilizing the experiences gained in industrial countries.

Notes

[1] The World Conservation Union, United Nations Development Programme, and World Wide Fund for Nature, *Caring for the Earth: A Strategy for Sustainable Living* (Gland, Switzerland, 1991), p. 137.

[2] Edward Goldsmith and Nicholal Hildyard, *The Earth Report - The Essential Guide to Global Ecological Issues* (Price Stern Sloan, Los Angeles, 1988), p. 81.

[3] *World Resources 1990-91*, A report by the World Resources Institute in collaboration with the United Nations Environment Programme and the United Nations Development Programme (Oxford University Press, 1990).

[4] Ibid., p. 163.

[5] Ibid., pp. 163, 166.

[6] Ciba-Geigy Ltd., "Annual report" (1989), p. 14.

[7] Material sent in support of responses to the BMS questionnaire.

[8] Material sent in support of responses to the BMS questionnaire.

[9] Union Carbide, "Health, safety and environmental protection" (n.d.), p. 12.

[10] *Environmental Manager*, vol.3, No. 4, November 1991, pp. 7-8, 12.

[11] *Environment Today*, vol. 2, No. 4, May 1991, pp. 3, 45.

[12] Toyota Motor Corporation, "Toyota and the environment" (1990), p. 21.

[13] Toyota Motor Corporation, "Toyota plant environmental measures" (1990), p. 7.

[14] Boehringer Ingelheim, "Annual report" (1988), pp. 20, 22.

[15] Sandoz International Ltd., "Refrain, recover, reduce" (1989), p. 35.

[16] Norsk Hydro A.S., "Norsk Hydro environmental report" (May 1990), p. 4.

[17] Degussa AG, "Annual report 1988/89", p. 14.

[18] Alusuisse-Lonza, "Thinking clean: the Lonza waste management concept" (1988).

[19] Imperial Chemical Industries, "ICI and the environment" (n.d.), pp. 23-24.

[20] AB Astra, "Astra and the environment" (n.d.), p. 8.

CHAPTER IX.

PROTECTION AND MANAGEMENT OF LAND RESOURCES

Land-based resources provide a large portion of the essential materials required to sustain today's society. Minerals, fuels, agriculture, and forestry are all are key components in the modern economy. Raw materials from land-based sources are also the basis of most corporate products and processes. Reliance upon those land-based resources, though, has resulted in a number of environmental ills, including desertification, soil loss, deforestation, and land degradation. Both the Benchmark Survey and UNCED featured land issues prominently in their examinations of environmental protection and sustainable development.

Forest depletion, particularly, has become a key land resource issue. Forests hold numerous vital plant and animal species as well as acting as a carbon sink to counteract the emission of greenhouse gases. Last year 17 million hectares of tropical forests were lost.[1] Corporate use of forests lands resulted in the cutting of 1.7 billion cubic meters of wood.[2] While local communities groups also use wood resources, particularly in developing nations, corporate activities are often more environmentally detrimental.[3] "Seldom does the gathering of wood for fuel result in the destruction of rich primary forests. Industrial cutting, on the other hand, is a major cause of primary forest destruction in both temperate and tropical nations". Commercial timber harvesting continues to increase; the market has expanded 50 per cent since 1965 and now supports an international forest-products trade of $85 billion.[4] The carrying capacity of forest lands to sustain that growth rate may not be sufficient.

The depletion of land resources affects ecological systems beyond the immediate soil and forest environments. Deforestation reduces the ability of the planet to respond to the build-up of greenhouse gases; tropical deforestation accounts for 20 to 30 per cent of the net annual increase in atmospheric carbon-dioxide concentrations.[5] Further, the loss of primary forested areas affects biodiversity through the ensuing displacement and disruption of plant and animal species. Industrial plantations often promote a single genetic tree species to maximize product output.

Corporations are likewise playing an increased role in world agricultural production. The structure of world agriculture is changing; family farms are being replaced by corporate holdings. In the United States, 29 corporations own over 21 per cent of the crop land.[6] Corporations control 51 per cent of fresh vegetable production, 85 per cent of the citrus crop, 97 per cent of broiler chickens, and 40 per cent of egg production.[7] Mono-culture farming practices have improved short-term efficiencies at the expense of long-term soil viability. The loss of soil nutrients and the contamination of land and water from pesticides and herbicides are likewise growing problems. Unsustainable agricultural practices such as mono-cropping and overgrazing are major causes of soil degradation and desertification.

Land disposal remains the primary refuse outlet for toxic and hazardous wastes such as PCBs, heavy metals, and dioxin. Over time those contaminants often migrate and result in other harm such as the poisoning of drinking water. Illegal disposal of these wastes near communities has compromised human health in a number of unfortunate incidents. Corporate responsibility in ensuring the safe disposal of wastes can help reduce the occurrence of such catastrophes.

The growing global concern over land resource damage has prompted attempts at national and international solutions. The World Banks's Tropical Forestry Action Plan (TFAP) has sought to promote sustainable uses of tropical forests. The International Tropical Timber Organization aims to have sustainable forest management as the basis for all international tropical timber trade by the year 2000. Agriculturally-related agreements such as the FAO Code of Conduct on the Distribution and Use of Pesticides have likewise helped to prevent damage to agricultural resources and human health. To be successful, the goals of those organizations and agreements rely upon corporate cooperation. Managing forest and agricultural resources on a sustainable basis is the only means by which the long-term viability of corporate investments and resources can be assured.

> **Agenda 21:**
>
> "Carrying out surveys and developing and implementing land-use plans for appropriate greening/planting/afforestation/forestrehabilitation" (11.14).
>
> "Carrying out investment analysis and feasibility studies, including environmental impact assessments, for establishing forest based processing enterprises" (11.23).
>
> "Formulating scientifically sound criteria and guidelines for the management, conservation and sustainable development of all types of forest" (11.22).

Forest issues were among the most disputed issues discussed at UNCED. Not accidently, the conference took place in the country where one third of the world's remaining rainforest exists. The Conference could not agree on a Convention on Forest Principles, but a chapter of Agenda 21 addresses the issue; it urges securing the multiple roles of trees, forests and forest lands, enhancing afforestation and reforestation activities, improving systems of monitoring forests, and assuming global responsibilities for the world's forest resources. The Conference also addressed land issues such as sustainable agriculture and combating desertification.

A. STATISTICAL FINDINGS

1. Sectoral activities

The large transnational firms analysed by the Benchmark Survey represent a range of corporate activities historically associated with the use of land resources. The extraction and production of mineral and fossil fuel resources, the harvesting and processing of forestry resources, the production and use of agricultural-based chemicals, and the processing and disposal of toxic substances are all activities which can result in severe land-resource degradation. Nearly one third of the companies surveyed engaged in agricultural activities; one third had some form of mining operations; and twenty per cent had activities involved in forestry.

2. Land pollutants

The corporations were asked to identify toxic and hazardous substance usage known to have the potential to degrade land resources. Despite the concerns raised over such hazards as dioxin and PCBs, specific corporate products and processes still involve these chemicals (see figure IX.1). Although PCBs had been largely restricted by legislation in the United States, the European Community and Japan since 1976, nearly one third of the corporations still utilized PCBs. Fourteen per cent of the firms reported utilizing corporate processes which produce dioxin by-products. (See annex table D.22.) Given that those large TNCs are the leaders in developing and using safe substitutes for these chemicals, these figures may represent conservative estimates for the overall use of such hazards. Further, nearly 10 per cent of the environmental representatives of those firms did not have sufficient data to comment on whether the firms utilized dioxin. If immediate centralized data are lacking for such high profile hazards as dioxin, managerial knowledge of other less-publicized (but also dangerous) hazards is probably less developed as well.

Over one half of the firms reported production of waste containing heavy metals. Once deposited in land disposal sites, heavy metals can compromise human health through a number of media, including the contamination of freshwater supplies. Radioactive waste materials were produced in 21 per cent of the surveyed corporations. Specialized test equipment often relies upon radioactive isotopes to accurately calibrate the measuring functions of these devices. While such instruments primarily use small amounts of low-grade radioactive materials, the fact that one fifth of the largest corporations handled radioactive substances is significant. Handling and leak-testing procedures are important even with low-grade materials. Further, the proliferation of radioactive isotopes in corporate production indicates radioactive waste disposal will continue to remain a key land hazard issue.

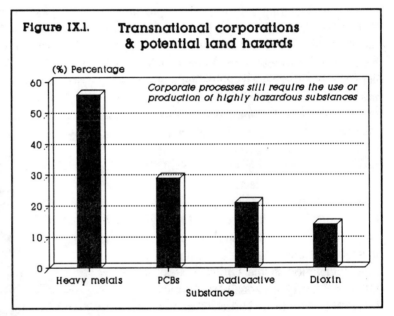

Figure IX.1. **Transnational corporations & potential land hazards**

Source: TCMD/DESD Benchmark Survey, 1990-91.

The United States Superfund Amendments and Reclamation Act (SARA) is often regarded as a milestone in legislation for controlling the generation of waste and its accompanying effects on land resources. Despite that legislation, North America-based firms generally reported higher usage rates of land-threatening hazards. North America-based firms were twice as likely to produce PCBs and heavy-metal wastes as their Asian and European counterparts. Possibly the reporting requirements dictated under

SARA Title III have forced United States-based management to be particularly aware of even small corporate outputs of such hazards. Other firms may also produce such chemicals, but a centralized environmental management staff may not be as aware of corporate-wide usage.

3. Policies and programmes

Approximately one half of the surveyed firms rated land-based environmental problems as one of their company's top five environmental concerns. Toxic-waste disposal is a topic closely related to land contamination and often the leading cause of land-based problems. Despite that relationship, toxic-waste disposal ranked considerably higher (83 per cent) than land pollution as one of the companies' top five environmental concerns. Toxic waste generation is a well-regulated field with a direct impact on corporate activities and public perception. Specific land issues such as soil loss and desertification may be perceived as global concerns beyond a corporation's control. However, specific sectors and processes, especially those involving agriculture, mining, and forestry, undertake activities directly affecting land quality and the growing problems of soil loss, desertification, and deforestation.

Articulating corporate strategies and goals for land management through policies indicates the degree to which land issues have progressed on the corporate agenda. Thirty-one per cent of the firms had developed land and soil quality policies beyond the requirements of national regulation. A similar number of firms had formalized policies regarding site selection (34 per cent), land transport (24 per cent), and land reclamation and rehabilitation (22 per cent). North America-based firms reported a higher number of land-related policies than either Asia- or Europe-based firms (see figure IX.2). Approximately half of the North America-based firms had articulated policies for land and soil quality and site selection. On the other hand, one quarter of the Asia- and Europe-based firms reported that such policies were not applicable to their operations. Again, the Superfund legislation in the United States may be largely responsible for the increased attention United States-based firms have directed toward land issues. The attention that SARA's reporting and compliance requirements have received may be responsible for United States firms' development of global corporate policies for land management.

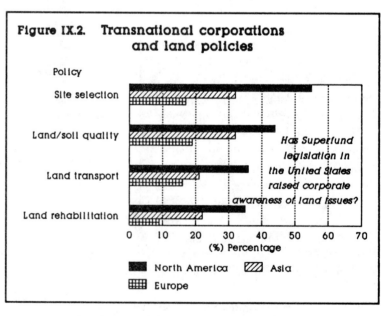

Figure IX.2. Transnational corporations and land policies

Source: TCMD/DESD Benchmark Survey, 1990-91.

Surprisingly, firms whose primary business line involved forestry, agriculture, or related products actually had fewer land-related policies than other sectoral groups. Only one fifth of those firms had soil and land quality policies which included provisions beyond national requirements. Nearly one half of the extractive-based firms, including corporations with mining operations, had developed such policies. The extractive-based sector likewise led other sectoral groups in policies for site selection, land reclamation and rehabilitation, and land transport. Although those extractive-based firms appeared as the leaders in land policy, 52 per cent of them did not have extensive policies for land reclamation and rehabilitation. The lack of explicit policy statements does not imply these large TNCs do not comply with governmental requirements. Rather, the results indicate the existence of a great potential to raise awareness of land issues within corporations. Policy statements can be an effective tool to integrate land preservation goals with the daily actions of managers and employees.

As was evident in most areas of the Benchmark Survey, the leading TNCs by sales revenues were also the leading firms in land management policies. The lower one third of corporations by sales were the most likely to regard land issues as being inapplicable to their operations. Of that lower one third by sales, over 40 per cent regarded land reclamation policies and land transportation policies as irrelevant to their operations. The relatively smaller firms may indeed have a narrower business scope and thus legitimately have little involvement in land management. A positive finding was that 41 per cent of the responding firms had either relocated operations for environmental reasons or had programmes in place to do so. Although the corporations re-

sponded at lower percentage rates on land and soil policy development, progressive steps were being taken.

4. Sustainable development programmes

Programmes and actions designed to ensure a sustainable future for land resources are beginning to gain popularity. Voluntary financing of afforestation programmes on corporate lands was being undertaken by 40 per cent of the TNCs surveyed. Recent calls to action by governments and international organizations to address the greenhouse gas problem may be prompting those tree-planting programmes. Asia-based (Japan) firms led the corporate afforestation efforts, with 57 per cent undertaking such programmes. (See figure IX.3.) The prominent Japanese efforts in afforestation indicated a progressive role for the firms in tackling world forestry problems. They may have been reacting to past criticism of

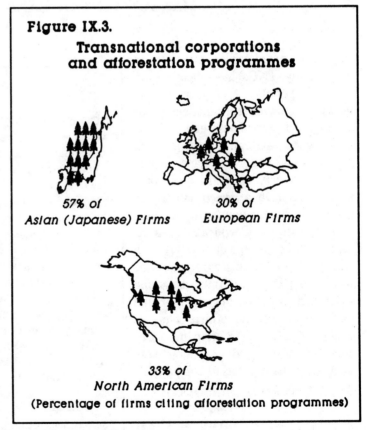

Figure IX.3.

Transnational corporations and afforestation programmes

57% of Asian (Japanese) Firms

30% of European Firms

33% of North American Firms

(Percentage of firms citing afforestation programmes)

Source: TCMD/DESD Benchmark Survey, 1990-91.

Japanese activities harvesting rainforest products in both Latin America and South-East Asia. Japan's consumption of tropical wood products is the largest in the world.[8]

For corporations operating in developing nations, several unique land issues have come to the forefront. The tragedy at Bhopal dramatized the need for safety zones around highly hazardous operations. Only 14 per cent of the surveyed corporations, though, had developed safety zones around their factories in developing nations. Japan-based firms led the other regions, with 24 per cent holding land to protect neighbouring communities. Similarly, extractive-based corporations led the other sectors. The Bhopal experience of **Union Carbide** may have influenced other firms to guard against such incidents. (See annex table D.25.)

The depletion of rainforests and wetlands is particularly acute in developing nations. Like safety zones, rainforest and wetland preservation programmes had been initiated by only 9.2 per cent of the firms surveyed. North America-based firms led corporate efforts in that area, with 21 per cent implementing rainforest or wetland programmes.

B. EXAMPLES OF CORPORATE PROTECTION AND MANAGEMENT OF LAND RESOURCES

As noted earlier, afforestation projects by TNCs have become remarkably popular. A number of Asia-based firms have received attention for dealing with greenhouse and soil-loss problems through tree-planting programmes. Pulp and paper firms, while extremely active in those projects, also have a vested interest in leading afforestation programmes. **Stone Container Corporation** reported that it had become quite aggressive with its afforestation programme. (See box IX.1.) In Latin America, **Stone Container** was making one of the largest reforestation efforts ever attempted there. As is often the case, environmental and long-term business interests do have points of compatibility.

Corporations such as **Oryx, Inc.** had developed other creative corporate approaches. **Oryx**, a multi-

> **Box IX.1. Stone Container Corporation and afforestation**
>
> "Our company, by design, does not own much timberland, but we have been aggressive in taking on responsibility as stewards of the public and private land that we harvest. One of our most import forestry programs is our Landowner Assistance Program (LOA). The program is a comprehensive plan of professional planting, growing and harvesting advice designed to help the landowner make informed decisions about his property and to realize the highest potential of his timberland. One of the important focuses of the program is reforestation, where we provide seedlings free of charge to participating landowners. Recent efforts have involved annual plantings of more than 40 million seedlings. Stone's LOA helps tremendously in improving the image and preserving the future of the forest products industry. As evidence of our success, this program was selected for the Forest Management "Environment Achievement" award by the American Paper Institute and the National Forest Products Association".
>
> *Source:* Stone Container corporate materials.

national oil and gas producer, reported that it had donated land for wildlife sanctuaries and had joined in cooperative efforts on programmes with the United States Department of Agriculture Forest Service. Such projects are often a mechanism by which corporations can foster favourable relations with the local communities in which they operate. **Texaco Inc.**, for instance, had launched a $2 million programme with the help of Louisiana State University to resolve soil erosion problems on Timbalier Island, a barrier island off the Louisiana coast near **Texaco's** Caillou Island producing field.

The firms innovative in environmental management are typically those which take a product-stewardship view of the company's role in managing products and processes. Analysing corporate impact upon the environment over the entire life and scope of the product is a common trait of many firms in the forefront of environmental efforts. **Amoco** stresses "stewardship and multiple land use" throughout its operations and strives to "preserve the best while balancing competing uses of vital resources". **Amoco** had made environmental considerations the focal point of a number of land-related decisions. Further, many firms such as **Amoco** were devoting increasing research and development efforts to land protection technologies (see box IX.2). Beyond correcting past land-related environmental problems, environmentally-aware firms were addressing these concerns proactively and integrating them into standard decision making. For instance, **Company Y**, in its

> **Box IX.2. Amoco and Land Stewardship**
>
> Amoco has undertaken a number of projects and programmes, such as its Safety and Integrity Program, supporting environmental protection of land resources.
>
> - Leak detection systems at service stations;
> - Establishment of systems to prevent accidental rupturing of pipelines and buried utility lines;
> - Investigation of former refinery sites for possible adverse effects on the local area;
> - Replacement of old pipes to avoid potentially catastrophic accidents.
>
> Amoco has likewise sought to introduce new technologies to minimize environmental harm:
>
> - Directional drilling which allows the firm to use only a small fraction of an area's land surface (in one example, only 2.5 per cent of the surface area) to produce oil and natural gas;
> - Utilization of special levees to prevent salt-water intrusions and seasonal flooding.
>
> *Source:* TCMD/DESD, Benchmark Survey, 1990-91.

"New Facility Assessment Policy", stressed the importance of collecting information about hazardous-material use, storage, and disposal, as well as the possible impacts of those hazards on the soil. Environmentally-leading firms strive to eliminate hazards before they occur rather than emphasize post-process clean-up.

C. SUMMARY

The Survey results indicate that managerial awareness of key land issues was often lacking, even if half the respondents found these issues important. Nearly two thirds of the TNCs surveyed had not yet developed extensive policies on land management.

Corporations with agricultural or forestry-based products were actually lagging behind other sectoral groups in areas such as land-policy development and integrated pest-management programmes. Land issues such as desertification and soil degradation were not explicitly reflected in any corporate environmental policy or programme reviewed by the Benchmark Survey.

Moreover, a relatively small percentage of firms was utilizing safety zones around manufacturing sites, particularly in developing nations. Addressing safety issues through process changes and emergency planning is a useful approach, but safety zones can provide an added margin of security. As unlikely as catastrophic process failure may be, anticipating the worse and implementing contingency solutions such as safety zones can prevent harm to local communities.

The widespread use of afforestation programmes is indicative of a certain corporate interest in these issues. Interestingly, corporations with virtually no involvement in the paper industry were undertaking afforestation programmes as frequently as more land-based firms. Tree-planting projects, though, had not been limited to the agricultural sector, which included the paper and pulp industry. Other sectors had undertaken such programmes in number nearly equal to the agricultural products sector. The service sector, for instance, was almost equally likely to have such programmes.

Tree-planting programmes are a tangible and easily recognizable act by which corporations can demonstrate environmental concern. They are also relatively straightforward in terms of execution. Afforestation produces other positive benefits as well; for example, the beautification of corporate lands increases employee morale. The task of governments and international organizations should be to identify other environmental activities which possess similar potential for positive corporate publicity, compatibility with other corporate goals, and simplicity.

Innovative land preservation policies and programmes were being initiated primarily by only the largest of TNCs. Relatively smaller firms (all of which had sales over $1 billion) were more likely to consider particular land issues as not applicable to their operations. Furthermore, North America-based corporations were , significantly more inclined to have policies on land management. High-profile legislation such as the SARA Title III in the United States, with its stringent disclosure requirements, might have been responsible for raising corporate awareness of land hazards.

Notes

[1] Worldwatch Institute, *State of the World 1991*, (New York, W.W. Norton, 1991), p. 74.

[2] Ibid., pp. 75-76.

[3] FAO, *Forest Products Yearbook 1988* (Rome, 1990).

[4] Worldwatch Institute, op. cit., p. 76.

[5] Ibid., p. 80.

[6] Jeremy Rifkin, *Entropy: Into the Greenhouse World*, revised edition (New York, Bantam, 1989), p. 154.

[7] Ibid., p. 155.

[8] Worldwatch Institute, op. cit., p. 78.

As a result of human activities from both inland and coastal areas, coastal and marine ecosystems and resources are rapidly deteriorating in many parts of the world. A wide range of activities on land contribute to the release of contaminants either directly to the sea or are carried by way of rivers and the atmosphere. Seaborne activities add the rest.

Urban, industrial, resort and agricultural development is often poorly planned and regulated. Run-off from land, also called non-point pollution, receives little regulatory attention even in developed countries. The coastal zone receives pollution both by direct discharge and via river systems. More than three quarters of marine pollution comes from land-based sources, via rivers, direct discharges, and the atmosphere, i.e., 40 per cent of contaminants arrive via rivers and 30 per cent via the atmosphere. The rest comes from shipping, dumping, and offshore mining and oil production.[1]

According to a report by the Group of Experts on the Scientific Aspects of Marine Pollution, the major marine contaminants, in order of importance, are: nutrients from urban sewage and rural runoff, microbial contamination from sewage, plastics from land and sea disposal, synthetic organic compounds such as pesticides and industrial chemicals, and oil from routine transport and spills. Plastics and pesticides have affected marine mammals even in remote islands.[2] Even though industry is not one of the most important contributors of contaminants to the oceans, it does contribute most of the arsenic, mercury, chlorinated hydrocarbons and other toxic chemicals.[3] For that reason, the Benchmark Survey chose to concentrate on this aspect of the environment in its study of TNCs, as well as the extensive history of intergovernmental activity on the protection of the oceans.

In terms of both tonnage and visual impact, the most important sea-based marine pollutant are crude petroleum and its derivatives. Of the approximately 600,000 tons of oil entering the oceans each year from maritime activities, less than 25 per cent is from major tanker accidents, although that type of release receives a great deal of publicity when it occurs. A much larger quantity of oil is discharged as a result of normal shipping operations.[4] The main sources of petroleum inputs into the marine environment are: transportation, 45.2 per cent; municipal and industrial waste discharge and run-off, 36.3 per cent; offshore oil production, 1.5 per cent; seeps and erosion, 7.7 per cent; and atmosphere, 9.2 per cent.[5]

Another source of marine pollution is disposal of wastes at sea. Large quantities of dredged spoils, sewage and industrial waste are dumped every year into the world's oceans. Transnational corporations are prominent in industries such as mining, metal and chemical processing or oil exploration, which create a significant part of such industrial waste.

Since direct dumping is now prohibited in most regional seas, the major dumping grounds are the Atlantic Ocean and the North Sea.[6] Although the London Dumping Convention has banned all dumping of heavy metals and persistent or carcinogenic wastes in all seas, many tons of heavy metals and persistent or carcinogenic wastes are still being dumped at sea legally under provisions that allow waste consignments to contain trace quantities of those banned substances.

Agenda 21:

"Apply preventive, precautionary and antici-patory approaches so as to avoid degradation of the environment, as well as to reduce the risk of longterm irreversible adverse effects upon it" (17.22).

"Prior environmental impact assessment, systematic observation and follow up of major projects, including the systematic incorpora-tion of results in decision-making" (17.6).

The point of departure for UNCED's delib-erations on ocean issues was that a coordinated institu-tional approach, integrating all relevant environmental and developmental aspects of ocean and sea resources, was essential. Among the priorities for action were the protection of the marine environment against the adverse effects of human land-based and sea-based activities. Industry activities with potential impact on the sea environment were oil exploitation, dumping, transport of hazardous substances, and effluent dis-charges. The conference also discussed the relationship between climate chance and sea levels.

A. STATISTICAL FINDINGS

The importance of the protection of the oceans ranked fifth among the seven UNCED themes presented to the participants in the Benchmark Survey. Only 36 per cent of the respondents found that issue significant. One half of these firms were based in Asia. (See figure X.1.)

A significant corporate activity which has direct impact on the well-being of the oceans is disposal of wastes into the seas. However, only ten per cent (15 firms) of the respon-dents stated that they engaged in such disposal and those firms were divided equally among the three regions. The sectoral breakdown, however, shows that firms in the extractive-based sector were more likely to engage in such an activity.

Shipping of oil is another activity with potentially detrimental effects on the oceans. Only 13 per cent of the responding firms were involved in shipping of oil. Half of those firms were in the extractive-based sector. (See annex table D.26.)

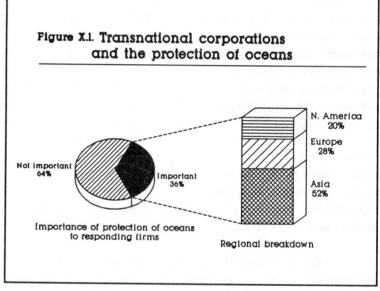

Figure X.1. Transnational corporations and the protection of oceans

Source: TCMD/DESD Benchmark Survey, 1990-91.

Fourteen per cent of the responding firms stated that they had marine transport policies. That may be directly related to the number of firms engaging in oil transport activities which necessitate such policies. Asia- and North America-based firms were more likely to have those policies. The extractive-based sector was far ahead of all other sectors in having such policies, which implies that those firms, in a line of business which involves frequent transport of sea pollutants, take their responsibilities in this area seriously. (See annex table D.27.)

Fourteen per cent of the respondents (17 firms) indicated that they released effluents into oceans or seawater tributaries in developing countries. Once again, the extractive-based firms (35 per cent) were more likely to do so than the other sectors. One oil company indicated that the effluent levels which they permitted in their developing-country operations were based on those of their home country. Another oil company stated that it released effluents into oceans through drilling operations (see annex table D.27).

B. EXAMPLES OF CORPORATE ACTIVITIES
PROTECTING THE OCEANS

Three of the four firms which indicated that they had programmes in place for the protection of the oceans were oil companies, and they did so in terms of policies for the prevention of oil spills or as a prompt urgent response in the case of an oil spill. The fourth company, **Broken Hill Proprietary Co. (BHP)** was involved in mining and metal processing.

BHP stated that the main source of discharges into rivers and marine environments was treated tailings from the processing of copper concentrates from mining operations. The company reported ensuring that the solid wastes were non-toxic and, in each instance, a detailed environmental monitoring programme had been established to make certain that there were no long-term deleterious effects resulting from the discharges. Drilling fluids and cuttings from offshore drilling operations were discharged into the ocean, provided they were not contaminated with diesel, oil etc. Formation water from oil recovery operations offshore was discharged into the ocean and oil content was monitored to make sure that it was within limits required by regulations. When treated wastewater from steel plants and other land-based operations was discharged into the marine environment, it was monitored to ensure compliance with strict regulatory requirements.[7]

Amoco Corporation stated that the company "thoroughly reviewed our oil spill and hazardous chemical response plans, updating and improving them as necessary. We tested these plans by conducting major exercise drills involving local, state, nation and in some cases international agencies, at our Texas City, Yorktown VA refineries, the Beaufort Sea, the North Sea and Louisiana". The company also reported that "in a separate program, we are voluntarily ceasing discharges of produced brine into coastal zone areas and putting oil spill containment equipment on coastal zone wells in critical areas".[8]

Texaco Inc., which placed high priority on preventing oil spills, had a "...company-wide response program to clean up spills promptly...". The company had created a world-wide Texaco Oil Spill Coordinating Committee, "...an oversight group that will ensure that we have highly trained personnel using the most up-to-date response plans and equipment". Since 1986, **Texaco** had also spent $100 million to replace underground steel gasoline tanks and lines with corrosion-resistant fiberglass systems. According to the company, the new tanks were equipped with the latest technology to minimize leaks as well as monitor detection devices.[9]

Chevron Corporation stated as one of the company's specific objectives "devising safer-operating procedures to reduce the number of petroleum spills, chemical releases and other accidents".[10] The **Sandoz Group's** Strategies on Safety, Environmental Protection and Industrial Hygiene, which were developed to implement the **Sandoz Group's** Principles for Safety and Environmental Protection, state that "...Sea dumping and export of wastes to developing countries are not acceptable".[11]

C. SUMMARY

Ocean issues will probably increase in importance in the near future due to the mounting environmental problems of oceans and coastal areas which stemming from multiple and diffuse sources, and thus remain unaddressed because of the lack of international cooperation. The Benchmark Survey provides little data illuminating ocean issues. As is evident in the examples from responding companies, there has been, and continues to be, some effort in containing oil spills and chemical releases, from improved oil transportation procedures to oil and chemical spillage preventive measures.

Unfortunately, companies outside the extractive-based sector have not implemented any precautions against the pollution of oceans. That could be an indication that some companies do not view ocean protection as an issue associated with their activities. Clearly, educational activity is required in this regard. It should be noted though, that polices to minimize the emission of wastewater and to conserve freshwater--activities which many corporations have in place--also contribute to limiting the pollution of oceans.

Most companies seeking to protect the ocean seemed to focus more on reactive plans rather than preventive plans, i.e., more firms cited having response plans and trained personnel in cases of accidents rather than working towards the elimination of oil spills, chemical discharges or other ocean pollutants.

Notes

[1] The World Conservation Union, United Nations Environment Programme and the World Wide Fund for Nature, *Caring for the Earth: A Strategy of Sustainable Living,* (Gland, Switzerland, 1991), p. 151.

[2] World Resources Institute, United Nations Environment Programme and United Nations Development Programme, *World Resources 1990-91* (Oxford, Oxford University Press, 1990), p. 179.

[3] *World Resources 1990-91,* op. cit., table 11.2, p. 182.

[4] "Protection of oceans, all kinds of seas including enclosed and semi-enclosed seas, coastal areas and the protection, rational use and development of their living resources" (A/CONF.151/PC/42/Add.6, 3 July 1991), p. 13.

[5] *World Resources 1990-1991,* op. cit., table 11.3, p. 186.

[6] E. Goldsmith and N. Hildyard, eds. *The Earth Report* (Price Stern Sloan, Los Angeles, 1989), p. 191.

[7] Broken Hill Proprietary Co., "Additional notes in response to UNCTC Benchmark Corporate Environmental Survey", unpublished.

[8] Amoco Corporation, "Annual report 1989", p. 24.

[9] Texaco Inc., "Environmental, health & safety review" (1990), p. 2.

[10] Chevron Corporation, "1990 report on the environment: a commitment to excellence", p. 4.

[11] Sandoz Technology Ltd., "Safety and environmental protection-principles and strategies (1988), p. 8.

CHAPTER XI.   ENVIRONMENTALLY SOUND MANAGEMENT OF BIOTECHNOLOGY

Biotechnology covers a broad field of applied science and related research that has emerged during the past 20 years. It includes a wide spectrum of activities ranging from old fermentation techniques to new expertise such as use of recombinant DNA and tissue-culture technologies. The newer developments have become possible through genetic engineering.

The most recent phase of biotechnology has been developed during the past 15 years within small firms and has either been financed through venture capital or funded by large corporations. There are problems in developing the new products which involve economic considerations in meeting regulatory requirements, and special aspects of intellectual property rights. Large corporations have been reluctant to make the capital investment themselves because of the initial risks arising from those problems. They have often provided the funding for such research, however, and when a particular process proves commercially successful, they buy the stock or marketing rights from smaller biotechnology firms. Transnational corporations have gradually taken over small biotechnology research companies and have increasingly used patents in biotechnology research to create a dominant role in the production and marketing of the research results. Thus, the Benchmark Survey targeted the management of biotechnology among TNCs.

Products resulting from biotechnology fall into three main groups in terms of value and volume: (a) very high-value medical products resulting mainly from genetic engineering; (b) an intermediate group of amino and organic acids which are used in the animal feed and food industry or as chemical feedstock; and (c) a group of low-value products resulting from the old fermentation processes, which have to be sold in large quantities and which compete against similar commodities produced by different means.[1] There is concern, however, about the environmental implications of biotechnology applications and uncertainty about the effects of biotechnology and genetic engineering on health and the environment, especially from the release of genetically-engineered organisms in the environment.

Some genetically-engineered organisms can assist in repairing environmental damage caused by other technologies. For example, micro-organisms produced through biotechnology have much to offer by way of minimization and abatement of environmental pollution. New organisms can be applied directly to manufacturing processes to manage waste at the source. Biotechnology offers the chemical industry the possibility of replacing pesticides, nitrate fertilizers and food additives with non-chemical-based products. Micro-organisms have already been used for recovery of metals from ore, and it is possible that they may be used in the future for recovery of oil reserves trapped in rock formations.

Conversely, genetically-engineered organisms and their products can have a negative impact on the environment. A number of corporations involved in biotechnology are concentrating their efforts in developing herbicide-tolerant crops which will withstand large amounts of the companies' produced herbicides. The world's leading pesticide companies, all major transnational corporations, are undertaking herbicide-tolerant plant research, as have virtually all major seed companies, many of which have been acquired by chemical companies.[2] Introduction of such plants, however, will probably result in the increased use of herbicides, which will bring a concomitant increase in environmental problems.

The risks of herbicide-tolerant plants in developing countries can be particularly serious. Nearly all major crops grown in developed countries are not native and have no wild relatives. In Asia and South America, however, where many of the main crops found in developed countries originated, wild relatives are common and frequently grown as weeds. Scientists are concerned that in those countries, herbicide-tolerant crops could cross-pollinate with their wild, weedy relatives and give rise to herbicide-tolerant crops.[3]

> **Agenda 21:**
>
> "Assist in exchanging information about the procedures required for safe handling and risk management and about the conditions of release of the products of biotechnology, and cooperate in providing immediate assistance in cases of emergencies that may arise in conjunction with the use of biotechnology products" (16.32).
>
> "Develop policies and mobilize additional resources to facilitate greater access to the new biotechnologies, particularly by and among developing countries" (16.40).

Controversy surrounds the use of bovine somatotropin (BST), a genetically-engineered growth hormone which controls the conversion of animal food into milk in cows. BST is being tested in the United States and is undergoing field trials in a number of developed and developing countries. It is already licensed for sale in Brazil, the Czech and Slovak Republics, Mexico, South Africa and former Soviet Union.[4] In addition to a number of social, economic and ethical concerns raised by the marketing of that animal drug, controversy also surrounds the safety of the product.

The environmental impacts of an industry based on genetically novel organisms are not easy to predict or to evaluate. The above-mentioned examples of how biotechnology can affect the environment can be summarized as follows: (a) direct effects of the release of genetically-altered organisms in the environment; (b) secondary effects on existing environmental problems such as herbicide use; and (c) tertiary effects on the structure of the economy, particularly the agricultural economy, which in turn could have environmental impacts. The implications for developing countries with agriculturally-based economies need to be considered. It is important to raise the level of public awareness on both the potential benefits and the detrimental consequences of biotechnology.

UNCED identified five priority areas which specifically address biotechnology research, development and use in relation to sustainable development. They seek to promote the environmentally sound application of biotechnology within an internationally agreed framework of safety and to establish appropriate enabling mechanisms. The areas are: (a) increased productivity of food, feed and renewable raw materials; (b) the improvement of human health; (c) the enhancement of environmental protection through biotechnology; (d) the enhancement of safety in biotechnology; and (e) the establishment of mechanisms for the environmentally sound application of biotechnology.

A. STATISTICAL FINDINGS

1. Sectoral and regional breakdown

Seventeen per cent of the respondents to the Benchmark Survey stated that they used bioengineering processes or manufacture products resulting from biotechnology. That low number is probably connected with the fact that biotechnology is a very specialized field in which only firms in certain sectors operate. The sectoral breakdown of the positive responses gives weight to that assumption; over 80 per cent of the firms involved in biotechnology belong in the agricultural and extractive-based sectors where the pharmaceutical, food and chemical firms are grouped.

The regional breakdown of the positive responses shows double the number of Europe- and Asia-based firms involved in biotechnology compared to North America-based firms. Since biotechnology is regulated quite extensively in all three regions, differences in the regulatory framework cannot be a likely explanation.

The sectoral breakdown of the firms involved in biotechnology within the three regions probably explains the regional difference. Among the eleven agricultural and extractive-based respondents working in biotechnology, only three were based in North America with the rest almost equally divided between the two other regions. That would mean that there were more respondents working in biotechnology based in Europe and Japan than in North America. (See figure X1.1.)

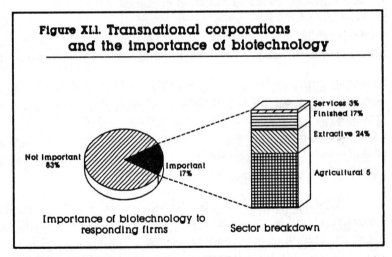

Figure X1.1. Transnational corporations and the importance of biotechnology

Not Important 83%

Important 17%

Importance of biotechnology to responding firms

Services 3%
Finished 17%
Extractive 24%
Agricultural 5

Sector breakdown

Source: TCMD/DESD Benchmark Survey, 1990-91.

2. Developing country issues

Among the respondents working in biotechnology, only three stated that they marketed genetically-engineered products in developing countries; another six firms indicated that they did not have sufficient data to respond to this question. Among the three which responded affirmatively, one firm marketed seeds; another marketed growth hormones manufactured in developing countries; the third respondent did not provide details. Even though the number appears to be very small, it translates to almost 30 per cent of all respondents involved in biotechnology. As it is unlikely that the regulatory mechanisms for overseeing the impact of marketing genetically-engineered materials in developing countries are very well-developed, the fact that those products have been marketed in developing countries raises concern. (See annex table D.28.)

B. EXAMPLES OF CORPORATE ACTIVITIES
UTILIZING BIOTECHNOLOGY

Although overall, the majority of the respondents to the Benchmark Survey did not rate the environmentally sound use of biotechnology very highly, 80 per cent of those finding the issue important belonged to the agricultural and extractive-based sectors. This indicated that firms involved in biotechnology did not take lightly the environmental implications of the subject.

Among the participants which indicated that they manufactured products or used processes involving biotechnology, **Imperial Chemical Industries (ICI)** had set up a pioneering scheme to clean up chemical waste by running it through effluent-eating bacteria living on the roots of reeds specially planted on previously derelict land. The reeds also formed a habitat for wildlife.

Through a method based on biological fermentation systems, **ICI** had also developed "Biopol", a new type of biodegradable plastic made from a family of polymers derived from sugar. The new product, which was both biodegradable and manufactured from a renewable raw material, sugar, could biodegrade harmlessly when buried or flushed away, but remained stable during normal use.

Another **ICI** product derived from biotechnology was an enzyme which neutralized potentially dangerous neuro-toxins which are a by-product of water treatment processes using polyacrylamides. The enzyme was a biological catalyst which broke down toxic acrylamide residues and converted them into harmless acrylic acid. **ICI** was examining possible ways of handling other difficult toxic-waste problems. Undesirable residues under scrutiny included those resulting from the production of polyvinyl chloride and PCBs at present disposed of by incineration.

Another participant to the Benchmark Survey, **Ciba-Geigy Ltd.** indicated that its main work in agricultural biotechnology was the development of new active substances for plant protection against agents, and the breeding of improved plant species for better harvests and increased resistance against pests and pathogens. In that regard, the company had been able to alter commercial maize seed lines by gene manipulation so that the newly introduced properties were inherited by subsequent generations. That allowed for the breeding of maize varieties with improved resistance to disease, pests and unfavourable climatic conditions.

Ciba-Geigy's stated policy was to use genetic engineering and biotechnology techniques whenever they could help people, animals or the environment. For ethical reasons, **Ciba-Geigy** contended that it did not work with human cells or embryos and rejected all experiments leading to manipulation of human genes or the alteration of the gene pool.[5]

Enso-Gutzeit OY reported that it had a research centre particularly active in the field of biotechnology. The biological process for the bleaching of wood pulp had been further developed, with the aim of improving pulp purity and reducing environmental loads.

C. SUMMARY

The development of biotechnology is, at the same time, a major opportunity for environmental protection and a threat. Owing to extremely high R&D costs, engaging in biotechnological projects is a major undertaking, and therefore TNCs play a central role.

The information on that issue collected through the survey was rather scarce. Taking into account that biotechnological problems will be a major issue of the future, more information is needed on TNC activities in this regard, especially in developing countries. What happens when TNCs apply biotechnological products in developing countries where only regulation of biotechnological products and processes is either weak or non-existent? Do corporations act prudently, using the highest existing standards, or do they have more lenient practices? Further research is clearly indicated.

Notes

[1] Kenneth Green and Edward Yoxen, "The greening of European industry", *Futures*, vol. 22, No. 5, June 1990, p. 476.

[2] Rebecca Goldburg, Jane Rissler, Hope Shand and Chuck Hassebrook, *Biotechnology's Bitter Harvest*, (report of the Biotechnology Working Group).

[3] Joel Keehn, "Mean green", *Buzzworm: The Environmental Journal*, vol. IV, No. 1 (January 1992), p. 35.

[4] International Organization of Consumers Unions, "Comments on environmentally sound management of biotechnology, on the progress report of the Secretary General of the Conference" (A/CONF.151/PC/67).

[5] Ciba-Geigy, "Facts and figures" (1991), p. 28.

CHAPTER XII.   CONSERVATION OF BIOLOGICAL DIVERSITY

A diversity of biological species is essential to maintain the planet's life-sustaining balance. Some 30 million different species are thought to exist, but scientists have only classified about 1.4 million.[1] Unfortunately, the demand for products and resources may result in the extinction of vital plants and animals before they are thoroughly analysed. A recent report concluded that "species are now being lost at an unprecedented rate--some 400 times faster than at any other period during recent geological time-- and the range of species affected is far wider than ever before".[2] Twenty-five per cent of the world's species are expected to be extinct or reduced to a tiny remnant by the middle of the next century.[3]

Biological species are not only a prime source of present corporate resources, but represent the future store from which new technologies and materials will emerge. The genetic variability of the natural world is the primary material source for new crops, medicines, fibers, and foods, hence the importance of biological resources to the Benchmark Survey of TNCs. World-wide, plant-derived drugs represented a market value of $40 billion.[4] Despite those pharmaceutical uses, only one per cent of the planet's 250,000 flowering plant species have been thoroughly examined for medicinal properties.[5] The continued destruction of rain forest lands may prevent the cataloguing of potentially lifesaving drugs. Rosy periwinkle, a rain forest plant, has already saved many children from leukemia. Export demands for hardwood products, crops and meat production have prompted rain forest deforestation. Other critical habitats such as wetlands and coral reefs likewise possess numerous species types. Those areas are also under pressure from industrial pollution and product resource needs.

Biological species are also becoming a key component in effective agricultural practices. Wild strains of domesticated plants have saved many crops from being completely destroyed by pests. A "useless" wild wheat plant from Turkey has been used to impact disease resistance to commercial wheat varieties worth $50 million annually to the United States alone.[6] Further, biological diversity is an important source of genes for improving cultivars through biotechnology.

Current agricultural practices have, in many instances, placed efficiency before the long-term sustainability of soil and species. Industrial plantings often promote a single genetic species to maximize product output. Such plantings, however, can upset predator relationships and result in disease and pest outbreaks. To combat those outbreaks, larger quantities of fertilizers, herbicides and pesticides are employed. Such solutions, though, may only further imperil species survival.

As consumer and industrial demand continues to grow, so, too, will the loss of biological diversity. Industrial product and process needs entail forest clear-cutting, oil and gas drilling, mining, and road-building. The location of resources often requires that such activities be undertaken in environmentally sensitive areas. Habitat loss and the accompanying effects on plant and animal species are clearly corporate concerns. The challenge facing corporations is to reconcile the short-term need for resources with the long-term promise those same resources hold for both corporate and environmental sustainability.

Issues related to biodiversity were highly disputed during UNCED. They overlapped the discussions on forests and those on patent and property rights. Whereas developing nations contended that they had a right to share the benefits of products derived from their biological reserves, some developed

Agenda 21:

"Take appropriate measures for the [fair and equitable] sharing of benefits derived from research and development and use of biological and genetic resources, including biotechnology, between the sources of those resources and those who use them" (15.4d).

"Develop policies to encourage the conservation of biodiversity and the sustainable use of biological and genetic resources on private lands" (15.5i).

"Introduce appropriate environmental impact assessment procedures for proposed projects likely to have significant impacts upon biological diversity" (15.5k).

nations opposed that view. The outcome was that several countries declined to sign the Convention on Biodiversity. But the Conference did agree on a complementary and reinforcing chapter of Agenda 21 on biological diversity which stated that more information was needed on biodiversity issues and that research and monitoring should be strengthened. Moreover, the benefits derived from utilizing resources from biological reserves should be spread and maximized. Finally, conservation efforts of biodiversity should be upgraded, and in that connection, capacities for managing biological resources should be enhanced, especially in developing nations.

A. STATISTICAL FINDINGS

Biodiversity is not a concern solely for governmental and non-profit wildlife organizations. The products, processes and services of the surveyed TNCs were based largely upon activities and raw materials directly affecting biological diversity. Further, the future supply of essential corporate resources for those firms depends upon the conservation of biological diversity. With nearly one quarter of the firms possessing mining operations, 19 per cent in agricultural production, 13 per cent in forestry operations, and 7 per cent in pharmaceutical products, the TNCs examined in the Benchmark Survey had a substantial business stake in conserving biological resources.

The corporations surveyed reported few of the specific activities most harmful to species survival. Few of the firms reported using agricultural resources derived from mono-cropping practices. Similarly, virtually none of the firms reported corporate operations involving drift net fishing. Given the nearly unanimous international disapproval of mono-cropping and drift net fishing, a low level of corporate involvement is not surprising.

International conventions have also been effective in eliminating such practices as drift net fishing. A 1989 United Nations resolution banned this fishing practice, in which threatened aquatic species are caught along with target commercial species. Taiwan and Japan, which had allowed drift net fishing, agreed to meet the resolution's June 1992 deadline.

Among the environmental issues examined in the Benchmark Survey, biodiversity ranked as the least likely to be among the firms' top five environmental concerns. Less than 10 per cent considered the conservation of biological diversity a key corporate environmental issue. That lack of recognition may have stemmed from unfamiliarity with the term "biodiversity". While biodiversity is a growing concern among the international community, the issue is not yet a top corporate priority. (See figure XII.1.)

Biodiversity may also be viewed as a more technically scientific discipline in comparison with broader environmental areas such as air and water protection. While genetic preservation is important to corporate materials and products, the effect upon corporations is less apparent than closely regulated air, land or water issues. As part of the global commons, plant and animal species may also be viewed as removed from direct corporate responsibility. As noted above, however, species preservation has direct economic implications for businesses.

1. Sustainable development policies and programmes

Relatively few of the surveyed firms reported programmes to help directly to conserve plant and animal species. Ten per cent of the

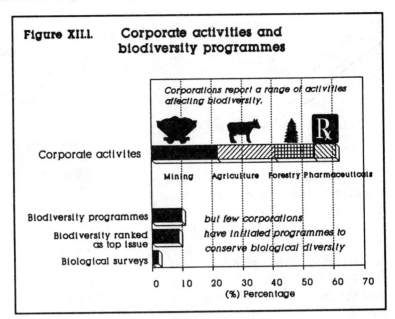

Figure XII.1. Corporate activities and biodiversity programmes

Source: TCMD/DESD Benchmark Survey, 1990-91.

firms reported conservation programmes directed at biodiversity. A slightly greater number, 16 per cent, had developed programmes to conserve endangered species. Since biodiversity includes programmes such as conservation of endangered species, the results again suggested a corporate unfamiliarity with the concept of biodiversity. Further, if large TNCs were unfamiliar with biodiversity, then the awareness level among small and medium-sized businesses would be most likely even less.

As previously noted in the land management discussion, corporations have made impressive efforts in afforestation. Those programmes can contribute significantly to biodiversity conservation by providing a habitat for endangered species. Surprisingly, the environmental officers of the firms which answered the questionnaire had not linked those programmes to species protection.

Firms based in North America were significantly more likely to recognize and undertake projects which protect biodiversity. One third of the North America-based firms cited programmes to conserve endangered species, while over 20 per cent directly noted involvement in biodiversity. The widely-known Endangered Species Act of the United States may have contributed to greater recognition of biodiversity issues by North American firms. While the Asia-based firms were leaders in afforestation projects (57 per cent) and wetland and rain forest programmes (24 per cent), only 2 per cent of the firms in that region reported programmes to conserve biodiversity. Thus, the Asia-based firms were leaders in programmes which would ultimately help conserve species, but recognition of that fact was minimal. (See figure XII.2.)

Nearly three quarters of the firms reporting biodiversity or endangered species programmes were involved in either extractive or agricultural-based industries. Thus, the industries with potentially the most detrimental impact upon threatened species were more inclined to develop specific programmes for their protection. Like the tree-planting projects discussed in the land management section, those programmes can be conducted simply and effectively, especially with the aid of non-profit conservation organizations and local governmental agencies. Overall, however, relatively few firms had taken direct action in biodiversity.

2. Developing country issues

As holders of some of the last untouched plant and wildlife areas, developing nations have gained much attention regarding biodiversity issues. Corporate activities such as mono-culture crop plantings and forest clear-cutting have been associated notoriously with developing nations. Given the near universal

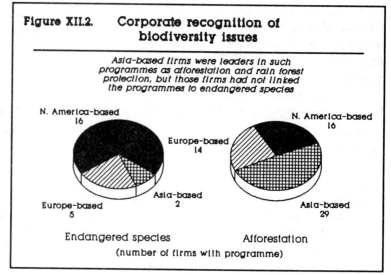

Figure XII.2. Corporate recognition of biodiversity issues

Asia-based firms were leaders in such programmes as afforestation and rain forest protection, but those firms had not linked the programmes to endangered species

Endangered species:
N. America-based 16
Europe-based 5
Asia-based 2

Afforestation:
N. America-based 16
Europe-based 14
Asia-based 29

Endangered species   Afforestation
(number of firms with programme)

Source: TCMD/DESD Benchmark Survey, 1990-91.

disapproval of mono-cropping and clear-cutting practices, it was a positive finding that two firms admitted using such techniques in developing nations.

Fewer than 10 per cent of the TNCs surveyed had conducted or were aware of corporate biological surveys in developing-country operations. Cataloguing species on corporate land is a first step to understanding the firm's impact upon plant and animal species. The lack of such cataloguing surveys again indicated that corporate actions to conserve biodiversity were still in a preliminary state. In the future, TNCs should be encouraged to establish biodiversity assessments similar to, or as a part of, overall corporate environmental auditing. (See annex table D.30.)

B. EXAMPLES OF CORPORATE BIODIVERSITY ACTIVITIES

Given the burgeoning corporate understanding of biodiversity issues, many of the surveyed firms were just then initiating biodiversity programmes. The first step has been to recognize the importance of species conservation to the firm's raw materials and products. Several firms had included plant and animal conservation themes in corporate policy statements. For those firms biological diversity had emerged as a principle central to the firm's operations. **Waste Management, Inc.** described biodiversity as one of its guiding principles:

> "The Company is committed to the conservation of nature. We will implement a policy of 'no net loss' of wetlands or other biological diversity on the Company's property".

Specific industries such as pharmaceutical, chemical and paper manufacturing have been among the first to see the relationship between the industry's future and biodiversity. **Imperial Chemical Industries (ICI)** reported it had designated the "preservation of important wildlife habitats" as a chief corporate concern. **Mo och Dormsjo AB (MoDo)** recognized the firm's activities "necessarily involve an impact on the environment." With 1,043,000 hectares of productive forest land, **MoDo** directly affected plant and animal populations. **MoDo** stressed, though, that the impact of the firm's activities would be controlled "so that important ecological processes are not disturbed. Forestry methods shall also ensure the continued existence of genetic diversity and multiplicity in the flora and fauna of the natural forests".

Like **MoDo**, **Ciba-Geigy Ltd.** recognized that its firm's activities could have negative effects on plant and animal species. To minimize the impact, **Ciba-Geigy** had incorporated species-saving concerns into the firm's research and development practices. Prompted by the inherent value of biological species to the firm's pharmaceutical operations, plant and animal welfare was considered in the firm's agricultural and chemical product lines as well. **Ciba-Geigy** had found that "environmentally sound chemistries" were cost effective.

"If, for example, our Agrochemicals Division were to succeed in developing herbicides which are more easily biodegradable, we would not only be doing justice to the environment, but also improving our own market potential. This convergence of interests between the pressing need to protect the environment on the one hand, and the legitimate economic interests of industrial concerns on the other, is a far better guarantee of a worthwhile future than could ever be provided by any number of laws or regulations."

Ciba-Geigy indicated that it was aggressively developing agricultural chemicals to "specifically attack the targeted pest without at the same time affecting plants or animals" and to "inhibit insect growth without unpredictable long-term effects such as resistance". Such products not only differentiated the firm from competitors but also minimized species disruption. For **Company O**, the recognition of wildlife preservation had also altered business practices. The company had promoted artificial hides for the seats of its luxury car models, for example.

A few leading firms in the conservation of biological diversity had initiated programmes and funds to directly enhance species survival. In several instances, those firms had teamed up with non-profit organizations or governmental agencies to support plant and animal life. **Company F** was supporting a United Kingdom Wildlife Trust to turn local marsh areas into wildlife refuges. **Company M** reported that it had donated the Asseek River estuary in British Columbia, Canada to the Nature Trust. The estuary is a critical habitat for several species of birds and animals. Additionally, the company had declared a moratorium on operations in environmentally-sensitive areas and had donated 40,000 hectares of primary forest land in New Zealand to permanent conservation. **Company P** had launched several projects with local communities and universities to preserve wildlife in areas where the firm operated. (See box XII.1.)

Beyond joint programmes with outside organizations, firms such as **Texaco** and **The Body Shop** had independently initiated conservation efforts. **Texaco** reported that it had dedicated corporate staff and resources to preserving and enhancing the 2,600 acres of wetlands surrounding the firm's Port Arthur, Texas, refinery. The **Texaco** wetlands now attract wading and shore birds from threatened areas elsewhere in coastal Texas.

Although not among the surveyed group of TNCs, The Body Shop stood out as an innovator and leader in environmentally sustaining activities, especially with regard to species conservation programmes. (See box XII.2.) This United Kingdom-based cosmetics and personal care retailer had grown rapidly to over 600 stores in 38 countries. The Body Shop's founder, Anita Roddick, attributed the firm's success to incorporating environmental and social concerns directly into company-wide values. Environmental programmes were the driving force behind stimulating employee enthusiasm and effectiveness as well as promoting consumer awareness of the store. In that sense, financial success and environmental protection were not only compatible but mutually dependent. Further, the Body Shop's efforts have demonstrated that all firms, regardless of size or sectoral activities, could contribute substantively to biological diversity and environmental sustainability.

C. SUMMARY

Few firms regard biological diversity as a corporate priority or have initiated programmes to help conserve species. Further, the results of the Benchmark Survey indicated a lack of familiarity with the issues associated with biodiversity. Fewer than 10 per cent of the large TNCs surveyed had conducted or were aware of corporate biological surveys. All firms should assess the impact of their products and processes upon plant and animal life.

The examples provided by the environmentally leading firms indicated that economic and biodiversity interests were indeed compatible. Species-saving efforts fostered both customer and employee goodwill as well as helping to preserve a natural resource which might be an important business asset in the future. Leading firms had used the species "friendliness" of the company's products and processes as a point of differentiation.

A few firms noted the importance of species-conservation in their guiding principles. A biodiversity policy statement can help integrate species conservation with the daily activities of managers and employees. By firmly stating a corporate concern for biological diversity to the firm's employees, customers and suppliers, a positive corporate value system regarding biodiversity can develop.

Box XII.1. Company P and Wildlife Protection

"Nestled amidst 6 million acres of [the company's] timberland resource base is an abundance of wildlife... We make sure to leave just the right trees for the various species in order to maintain the forest ecosystem. But we do more than just share the forest with these creatures; we help in the research and management of wildlife and their habitats."

[the company's] programmes include:

- Since 1981 [the company] has been working with the Peregrine Fund. The company now co-sponsors a peregrine release programme with the state of Washington. The firm's contribution to peregrine restoration has amounted to over a quarter of a million dollars.
- [the company] has contracted nearly 100,000 acres of company timberland to the state of Louisiana for co-operative wildlife management areas.
- The company manages a wetlands preservation zone on its Maine timberlands to protect riparian wildlife.
- The company has initiated a major elk management programme which addresses habitat issues. By working with the Oregon Department of Fish and Wildlife and University of Idaho researchers, the firm is developing long-range management guidelines for elk.

Source: Material submitted in support of responses to the BMS questionnaire.

Box XII.2. The Body Shop: "Trade Not Aid"

Through its "Trade Not Aid" programme, The Body Shop seeks to not only protect plant and animal species but also ensure the survival of indigenous peoples.

- The Body Shop has sought to save plant and animal species in the Brazilian rainforest by promoting sustainable uses of rainforest products. The firm has arranged to purchase brazil nut oil from the Kayapo Indians, a rainforest tribe. This trade helps the Indians and rainforest plant and animal species to survive against encroaching development.
- The company also set up trade with Nepalese paper makers to help save an endangered shrub called lokta. By identifying local alternatives to the lokta plant, The Body Shop has protected the lokta and stimulated needed economic growth.
- Through its "Stop the Burning" campaign, The Body Shop has publicized the plight of the rainforest to millions of consumers.

The Body Shop has also integrated plant and animal concerns into the firm's underlying principles: "Ensure products do not use materials from threatened species or threatened environments".

Source: The Body Shop.

A few environmentally leading firms have gained considerable public attention from biodiversity programmes. As noted, sponsoring projects to conserve biological species can be relatively simple and economical, particularly with the assistance of non-profit organizations and governmental agencies. Further, corporate examples have proven that those programmes can be undertaken successfully regardless of the firm's size or sectoral activities.

Direct action by corporations to preserve animal and plant species is a visible means of contributing to a significant global problem. Adopting biodiversity as a corporate priority is an opportunity for corporations to demonstrate publicly an ethical position on species preservation.

Notes

[1] United Nations Environment Programme, *Saving Our Planet: Challenges and Hopes* (Nairobi, 1992), p. 53.

[2] Edward Goldsmith and Nicholas Hildyard, eds., *The Earth Report* (Price, Stern, Sloane, Inc., 1988), p. 153.

[3] World Conservation Union, United Nations Environment Programme, and World Wide Fund for Nature, *Caring for the Earth: A Strategy of Sustainable Living* (Gland, Switzerland, 1991).

[4] United Nations Environment Programme, *Saving Our Planet: Challenges and Hopes* (Nairobi, 1992), p. 56.

[5] Joseph Wallace, "Rainforest Rx," *Sierra*, July/August 1991, p. 37.

[6] United Nations Environment Programme, op. cit., p. 56.

Whereas Part One provided an analysis of the Benchmark Survey data along functional management categories, Part Two analysed the data in relation to specific environmental problems discussed at UNCED. The analysis shows that there is a close relationship between the issues that have received much regulatory attention in recent years and the issues that have high priority on the corporate agenda. Of the seven issues discussed at UNCED targeted by the BMS of TNCs--atmosphere, toxic waste, freshwater, land, biodiversity, biotechnology, and oceans--corporations give high priority to atmosphere, toxic waste and freshwater. That became evident both when firms were asked to rank those issues in order of importance and in the concrete management practices reported in response to the questionnaire. The apparent explanation for the corporate interest in the issues is that they are the areas where the regulatory interest has been high in recent years or is likely to be intensified in the near future.

Even if most corporate activities can be related to local or national regulatory initiatives, international regulation seems to influence the activities of TNCs. Thus, the numerous examples of corporate CFC reduction programmes indicated that the Montreal Protocol had had a remarkably catalytic effect on corporations in that area. The relative success in inducing the corporate community to phase out CFC gases under the Montreal Protocol suggests that future international environmental initiatives should be focused on relatively specific problem areas, and that a combination of voluntary agreements and follow up regulation should be utilized. That will not only give corporate leaders a chance to develop technological and managerial fixes on a given environmental problem; it will also allow governments and the international community to adapt environmental regulation to the technological possibilities.

On an other level, international criticism of corporate conduct in specific areas seems to have had an effect as well. For example, it is probable that the fact that numerous Japanese corporations have afforestation programmes is related to the widespread international criticism of the conduct of Japanese forest corporations in South East Asia. Similarly, the oil industry's policies and programmes for protection of oceans point in that direction.

In areas such as water and energy conservation, corporate ingenuity has produced impressive results. The Benchmark Survey thus offers many examples of corporations that have obtained 90 per cent or more reductions in emissions and resource consumption. Those are also areas where corporations can obtain huge savings by preventing pollution. Taxation of natural resources such as water and energy could further encourage the corporate community to find ways of reducing the consumption of these resources.

Interestingly, there are significant regional variations in the way corporations choose to address the seven targeted issues. Clearly, the United States Superfund legislation has encouraged North American enterprises to take a special interest in land issues, whereas European corporations, in the wake of several serious chemical accidents on that continent, seem to concentrate on management of toxic and hazardous waste. All TNCs, independent of their home region, take an interest in issues related to atmospheric protection. That reflects the political concern in recent years in regard to issues such as sulfur rain, ozone depletion, air pollution in major cities and climate change.

One of the most positive findings of the Benchmark Survey is that corporations are employing innovative measures to curb specific environmental problems. Some corporations have chosen to address global environmental problems, such as climate change, even though no national or international regulation currently exists. Many corporations have programmes for the conservation or re-establishment of biological reserves such as forests and wetlands. That kind of activity presents the greatest potential for the achievement of Agenda 21 sustainable development goals.

PART THREE

CHAPTER XIV.   INTEGRATING SUSTAINABLE DEVELOPMENT IN CORPORATE DECISION-MAKING

The UNCED process has brought the international community a long way towards understanding the basic challenges that face humanity. It is now clear that environment and development are not adversarial but complimentary considerations, that development cannot take place at the expense of the environment, and that long-term solutions to environmental problems have a development dimension. In all parts of the world, environmental questions are becoming an increasingly important part of the political agenda, and the difficult process of integrating environmental considerations in economic and social decision-making is taking off, albeit slowly.

Transnational corporations are among the entities that can contribute significantly to sustainable development. They are especially well positioned to transfer environmentally sound technology and management experience to developing nations. In order to assess the current state of environmental management in TNCs, as well as the potential of TNCs in sustainable development, the Transnational Corporations and Management Division (TCMD, of the United Nations Department of Economic and Social Development (DESD) [now the UNCTAD Programme on Transnational Corporations] undertook the Benchmark Corporate Environmental Survey. The data were gathered in the period 1990-1991 from 210 of a target population of 794 TNCs with annual sales over $1 billion (a response rate of 27 per cent). The sample was divided into three distinct geographic regions (North America, Europe and Asia), four industrial sectors (agricultural, extractive, finished products and services) and three equally large divisions grouped by sales.

A. THE RESULTS OF THE BENCHMARK CORPORATE ENVIRONMENTAL SURVEY

The Benchmark Survey confirms that TNCs possess a great wealth of ideas and practices to draw from, and that some corporations have started seriously to consider their role in sustainable development and to integrate environmental concerns in decision-making. As demonstrated by the analysis presented in Part One of this report, most TNCs have incorporated EH&S policies into some level of their management structures. To a measurable degree, TNCs are beginning to link EH&S considerations with business objectives, at least in their policy statements. Activities such as environmental audits, safety procedures, disclosure of EH&S information and training programmes are widely undertaken by the TNCs that made up the survey sample, and many corporations have established highly sophisticated EH&S organizations.

The relatively innovative responses of some TNCs to specific environmental problems, detailed in Part Two of this report, demonstrate the potential of corporate management to contribute to sustainable development. The ground-breaking work some of the responding corporations in afforestation, resource and energy conservation, recycling, waste management, pollution control and climate change provides an impetus for other corporations to consolidate and expand environmental management in those areas.

The level of sophistication in EH&S management, however, varies significantly among the respondents. Some corporations have as many as fifteen or more company-wide EH&S policies and programmes in place, while one quarter of the respondents have none. Some corporations are consistently innovative, while others are followers, having only a bare minimum of policies and practices. Some corporations are active, seeking to seize future "green" business opportunities, while others focus merely on compliance with existing regulations. Some corporations have developed biodiversity protection and afforestation projects, while others are still engaged in extremely environmentally destructive activities such as dumping waste in the sea or drift net fishing. Despite the significant evidence of corporate commitment to environmental management, there remains a considerable need for corporations to address global environmental problems and to concentrate more attention on policies for overseas operations, particularly those in less developed countries.

One factor that appears to be instrumental in expanding corporate environmental activity is strong leadership and the direct involvement of boards of directors and chief executive officers. The fact that some corporations have chosen to be leaders in the field, with the opportunities that gives them, indicates to the followers, who only react to outside pressures and initiatives, the path for future corporate development. There is a wide gray zone between governmental regulations and corporate altruism that merits exploration by corporations, and might prove profitable both in terms of public relations and in terms of market shares. Such a venture requires a commitment from the leadership of the corporation. Leading-edge corporations look beyond short-term interests and include long-term considerations in their decision-making. They recognize that the viability of an enterprise depends not only on success in the market-place but also on the response to political and social concerns.

Ultimately, however, the potential of corporate discretion to contribute to sustainable development is limited. Each corporation operates under a specific set of conditions that constrain its choice of management practices. The nature of the industry in which the corporation is active, the size of the corporation, the dispersion of its activities, all influence the management practices that the corporation is able or willing to adopt. The conditions of production in a declining metals industry are markedly different from those in the dynamic computer industry. The EH&S responsibilities of a chemical corporation cannot be compared to those of a service company. The need for a positive EH&S image in an oil company operating in 40 countries will be much greater than in an oil corporation with little activity outside its home base. Consistent with that, the Benchmark Survey findings indicate significant variations in the management paths that different sectors and sales groups have chosen. Those TNCs in extractive-based industries--primarily chemical and oil industries--are leading in both safety procedures and resource management, due to their collective experiences of catastrophic environmental accidents. The computer and pharmaceutical industries, on the other hand, seem to have advanced in environmental management because their dynamic progress provides the resources and strategic potential for investing in long-term environmental programmes. Similarly, the larger the corporation, the more likely it is to have more advanced policies and practices; not only do economies of scale facilitate that process, but the stakes are also higher if disaster strikes.

Perhaps the most important factor influencing and constraining the scope and content of corporate EH&S management activities is the regulatory environment of the corporation, that is, the regulations and laws, the court system, the political culture and the traditions of cooperation between industry and state. Thus, the Benchmark Survey reveals significant variation among the respondents depending on the home region of the corporation, although companies in the three major regions face largely similar environmental problems. That clearly indicates that the actions of governments do make a difference for corporate behaviour and further suggests that in order to move TNCs towards more sustainable development management, governments and international organizations must create the right kind of incentive structures.

The importance of governments in encouraging improved corporate environmental management was clearly acknowledged by UNCED. Thus, Agenda 21 recommends that governments reorient their policies to "implement an appropriate mix of economic instruments and normative measures such as laws, legislation and standards in consultation with business and industry, including transnational corporations" (30.8); to "establish effective combinations of economic, regulatory and voluntary (self-regulatory) approaches" (8.32a); to "establish a policy framework that encourages the creation of new markets in pollution control, and environmentally sounder resource management" (8.32d); and to "explore the use of economic instruments and market mechanisms in consultation with business and industry, including transnational corporations" (8.33). Furthermore, Agenda 21 states that "facilitating and encouraging inventiveness, competitiveness and voluntary initiatives are necessary for stimulating more varied, efficient and effective options" (30.4). In alignment with those Agenda 21 recommendations, the following sections will provide a framework, based on the findings of the Benchmark Survey, for analysing the dynamic relationship between governmental action and corporate EH&S management, and will suggest different ways in which governments, in collaboration with business and industry, including TNCs, can reorient their policies to encourage improved corporate EH&S management.

B. A FRAMEWORK FOR ANALYSING THE RELATIONSHIP BETWEEN CORPORATE MANAGEMENT PRACTICES AND GOVERNMENTAL/INTERNATIONAL ORGANIZATION INITIATIVES

The Benchmark Survey demonstrates that corporations have chosen markedly different ways of addressing the environmental challenge. It suggests that at least four different management approaches are being utilized by the respondents. The lowest level in the evolution of corporate management practices is oriented towards compliance with regulations: *compliance-oriented management*. A second type of management goes beyond mere compliance, and engages in prevention of pollution and the reduction of resource use: *preventive management*. A third type of environmental management integrates EH&S protection in the overall business strategy and seeks to seize the business opportunities of growing green markets: *strategic environmental management*. Finally, the analysis of the survey data indicates that a handful of corporations have started considering their role in sustainable development in a more fundamental way and have begun to adopt programmes related to developing countries and protection of the global commons. That highly advanced level of EH&S management is designated here as *sustainable development management*. To each of these management levels belongs a distinct set of government actions. The following sections will describe the features of the four levels of environmental management, as well as the accompanying activities of governments and international organizations that are required to support and encourage a particular type of management. The discussion is summarized in box XIV.1.

Box XIV.1. Four levels of corporate EH&S management		
Management type	Corporate activities	Supporting governmental activities
I. Compliance-oriented management (The reactive corporation)	End-of-pipe solutions. Abatement procedures. Monitoring. Compliance reports. Training. Emergency response.	Command and control. Realistic regulations. Involvement of business in designing regulations. Inform on regulations. Tough enforcement.
II. Preventive management (The lean and precautionary corporation)	Internal audits. Pollution prevention. Waste minimization. Public information. Energy conservation. Green accounting.	Increased liabilities. Waste treatment requirements. Restrictive landfills policy. Community right-to-know. Energy conservation. Taxation.
III. Strategic environmental management (The opportunity-seeking corporation)	Public dialogue. External audits. Disclosure. Integration of EH&S in planning. Cradle-to-grave policy. Green R&D. Setting EH&S targets.	Stable regulatory build-up. Green labelling programmes. Support of consumer and green investor groups. Market means of regulation. Voluntary regulations. R&D tax-breaks.
IV. Sustainable development management (The responsive corporation)	Developing country programmes. Ethical sales policies. International disclosure. Climate change policies. Afforestation programmes. World-wide policies. International auditing.	International information dissemination. Integration of SD objectives in decision-making. International harmonization of environmental regulations and/or standards. International taxation.

1. Compliance-oriented management

(a) Corporate activities

In most industrialized countries environmental protection is a well-established discipline. More than 20 years have gone by since environmental laws were first enacted, and environmental laws are in place in some countries for most types of industrial pollution. Practice, however, has not always followed the letter of the law. Many countries have experienced serious problems in the implementation of environmental regulations, partly because statutory environmental requirements have been too ambiguous and thus subject to wide interpretation in the implementation phase, and partly because lenient or non-existent enforcement--often politically dictated--has given corporations the impression that environmental standards are open to negotiation.

Thus, it is not inconsequential when corporations pledge compliance with regulations and gear their EH&S practices accordingly, as many of the respondents to the Benchmark Survey stated that they had done. The significance of a compliance pledge is highlighted when one considers the volume of EH&S regulations that a typical corporation in an industrialized country must observe. For example, the European Community has issued more than 300 environmental laws. In addition, Europe-based corporations have to observe national legislation. In the United States, the operations of IBM's Mannassas plant are covered by some 15,000 pages of state and federal environmental regulations.

According to the Benchmark Survey, most of the respondents have compliance activities such as monitoring, control procedures and regular compliance reports in place, and many explicitly pledge in their policy statements to comply with regulations. Moreover, half the respondents reported that they had annual meetings with local environmental officials, an important aspect of the local application of environmental laws and regulations. The training of employees is also crucial to ensure compliance with regulations as well as with internal guidelines and policies; between 60 and 80 per cent of the respondents stated that they engaged in specific EH&S training, performance evaluation and awareness-raising activities.

Compliance-oriented management in developing nations is particularly important, as effective enforcement procedures have not yet been established in many of them.[1] Here, the Benchmark Survey produces disappointingly few examples of corporations explicitly referring to international compliance in their policy statements, even though more than half the corporations had activities in developing countries.

(b) Supportive tasks for governments

The Benchmark Survey results indicate that the establishment of regulations in the home country is the single most important factor in the development of corporate-wide global EH&S policies and programs. However, merely establishing regulations is not sufficient. Weak enforcement procedures, political leniency and ill-designed regulations seriously cripple the effectiveness of environmental regulation. Thus, it is crucial that governments establish effective enforcement procedures so that corporations have an incentive to adhere to the requirements of the law. Requiring mandatory compliance reports on a regular basis, as is currently the case in many countries, is one way of encouraging corporations to establish compliance procedures and practices, and to ease enforcement.

Furthermore, governments and international organizations can further encourage corporate compliance by disseminating information on relevant national regulations and, in general, by keeping regulations as simple, flexible and realistic as possible. There is no point in setting up strict environmental regulations if soon after the *raison d'être* of these regulations is undermined by new scientific evidence, or simply turns out to be economically unfeasible. In many cases, policy makers could benefit from listening to industry when designing new regulations. In addition, compliance can be achieved with much lower enforcement costs if a prior understanding with industry is reached.

Compliance can also be encouraged by reform of the legal system. In the United States, environmental damage is increasingly seen as a criminal offense. The past five years have seen a 33 per cent annual increase in environment-related prosecutions in the United States. In some cases, senior officials have gone to prison, held liable for the illegal actions of subordinates. Other countries have seen a similar trend

> **Box XIV.2. The Task for Governments**
>
> "The political authorities have to create and implement environmental standards, because it is not the task of industry to create a clean environment. The task and purpose of industrial activity is to earn money for the stockholders, to employ people and to comply with environmental regulation" (Umberto Colombo, Officer responsible the WCEDs work on industry and environment).

towards tough prosecution of environmentally non-compliant corporations. Notwithstanding the fact that criminalization of environmental offenses is effective in bringing about a certain behaviour, it is not an entirely desirable means of enforcing regulations, with the possible exception of cases of highly dangerous and toxic pollution. Criminal prosecution of environmental offenses tends to increase transaction costs unduly, and tends to focus corporations, as well as regulators, on proxy measures instead of environmental objectives.

2. Preventive management

(a) Corporate activities

Whereas compliance-oriented management is essentially the corporate behaviour of reacting to direct regulatory initiatives, changes in EH&S management practices will often be dictated by more indirect factors such as growing costs of waste disposal, raw materials or insurance. Huge amounts of money are being saved by corporations that establish programs to reduce their potential liabilities and costs.[2]

Most of the participants in the Benchmark Survey seem to have moved beyond mere compliance and are engaged in preventive management. They appear to be seeking to anticipate and prevent short-term costs and liabilities through EH&S management procedures or through new production processes and products. Many corporations refer to "product stewardship" and "precautionary and preventive management" in their policy statements, and between 60 and 80 per cent of the responding corporations have EH&S policies and programmes in areas such as waste-reduction, energy conservation, and accident prevention, all areas where there is potential for major savings. The supplementary material attained through the survey provides many examples of the gains from preventive management. For example, **Chevron** reports that over a period of three years its "SMART" program (Save Money and Reduce Toxics) has reduced hazardous waste by 60 per cent and saved the corporation more than $10 million in disposal costs. Similarly, **Toyota** has established programs to minimize wastewater with the result that 98 per cent of used water is reclaimed.

Preventive EH&S management relies on keeping management well informed on the state of EH&S issues in the corporation in order to prevent major accidents or liabilities. This is done through procedures such as auditing or assessments of risks and hazards. The Benchmark Survey indicates that between 60 and 70 per cent of the respondents have hazards assessment procedures or conduct environment and safety audits, and the supplementary material reveals that some corporations have developed highly complex systems for EH&S auditing. Costing environmental impact is another way of keeping management informed on the environmental impacts of a given activity. New information technologies have dramatically enhanced the possibilities of measuring and quantifying environmental impacts. When accounting procedures that take into account the abatement and clean up costs are in place, they will often reveal that some products actually give the corporation a net loss. One of the more positive findings of the survey is that almost one third of the respondents report having environmental accounting procedures, although it should be noted that no supplementary material substantiated this claim.

Not surprisingly, the industry with the highest liabilities -- the chemical industry -- proves to be more engaged in preventive management activities than other industries. It seems that this industry, encouraged by the Chemical Manufactures Association's "Responsible Care" program, has initiated and developed elaborate preventive management practices. Interestingly, it seems that many non-chemical corporations have been inspired by the chemical industry to establish their own environmental management programs and practices.

(b) Supportive tasks for governments

In recent years a new generation of environmental regulation has been developed. Whereas first generation regulations were directed towards solving local and acute environmental problems through end-of-pipe and filter solutions, pollution permits and outright prohibitions on certain pollutants, the new generation of regulatory initiatives has been aimed at pollution prevention.

One way that governments encourage preventive management in corporations is to increase the penalties for accidents or serious pollution. According to the Benchmark Survey, the second most important factor instigating corporate EH&S programs after regulations is litigation against the company. Twenty per cent of the respondents cited this factor as influential. This is particularly the case for North America-based corporations, where one third of the respondents cited this factor as important. Notably, North American corporations are also more inclined to have preventive management practices such as audits, risk assessments and related preventive activities than other regions. This suggests that the rather severe penalties that characterize United States EH&S regulation, and in particular the Superfund legislation, have a significant impact on the scope and content of EH&S management. Furthermore, United States courts tend to award plaintiffs huge financial rewards, which has a strong deterrent effect on corporate behaviour. The implication of this finding seems to be that government policy aimed at increasing the liabilities of environmentally unwarranted behaviour will be effective in encouraging the establishment of preventive EH&S practices. Increasing the ability of citizens to challenge corporations, for example by enacting legislation that, to a higher degree, places the burden of proof on corporations, can also work as an incentive for corporations to prevent pollution.

Another way of rewarding corporations that prevent pollution (and discouraging environmentally undesirable behaviour by corporations) is through taxation of environmental vices or the removal of subsidies for environmentally detrimental activities such as mining, logging, water use or energy consumption. The Benchmark Survey exhibits several examples of significant reductions in energy use, water consumption and waste production among the responding companies. It is probable that these initiatives have been spurred by rising prices of energy, water and waste disposal in the last one or two decades, rather than by environmental regulations. In general, governments can utilize market-oriented measures to a higher degree than they have in the past, as recommended by UNCED. For example, the creation of markets for pollution permits in certain areas of pollution prevention could lead to a more optimal allocation of pollution costs among corporations and give individual corporations as much leeway as possible in choosing the means of environmental action.

Finally, governments could continue to encourage the establishment of preventive practices by requiring corporations to acquire and disclose information on potentially dangerous activities.[3] Mandatory audits would force corporations to be more responsive to the environmental problems arising out of their operations. Furthermore, it seems that legislation requiring corporations to inform workers and neighbors of environmental risks has a deterrent effect on environmentally detrimental corporate activities. For example, there are indications that so called "Right-to-Know" legislation requiring corporations to inform workers and surrounding communities on chemical hazards has encouraged voluntary limitations on releases of hazardous chemicals.

3. Strategic environmental management

(a) Corporate activities

Using EH&S management strategically and integrating EH&S objectives in the overall business strategy demand a much more firm commitment from corporations than preventive management does. Corporations that exercise preventive management concentrate on doing what is minimally necessary to create lean production and reduce liabilities. Strategic EH&S management demands a comprehensive reorientation of the corporation's planning, R&D and investments. Corporations employing strategic management believe that a clear dedication to environmental protection and a comprehensive integration of this philosophy in all aspects of the corporation's

> **Box XIV.3. Aligning Social Policy and Business Strategy**
>
> "Increasingly, corporate America is searching for new ways to replace piecemeal social initiatives with more integrated social policies, and to align these policies with fundamental business strategy. Such an alliance, if successful, has enormous social and economic implications. Companies would not only become more skillful agents with social change, they would become more competitive in the emerging global economy" (Hutton, 1992, p. 32).

activities is a logical step for an expanding enterprise. They anticipate that in the long run it makes good economic sense to ride on the green wave. They realize that environmental protection is not a distraction, an unwelcome factor hampering the success of the corporation, but an integrated part of its success. Furthermore, they see the potential of the rapidly growing market of environmental services and equipment. Corporations such as **Amoco, Imperial Chemical Industries** or **Noranda, Inc.** have, at least in their policy statements, acknowledged the close linkage between EH&S protection and a successful business enterprise.

Strategic management demands a clear dedication from top management and an integration of EH&S objectives in all key operating activities. The Benchmark Survey indicates that Japan-based corporations are ahead of European and North American TNCs in this regard. Personnel from top management, strategic planning and market research of Japanese corporations are more involved in initiating environmental programmes than is the case in other regions. Furthermore, Japanese corporations are significantly more inclined to have environmental R&D than either European or North American corporations. Environmental R&D in new products and production processes are a clear indication that corporations are willing to risk substantial resources in order to capture new green markets.

Another clear indication that a company has a strategic approach to environmental protection is when it adopts a "cradle-to-grave" philosophy, which implies that environmental and resource concerns are integrated into all phases of a product's life cycle through all levels of production. Cradle-to-grave management will, in many cases, be a natural extension of "total quality management" (TQM) that many corporations already implement.[4] Some of the respondents, such as **Xerox Corporation** and **AB Volvo**, report that they have adopted a cradle-to-grave or life-cycle philosophy.

Corporations using strategic EH&S management understand the importance of maintaining good public relations. By developing and publishing EH&S policies and guidelines, and by investing in EH&S activities, they seek to appease the public and appeal to green consumers, ethical investors and politicians who are increasingly responsive to environmental concerns of their constituencies. As many corporations, especially in the chemical industry, have experienced, public goodwill is an important business asset.[5] A flawed environmental reputation can not only lead to consumer boycott and regulatory action, it can also hurt employee morale and recruiting prospects. The purpose of an active public relations strategy is to maintain the corporation's long-term viability by matching the demands of stakeholders. If a green strategy succeeds, it can become a crucial point of differentiation for the corporation. The current crises of the atomic industry illustrate what can happen to an industry if it does not succeed in that strategy.

One of the corporations responding to the Benchmark Survey, **Norsk Hydro,** seeks public acceptance by allowing external auditors to assess the conduct of the company. External auditors can provide real accountability and help build trust between corporations and the public. About one third of the respondents reported that they disclose EH&S information, although it should be noted that the respondents offered little information on the scope and content of

> **Box XIV.4 "Track Us Don't Trust Us"**
>
> "We first want the public to track us. Eventually we hope trust will come. We'll tell people our goals, what's working and where we fell short" (Bob Kennedy, Chairman of Union Carbide).

the disclosure procedures. Numerous corporations have community outreach activities such as cooperation with environmental groups, an important element in corporate confidence-building.

Finally, corporations using strategic EH&S management realize that by having progressive and innovative EH&S procedures, they make a preemptive strike against future regulations. Good public relations will build political capital that can be used to influence or prevent future environmental regulation, thus further improving a corporation's market position. Therefore, it is likely that these corporations also engage actively in a dialogue with regulators, politicians and business associations in the formulation of new legislation and industrial guidelines. Thus, corporations such as **Chevron Corporation** or **Caterpillar Inc.** explicitly state in their policy statements that they seek opportunities to participate in the formulation of future regulations.

(b) Supportive tasks for governments

To encourage the integration of environmental concerns in the overall business strategy, it is important that governments expand environmental regulation incrementally. This allows corporations to have a long-term and predictable investment horizon and enables them to reap the benefits of R&D investments. In general, governments can pursue environmental objectives by setting up short-term, mid-term and long-term environmental targets and then use a mix of voluntary agreements and government regulations to reach those goals.

Governments could further support the expansion of green financial markets by encouraging financial institutions such as banks and investment firms to adopt environmental guidelines for lending and investments. There already exists a considerable lending and investment portfolio that requires certain environmental criteria to be met before capital is committed.

Governments could develop and better coordinate accounting and disclosure procedures to enable stakeholders to assess the natural resources depletion of a corporation. In this connection it also is crucial that ways of making EH&S commitments and targets are standardized so that the public is allowed to compare different corporate achievements. Currently the United States Environmental Protection Agency (EPA) is preparing an "Environmental Leadership" programme to encourage corporate environmental leadership by developing performance measures and disclosure standards that enable the public to identify environmental leaders. Agenda 21 strongly recommends such initiatives as well.

Green consumerism can be encouraged by enabling consumers to evaluate the environmental content of a product. Efforts to create labelling laws and harmonize labelling and marketing practices has been undertaken at the international level by the International Organization for Standardization (ISO). If these efforts do not succeed in giving eco-labelling credibility, consumers might well be discouraged from buying "green".[6]

Recent years have seen a dramatic rise in governmental initiatives to encourage recycling. In Germany, new recycling laws require producers to take back a variety of products when used, and to recycle packaging. By 1995, German firms will be required to recycle 80 per cent of what they collect. Such legislation can encourage corporations to adopt cradle-to-grave policies.

Government cooperation with the most progressive segments of industry in setting and implementing EH&S standards can also encourage strategic environmental management. Europe and Japan, especially, have a long-standing tradition for institutionalized involvement of business in environmental decision-making. Recently, the United States EPA has also developed programmes that seek to involve corporate leaders in setting EH&S standards, for example, the "33/50" and "Green

Lights" programmes. Under the "33/50" programme, 600 United States corporations have signed up to voluntarily reduce emissions of 17 different toxic substances by 33 per cent by 1992 and by 50 percent by 1995. The "Green Lights" programme encourages voluntary reduction in the consumption of energy. Cooperation between governments and the industry on R&D in environmentally sound technologies and products, such as developing cars that are radically cleaner than today's cars, could also encourage corporations to assume a leadership role in environmental protection.

4. Sustainable development management

(a) Corporate activities

Compliance management, preventative management and strategic environmental management all contribute to sustainable development. They all help to preserve the global resource base and prevent adverse environmental impacts, and they are all part of the sustainable managed enterprise. But apart from these types of practices, the UNCED process has pointed towards some additional corporate activities that can be characterized as genuine sustainable development activities.[7]

First, sustainable development management, according to UNCED, implies a special consideration for the particular conditions of developing countries in corporate environmental conduct. Agenda 21 suggests that corporations establish world-wide policies on sustainable development. Moreover, Agenda 21 recommends that corporations recognize the special conditions in developing countries and that they develop explicit policies and procedures for developing countries, such as specifically designed training programs, in-house standards in the absence of host-country standards, technology cooperation schemes, and a special consideration for local communities and cultures.

The Benchmark Survey has identified almost no direct developing country references in the policy statements submitted by the respondents and only very few examples of specific developing country programs. A few corporations have specific training and sponsoring activities in developing countries. A handful of the respondents, such as **Cargill Company**, pledge to use the same EH&S standards globally, and corporations like **Ciba-Geigy** and **AB Volvo** indicate that they have established procedures for world-wide environmental auditing.

> **Box XIV.5 A Business Definition of Sustainable Development**
>
> "Sustainable Development means conducting business in a way which meets the needs of the enterprise and its stakeholders today, while protecting, sustaining and enhancing the human and natural resources needed tomorrow" (IISD,1992, p. 11).

Second, a commitment to sustainable development requires an explicit accounting of the corporation's role in dealing with global environmental problems, such as pollution of the oceans and the atmosphere, or the destruction of the rainforest: issues that were at center stage at UNCED, and are addressed in several chapters of Agenda 21. The Benchmark Survey has identified quite a few examples of corporations that have assumed such responsibilities. **Waste Management** and several pharmaceutical corporations have a policy of no net loss of biodiversity. **Sandoz** states that sea-dumping is not acceptable. About 20 per cent of the respondents have activities related to renewable energy sources. Many corporations have afforestation programs, and some of them, especially Japan-based corporations link them to greenhouse gas problems. However, few corporations link their afforestation programs to biodiversity problems. One of the most encouraging findings is that many corporations have programs for phasing out the use of CFC gases. Obviously, the Montreal Protocol has had a strong impact on the corporate agenda. This suggests that when given a tangible and simple course of action the business community can respond with impressive positive environmental contributions, even in the case of rather diffuse and global environmental problems.

Finally, an expansion of international cooperation on issues related to business and environment seems to be an integral part of sustainable development management. One corporation in particular seems to have given this aspect of sustainable development management consideration. **Amoco** states its belief that "United States business also should become more active in helping formulate the global environmental philosophy that almost certainly will be reflected in future international agreements".[8] Individual corporations can best contribute to the process of defining and coordinating international environmental standards by participating actively through their industry associations. It is a positive sign to see how the UNCED process has brought corporations together under different organizational umbrellas to contribute to the sustainable development discussions. New organizations have been formed and well-established organizations, like the ICC are investing substantial resources in influencing the process. According to a post-UNCED survey conducted by TCMD, close to 1,000 TNCs out of an estimated 35,000 TNCs world-wide, took part in the preparations for UNCED in one way or another. However, this survey also concluded that only about 40 corporations participated in a broad range of activities in preparation for UNCED.[9] Efforts must be undertaken to ensure that more corporations are involved in the process of defining the practical implications of Agenda 21 for business and in its implementation.

At present, assuming responsibility for these genuine sustainable development problems seems beyond reach for most corporations, however. The investment horizon for sustainable development programmes and policies will often be very long, even generational. Most corporations feel they cannot afford to make substantial investments in areas where the prospective pay-offs are as illusive as they seem to be in the area of sustainable development management. Therefore, supportive governmental and international organizations' activities aimed at changing the incentive structure surrounding sustainable development issues are absolutely crucial.

(b) Supportive tasks for governments

At least three categories of international initiatives would encourage major corporations to move towards genuine sustainable development management.

When asked what role they wanted the United Nations to play in the future, the majority of the corporations responding to the Benchmark Survey requested the United Nations to harmonize environmental standards. Seen from the perspective of the individual TNC, harmonized EH&S standards make it easier to do business across borders. International cooperation on setting EH&S standards is equally important to avoid the environment becoming a point of competition among nations. Already, there are indications that some countries design environmental regulation in a way that amounts to industrial policy and that environmental regulation is made to work as a protective measure for the national industry. Agenda 21 addresses the relationship between environment and trade in a separate section on "Making Trade and Environment Mutually Supportive" (ch. 2.B.) The message in this section is that international coordination of environmental regulations dealing with global environmental problems is crucial to curb an environmentally spurred trade war, and that measures should be taken to ensure that environment-related regulations and standards do not constitute a disguised restriction on trade.

As part of efforts to harmonize international environmental standards, assistance of industrialized countries to developing countries in establishing industrial EH&S regulations has to be upgraded. Many industrialized nations have experienced the pitfalls of implementation of environmental regulations, and their mistakes should not be repeated in developing countries. The United States EPA's assistance to the Mexican environmental protection agency as part of the North American Free Trade Agreement can serve as a model in this regard. It should be noted that international coordination of EH&S regulations does not necessarily imply the establishment of new environmental law. Non-binding international guidelines from industry associations and international organizations could, to some extent, serve the same purpose. Therefore, governments and international organizations could benefit from far closer coordination with industry associations in designing industrial guidelines and codes of conduct.

Secondly, gathering and disseminating information internationally on industrial activities in developing countries, especially those of TNCs, would encourage sustainable development management. In fact, many of the recommendations in Agenda 21 deal with improving information-gathering and dissemination. International exchange of information on corporate practices through clearing-houses and databases can both encourage environmentally sound activity and discourage environmentally unsound practices. International organizations could also develop and harmonize international reporting standards, thereby encouraging the work of international "watch dogs" such as Friends of the Earth or the Third World Network.

Thirdly, the international community could ensure that the exploitation of natural resources in the global commons are quantified and priced. This can be done, for example, by establishing international taxation of carbon dioxide or timber trade, or by establishing international environmental regulations. This, in turn, could encourage corporations to establish policies on these issues. For example, the determined corporate effort to phase out CFCs documented in the Benchmark Survey is no doubt inspired by hefty taxes on ozone depleting chemicals in many industrialized nations. Finally, the international community could recognize the rights of developing nations to get a share of the benefits of products derived from their bio-resources, thus encouraging those nations to protect their bio-resources before they vanish.

C. PARTNERSHIPS FOR SUSTAINABLE DEVELOPMENT

The analysis in Part Three of the dynamic relationship between governmental action and corporate EH&S activities points towards two major conclusions for future partnerships on sustainable development. Firstly, the analysis suggests that in collaboration with TNCs, governments and international organizations can do a great deal to improve corporate EH&S practices and move forward towards sustainable development management. Governments and international organizations must carefully evaluate policies and regulatory instruments in order to find the means that bring about the optimal corporate response in a given situation. In some areas, especially in areas of highly dangerous and risky productions, it is preferable to employ command-and-control approaches to environmental problems that conform to the compliance-oriented management activities ongoing in corporations. In other cases, however, governments will be better off by encouraging practices, through incentives, that prevent pollution from occurring in the first place. Compared to command-and-control measures, incentives give corporations more freedom to chose the means of achieving an environmental goal and place less strain on the administrative apparatus of the government. Ideally, governments should find instruments that unite the societal preferences for sustainable industrial activity with corporate profitability. To help persuade corporations that green strategies are profitable, governments and international organizations can encourage the expansion of green markets and reward environmental leaders. Still, it is only the vanguard of corporations that conceives of environmental protection as a business opportunity,[10] but the attitude might rapidly change as or if these corporations prove successful.

The second major conclusion drawn from the analysis of Part Three is that the action of governments and international organizations can and should be informed by the wealth of initiatives and ideas, which, as documented in the Benchmark Survey, is present in the business community. In particular, consulting with business is crucial as the international community searches for ways of dealing with joint environmental and developmental challenges. In a situation where the precise implications of sustainable development for corporate management is rather murky, it is absolutely essential that governments and international organizations mobilize the innovative potential already present in the corporate community to find ways of addressing these issues. UNCED clearly acknowledged the importance of cooperation with the business community, and many recommendations of Agenda 21 stress this partnership concept. For example, the Agenda states that business should "be full participants in the implementation and evaluation of Agenda 21" (30.1); that "United Nations organizations and agencies should improve mechanisms for business and industry inputs, policy and strategy formulation processes to ensure that environmental aspects are strengthened in foreign investments" (30.28); and, that "Governments, business and industry, including transnational corporations, should strengthen partnerships to implement the principles and criteria for sustainable development" (30.7).

The UNCED process demonstrates that some corporations are willing to engage in serious dialogue with the international community on global environmental and developmental issues. The relatively high response rate to the Benchmark Survey confirms this. What is emerging from the UNCED process may be the contours of new modalities for international corporation between businesses and governments and international organizations on sustainable development issues. The Benchmark Survey may well be the beginning of a process where the United Nations, in conjunction with the corporate community, seeks to find structured ways of collecting and disseminating information on EH&S practices of the corporate environmental leaders, thus potentially inspiring other corporations to undertake similar activities and to move ahead towards sustainable development management.

Notes

[1] For example, one of the concerns that has been raised in connection with the North American Free Trade Agreement is that United States-based corporations might by-pass Mexican environmental regulation. Pledges by major United States corporations to meet Mexican statutory requirements could address this concern, to some degree.

[2] It is estimated that just the cleaning up of hazardous waste sites alone will cost the industry anywhere between $300 billion and $700 billion during the next ten years. As a result, corporations are facing increasing insurance premiums, and this in turn encourages the industry to further minimize its impacts on the environment.

[3] United Nations Center on Transnational Corporations, *Transnational Corporations and International Disclosure*, (New York, United Nations, 1991).

[4] The close relationship between the two concepts has prompted the Global Environmental Management Initiative (GEMI) to launch a programme on environmental TQM.

[5] For example, after Bhopal, Union Carbide was forced to cancel several projects, including the building of plants in Scotland, and in Washington and Connecticut in the United States due to public opposition.

[6] In a recent survey of 1,000 adults by the New Jersey-based Environmental Research Institute, half said they view environmental claims as mere gimmickry. A 1990 report by Cambridge Reports found that 89 per cent of the respondents maintained that "government needs to establish national advertising and labelling standards" (Business International, 1992: p. 217).

[7] The precise implications of sustainable development for a business enterprise are still rather unclear. Amidst surveying the sustainable development literature, a United States expert on business management issues, Tom Gladwin, assessed that "the concept of sustainable development is still quite embryonic, generally being discussed and written about in broad conceptual, rather abstract, macrolevel and fuzzy ways." (*National Wildlife Foundation*, 1992, p. 94)

[8] Amoco Corporation, *Span: For the Future of Our Planet*, 1990, Number 3, p. 30.

[9] TCMD, *Follow-up to the United Nations Conference on Environment and Development as Related to Transnational Corporations* (E/C.10/1993/13) (New York, United Nations, 1993).

[10] This conclusion is supported by McKinsey's study among more than 400 CEOs. It was found that a large majority of the respondents adopts an operational focus in environmental matters. These respondents consider compliance with regulations and prevention of incidents as their top two environmental concerns. But the survey also found that enhancing corporate image, integrating the environment into corporate strategy and realizing new environment-related market opportunities occupy much lower positions on the corporate agenda (McKinsey & Co., 1991, p. 7).

SELECTED BIBLIOGRAPHY

Booz-Allen & Hamilton. *Corporate Environmental Management: An Executive Survey*. U.S.A., 1991.

Bowonder, B., S. Arvind and B. Venkata Rao. *Institutionalization of Ecological Management Practices in Indian Industries*. Hyderabad, Centre for Energy, Environment and Technology, 1992.

Bradshaw, Thorton and Vogel, eds. *Corporations and their Critics: Issues and Answers to the Problems of Corporate Social Responsibility*. New York, McGraw-Hill, 1981.

Brown, H., J. Himmelberger and A. White. "Development - environment interactions in the export of hazardous technologies: A comparative study of three multinational affiliates in developing countries", *In Technological Forecasting and Social Change*. (Forthcoming)

Business International Corporation and Arthur D. Little. *Managing the Global Environmental Challenge*. New York, Business International Corporations, 1992.

Cahan and Smith. "The greening of corporate America." *Business Week*, April 23, 1990.

Cairncross, Frances. *Costing the Earth: The Challenge for Governments; The Opportunities for Business*. Boston, Harvard Business School Press, 1992.

Chemical Manufactures Association (CMA). *An Industry Survey of Chemical Company Activities to Reduce Unreasonable Risk*. Washington D.C., CMA, February, 1983.

"Cleaning up, a survey of industry and the environment", *The Economist*, September 8, 1990.

Deloitte & Touche. *The Environmental Transformation of U.S. industry: A Survey of U.S. Industrial Corporations Environmental Strategies, Management Policies and Perceptions*. Stanford, Stanford University Graduate School of Business Public Management Program, 1990.

P. Dicken. *Global Shift: The Internationalization of Economic Activity*. N.Y, Guilford Press, 1992.

Dillon and Fisher. *Environmental Management in Corporations: Methods and Motivations*. Massachusetts, Tufts University Center for Environmental Management, 1992.

Flaherty, M. and A. Rappaport. *Multinational Corporations and the Environment: A Survey of Global Practices*. Massachusetts, Tufts University Center for Environmental Management, 1991.

Frederick, W., K. Davis and J.E. Post. *Business and Society: Corporate Strategy, Public Policy, Ethics*. New York, McGraw-Hill, 1988.

Friedman, F. B. *Practical Guide to Environmental Management*. Washington, D.C., Environmental Law Institute, 1991.

Gladwin, T. *Environment, Planning and the Multinational Corporation*. Greenwich, Connecticut, Jai Press, 1977.

_____. *Building the Sustainable Corporation: Creating Environmental Sustainability and Corporate Advantage*. National Wildlife Federation, 1992.

International Institute for Sustainable Development (IISD) and Deloitte & Touche. *Business Strategy for Sustainable Development: Leadership and Accountability for the '90s.* Canada, IISD, 1992.

Keidanren. *Towards Preservation of the Global Environment. Results of a Follow-up Survey on the Subject of the Keidanren Global Environmental Charter.* Tokyo, Keidanren, 1992.

Arthur D. Little. *Environmental Health and Safety Policies: Current Practices and Future Trends.* Cambridge, Massachussets, Arthur D. Little, 1988.

Lund, Leonard. *Corporate Organization for Environmental Policy-making.* New York, The Conference Board, 1974.

Lundqvist, Lennart. *The Hare and the Tortoise: Clean Air Policies in the United States and Sweden.* Ann Arbor, University of Michigan Press, 1980.

McKinsey & Company. *The Corporate Response to the Environmental Challenge.* Amsterdam, McKinsey & Company, 1991.

National Wildlife Federation. *Building the Sustainable Corporation: Creating Environmental Sustainability and Corporate Advantage.* Paper based on "Synergy 92" conference held in California in January, 1992.

Pearson, Charles S. *Down to Business: Multinational Corporations, the Environment and Development.* Washington D.C., World Resources Institute, 1985.

Sarokin, D. *Toxic Releases from Multinational Corporations: Does the Public have a Right to Know.* Washington, D.C., Friends of the Earth, 1992.

Schmidheiny, Stephen. *Changing Course: A Global Business Perspective on Development and the Environment.* Geneva, Business Council of Sustainable Development (BCSD), 1992.

Smart, Bruce. *Beyond Compliance, A New Industry View of the Environment.* Washington, D.C., World Resources Institute, 1992.

United Nations Centre on Transnational Corporations. *Environmental Aspects of the Activities of Transnational Corporations: A Survey.* New York, United Nations, 1985.

_____. *Preliminary results of the Benchmark Survey, Report I-IV.* New York, United Nations, 1991.

_____. *Transnational Corporations and Sustainable Development: Recommendations of the Executive Director.* (E/C.10/1992/ 2), New York, United Nations, 1992.

United Nations Conference on Environment and Development. *Agenda for the 21st Century. A/CONF.151/26 (Vol I-III).* New York, United Nations, 1992.

Transnational Corporations and Management Division. *World Investment Report; Transnational Corporations as Engines of Growth.* New York, United Nations, 1992.

Vogel, David. *National Styles of Regulation: Environmental Policy in Great Britain and the United States.* London, Cornell University Press, 1986.

Willums, J. O. and U. Goluke (International Chamber of Commerce, ICC). *From Ideas to Action, Business and Sustainable Development*. Oslo, Gyldendal, 1992.

World Commission on Environment and Development. *Our Common Future*. New York, Oxford University Press, 1987.

ANNEX A:
QUESTIONNAIRE

UNITED NATIONS CENTRE ON TRANSNATIONAL CORPORATIONS

Benchmark Corporate Environmental Survey

UNITED NATIONS
New York, 1990

Benchmark Corporate Environmental Survey

(Company publications can be attached as replies when it is easier for the respondent)

1.   a.   Name of company and address of headquarters :

_____

_____

_____

     b.   Name(s), title(s), telephone and fax number(s) of respondent(s):

_____

_____

_____

     c.   Please check in box if you do not wish the company's name to be used in the final report   ☐

2.   Senior Environmental Officials :

     a.   Name and title of the senior corporate official on environmental matters:

_____

_____

_____

     b.   To whom in the company does the senior corporate official on environmental matters report?

_____

_____

_____

     c.   What committee of the board of directors, if any, reviews environmental issues?
         If there is a designated environmental director on the board of the company, please provide
         the director's name.

_____

_____

_____

3.   Major sectors of industrial activity (please provide the major industrial sectors of the firm based on their
     1989 sales):

     largest sector   second largest sector   third largest sector

     _____   _____   _____

     other sectors

     _____   _____   _____

4.   Corporate Environmental Information:

    a.   Does the corporation have a formal published international   Yes / No   Attachment No.____
          environmental policy or programme?

    b.   Does the corporation publish a separate environmental report or does Yes / No   Attachment No. ____
          the annual report contain a section on the environment?

    c.   Does the management prepare a separately identified annual   Yes / No   Attachment No. ____
          statement on environmental affairs for the corporate board?

    d.   Does headquarters publish an environmental bulletin or newsletter   Yes / No   Attachment No._____
          for managers throughout the company?

    e.   Has the company prepared a special public briefing/brochure   Yes / No   Attachment No. _____
          on its environmental performance?

    f.   What channels exist for local management to bring potentially serious environmental problems to the
          attention of the corporate headquarters?

          _____
          _____
          _____

    g.   What channels exist for local management to bring environmental emergencies to the attention
          of corporate headquarters?

          _____
          _____
          _____

5.   Do you have specific <u>company-wide</u> environmental policies and standards, beyond those required by national
    law or regulations, in the following areas: (Mark with * those which the company does not categorize as
    "environmental" activities.)

		Not applicable	Yes	No	Attachment No.
a.	Air quality/pollution	☐	☐	☐	____
b.	Water quality/pollution	☐	☐	☐	____
c.	Soil quality/pollution	☐	☐	☐	____
d.	On- and off-site pollution monitoring	☐	☐	☐	____
e.	Greenhouse gas generation reduction	☐	☐	☐	____
f.	Noise pollution	☐	☐	☐	____
g.	Toxic substances in general	☐	☐	☐	____
h.	Specific hazardous compounds	☐	☐	☐	____
i.	Storage tanks	☐	☐	☐	____
j.	Site selection	☐	☐	☐	____
k.	Land reclamation/rehabilitation	☐	☐	☐	____
l.	Radiation protection	☐	☐	☐	____
m.	Accident prevention	☐	☐	☐	____
n.	Emergency preparedness	☐	☐	☐	____
o.	Waste disposal	☐	☐	☐	____
p.	Waste reduction/technologies	☐	☐	☐	____
q.	Worker health and safety	☐	☐	☐	____

5.   (continued)   Not applicable   Yes   No   Attachment No.

    r.   Marine transport   ☐   ☐   ☐   _____
    s   Land transport   ☐   ☐   ☐   _____
    t.   Environmental impact assessment ☐   ☐   ☐   _____
    u.   Disclosure of product-risk   ☐   ☐   ☐   _____
         information
    v.   Disclosure of process-risk   ☐   ☐   ☐   _____
         information
    w.   Other (specify _____)

6.   Has the company prepared its own standardized version of the following procedures and programmes for use throughout the firm?

                                        Not applicable   Yes   No   Attachment No.

    a.   Pollution monitoring techniques   ☐   ☐   ☐   _____
    b.   Environmental audit procedures   ☐   ☐   ☐   _____
    c.   Environmental impact assessment   ☐   ☐   ☐   _____
         procedures
    d.   Waste handling procedures   ☐   ☐   ☐   _____
    e.   Safety audit procedures   ☐   ☐   ☐   _____
    f.   Hazard assessment procedures   ☐   ☐   ☐   _____
    g.   Accident prevention plans   ☐   ☐   ☐   _____
    h.   Emergency response systems   ☐   ☐   ☐   _____
    i.   Worker safety training programmes ☐   ☐   ☐   _____
    j.   Management safety training   ☐   ☐   ☐   _____
         programmes
    k.   Contents of material and   ☐   ☐   ☐   _____
         data safety sheets
    l.   Contents of product labels and   ☐   ☐   ☐   _____
         safety instructions
    m.   Other (specify _____)

7.   Does the company utilize any of the following voluntary international guidelines, or incorporate sections of them, as internal company standards?

| | | In Use | | |
	Not applicable	Yes	No	Implemented (year)
a. UNEP's Environmental Guidelines	☐	☐	☐	_____
b. UNEP's APPEL Programme	☐	☐	☐	_____
c. FAO's Code for the Safe Marketing and Use of Pesticides	☐	☐	☐	_____
d. ILO tripartite Agreement on Multinational Enterprises	☐	☐	☐	_____
e. ILO's Code of Practice on Accident Prevention	☐	☐	☐	_____
f. International Chamber of Commerce Environmental Guidelines	☐	☐	☐	_____
g. OCED Guidelines on Multinational Enterprises	☐	☐	☐	_____
h. CEFIC Guidelines for the Safe Transfer of Technology	☐	☐	☐	_____

7. (continued)

		Not applicable	In Use Yes	No	Implemented (year)
i.	CEFIC Guidelines for the Safe Storage of Chemicals	☐	☐	☐	_____
j.	CMA's Responsible CARE	☐	☐	☐	_____
k.	ISO Technical Environmental Standards	☐	☐	☐	_____
l.	Sectorial Trade Associations Guidelines (attachment # _____)	☐	☐	☐	_____
m.	Other voluntary guidelines in use (attachment # _____)	☐	☐	☐	_____

8. What other measures are important components of the company's international environmental programme? (Please append a description of each programme as an attachment.)

		Not applicable	Yes	No	Attachment No. if necessary
a.	Safety and environmental audits	☐	☐	☐	_____
b.	Energy conservation	☐	☐	☐	_____
c.	Green labelling	☐	☐	☐	_____
d.	Environmental accounting	☐	☐	☐	_____
e.	Safety standards for joint venture partnerships and subcontractors	☐	☐	☐	_____
f.	Workers' participation in setting health, safety and environment committees	☐	☐	☐	_____
g.	Educating staff on the environmental impact of the firm's operations	☐	☐	☐	_____
h.	Community participation in emergency planning	☐	☐	☐	_____
i.	Site relocation for environmental reasons	☐	☐	☐	_____
j.	Annual meeting between headquarters and local environment officials	☐	☐	☐	_____
k.	Contributions to local environmental and nature societies	☐	☐	☐	_____
l.	Other (specify _____)				

9. Measurement of international progress in environmental performance:

   a. What are the major topics of attention in the firm's environmental auditing? (Attachment No._____)

   b. On what schedule does the firm perform environmental audits in plant sites outside the home country?

   c. If the firm compiles comparative performance data on individual plant sites outside the home country, please indicate the variables measured: (Attachment No._____)

10. Please indicate the extent to which the different divisions/functions of your corporation are concerned with environmental issues:

Division/function	Tends to initiate environmental programmes	Tends to implement environmental programmes	Tends not to be involved in environmental programmes
Top management	☐	☐	☐
Production	☐	☐	☐
Strategic Planning	☐	☐	☐
Marketing	☐	☐	☐
Market Research	☐	☐	☐
Research & Development	☐	☐	☐
Human Resources	☐	☐	☐
Accounting	☐	☐	☐
Public Relations	☐	☐	☐

11. Corporate environmental targets :

   a. Which corporate-wide targets does the company have for reducing environmental damage ? (e.g. reduction in CFC use, carbon dioxide emission, energy consumption, waste generation, etc.)   (Attachment No._____)

   b. If new corporate-wide policy options related to environmental issues are under consideration, when could UNCTC receive a report on the new directives?

12. Historical background of the corporate environmental policy and programme:

   Which of the following provoked a change in your overall, company-wide environmental policy or programme?

   a. _____ changes in legislation in your home country

      year(s) and topic(s):

   b. _____ changes in legislation in a host country

      year(s) and topic(s):

   c. _____ environmental accidents at your premises

      year(s) and event(s):

12. (continued)

    d.   _____ environmental accidents at other companies

        year(s) and event(s):

    e.   _____ environmentally related legal actions involving your company

        year(s) and topic(s):

    f.   _____ environmentally related legal actions involving other companies

        year(s) and topic(s):

    g.   _____ consumer related events (e.g. boycotts)

        year(s) and topic(s):

    h.   _____ worker related events

        year(s) and topic(s):

    i.   _____ other

year(s) and topic(s):

13. Information regarding those corporate activities that have the potential for serious detrimental effects on the environment. Please indicate whether any of the company's operations presently involve any of the following products, processes or activities.

		Yes	No	Data insufficient at headquarters	Attachments No.	Page No.
Related to raw materials used in manufacturing						
a.	Asbestos	☐	☐	☐	_____	____
b.	Other known carcinogens	☐	☐	☐	_____	____
c.	Chlorofluorcarbons and related compounds					
d.	Mono-crops from developing countries	☐	☐	☐	_____	____
e.	Non-renewable natural resources	☐	☐	☐	_____	____

13.   (continued)

	Yes	No	Data insufficient at headquarters	Attachment No.	Page No.

Related to process safety

f. Plant sites covered by the Seveso Directive (EEC) — ☐ ☐ ☐ _____ ___
g. Plant sites covered by the SARA title 3 (USA) — ☐ ☐ ☐ _____ ___
h. Plant sites within 10 miles (15Km) of an international border — ☐ ☐ ☐ _____ ___
i. Bioengineering processes — ☐ ☐ ☐ _____ ___

Related to storage and packaging

j. Use of large below ground storage tanks — ☐ ☐ ☐ _____ ___
k. Use of plastic packaging — ☐ ☐ ☐ _____ ___

Related to specific sectors

l. Agriculture — ☐ ☐ ☐ _____ ___
m. Forestry — ☐ ☐ ☐ _____ ___
n. Mining — ☐ ☐ ☐ _____ ___
o. Drift net fishing — ☐ ☐ ☐ _____ ___
q. Tourism — ☐ ☐ ☐ _____ ___
r. Road transport — ☐ ☐ ☐ _____ ___
s. Nuclear power — ☐ ☐ ☐ _____ ___
t. Oil shipping — ☐ ☐ ☐ _____ ___

Related to product safety

u. Organochloride pesticides — ☐ ☐ ☐ _____ ___
v. Organophosporous pesticides — ☐ ☐ ☐ _____ ___
w. Carbamate — ☐ ☐ ☐ _____ ___
x. Military armaments — ☐ ☐ ☐ _____ ___
y. Products derived from biotechnology — ☐ ☐ ☐ _____ ___
z. Products containing CFCs — ☐ ☐ ☐ _____ ___

Related to waste disposal and emissions

aa. Heavy metals (e.g. lead, cadmium, chromium) — ☐ ☐ ☐ _____ ___
ab. Radioactive waste — ☐ ☐ ☐ _____ ___
ac. PCBs — ☐ ☐ ☐ _____ ___
ad. Dioxins — ☐ ☐ ☐ _____ ___
ae. Oxides of Sulphur (e.g.SO_2) — ☐ ☐ ☐ _____ ___

13. (continued)

		Yes	No	Data insufficient at headquarters	Attachment No.	Page No.

af. Oxides of nitrogen (e.g. N0x) — ☐ ☐   ☐   _____   _____

ag. Volatile organic compounds — ☐ ☐   ☐   _____   _____

ah. Disposal of waste outside the country of origin — ☐ ☐   ☐   _____   _____

ai. Ocean disposal of wastes — ☐ ☐   ☐   _____   _____

14. New facilities acquisition process :

a. What role does the environmental office have in the firms's acquisition process? Attachment No. _____

b. What are the major environmental topics in the firm's review of a company before its potential acquisition ? Attachment No. _____

15. Public perception issues :

a. What does the influential public on a global basis see as the corporation's most serious environmental problem(s) ?

b. What does the company itself see as its most serious environmental problem(s) on a global basis?

c. What does the company see as its major international environmental public relations problem(s)?

16. Approximate annual gross corporate-wide environmental expenditures and savings from environmental initiatives:

	Expenditures	Savings	Data not available at headquarters
1988	_____	_____	_____
1989	_____	_____	_____
1990 (est.)	_____	_____	_____

Accounting definitions used for environmental activities are in attachment no. _____

17. Approximate value of direct donations (e.g. in cash and/or technology) and in-kind outside contributions (e.g. in services, use of facilities, and/or staff time) for environmental protection:

	Direct donations	In-kind contributions	Data not available at headquarters
1988	_____	_____	_____
1989	_____	_____	_____
1990 (est.)	_____	_____	_____

   Definitions and descriptions of supported programmes are in attachment no. _____

18. International environmental management

   a. Does your company have formal arrangements for allocation of responsibilities on environmntal management between corporate headquarters and controlled affiliates? (e.g., Majority owned subsidiaries)   Yes / No   Attachment No. _____

   b. Does your company have formal arrangements for allocation of responsibilities on environmental management between corporate headquarters and non-controlled affiliates? (e.g., licensors)   Yes / No   Attachment No. _____

   c. If the company has a specific staff arrangement for international environmental matters, please provide the composition of its professional staff, its structure and its reporting structure.   Attachment No. _____

19. Personnel practices for plant management and supervisors:

   a. Does the company operate any incentive schemes at the plant level to induce staff to contribute to the company's environmental objectives?   Yes / No   Attachment No. _____

   b. In general, is environmental protection or health and safety responsibilities a part of an employee's job description?   Yes / No   Attachment No. _____

   c. In general, are environmental performance and safety records part of staff's performance evaluations?   Yes / No   Attachment No. _____

20. The United Nations General Assembly has identified nine environmental themes for the 1992 United Nations Conference on Environment and Development. Please indicate which are the five most important issues for your company.

   a. _____ Atmospheric protection
   b. _____ Protection of freshwater resources
   c. _____ Protection of oceans
   d. _____ Protection and management of land resources
   e. _____ Conservation of biological diversity
   f. _____ Environmentally sound management of biotechnology
   g. _____ Environmentally sound management of toxic wastes and chemicals
   h. _____ Improvement of the environment of the urban and rural poor
   i. _____ Protection of human health

21. Developing country aspects:

The following questions focus on specific aspects of these themes in relation to the firms' activities in developing countries.

	Yes	No	Data insufficient at headquarters	Attachment & Page No.
Atmospheric protection:				
a. Does the company use CFCs or related products at their plant sites in developing countries ?	☐	☐	☐	_____
b. Does the company monitor its stacks for air emission components in developing countries?	☐	☐	☐	_____
Protection of freshwater resources:				
c. Are any of the company's plants located in the immediate vicinity of drinking water supplies in developing countries ?	☐	☐	☐	_____
d. Are any of the company's products particularly hazardous to drinking water supplies in developing countries?	☐	☐	☐	_____
Protection of oceans:				
e. Does the company release effluents into oceans or seawater tributaries off developing countries ?	☐	☐	☐	_____
Protection and management of land resources:				
f. Does the company hold land for safety zones in developing countries?	☐	☐	☐	_____
g. Does the company have programmes for wetland and rainforest protection in developing countries?	☐	☐	☐	_____
Conservation of biological diversity:				
h. Does the company practice mono-cropping or clear-cutting in developing countries?	☐	☐	☐	_____
i. Is the company aware of any survey on biological species on its undeveloped land in developing countries?	☐	☐	☐	_____
Environmentally sound management of biotechnology:				
j. Does the company market any genetically engineered products in developing countries ?	☐	☐	☐	_____
Environmentally sound waste management:				
k. Does the company have procedures for monitoring the disposal of hazardous waste generated in plants in developing countries ?	☐	☐	☐	_____

21.   (continued)

	Yes	No	Data insufficient at headquarters	Attachment No & Page No.

Improvement of the environment of the urban and rural poor:

l.   Has the company made provisions for infrastructure, housing, or services for its workforce in developing countries?   ☐ ☐ ☐ _____

Protection of human health and control of toxic chemicals:

m.   Does the company have a toxic education programme for its workforce or for the surrounding communities in developing countries?   ☐ ☐ ☐ _____

22.   Sustainable development has focused corporate direction on ways to merge growth and environmental protection: Please indicate whether any of the following activities describe present corporate programmes or practices: (NA - not applicable)

	NA	Current Activities Yes	No	Under consideration Yes	No	Data insufficient at headquarters	Attachment No & Page No.

Company undertakes environmentally-oriented R & D

a.   For new methods of pollution control   ☐ ☐ ☐ ☐ ☐ ☐ ____
b.   For tropical health problems   ☐ ☐ ☐ ☐ ☐ ☐ ____
c.   For energy efficiency production methods   ☐ ☐ ☐ ☐ ☐ ☐ ____
d.   For reduction in greenhouse gas generation   ☐ ☐ ☐ ☐ ☐ ☐ ____
e.   Other _____

Company utilizes
f.   Integrated pest management   ☐ ☐ ☐ ☐ ☐ ☐ ____
g.   Renewable energy sources (e.g. solar, photovoltaic)   ☐ ☐ ☐ ☐ ☐ ☐ ____
h.   Recycling   ☐ ☐ ☐ ☐ ☐ ☐ ____
i.   Other _____

Company undertakes programmes to conserve

j.   Water resources   ☐ ☐ ☐ ☐ ☐ ☐ ____
k.   Non-renewable resources   ☐ ☐ ☐ ☐ ☐ ☐ ____
l.   Energy supplies   ☐ ☐ ☐ ☐ ☐ ☐ ____
m.   Biodiversity   ☐ ☐ ☐ ☐ ☐ ☐ ____
n.   Endangered species   ☐ ☐ ☐ ☐ ☐ ☐ ____
o.   Other _____

Company provides public access

p.   To results of environmental R & D   ☐ ☐ ☐ ☐ ☐ ☐ ____
q.   To corporate lands for nature walks   ☐ ☐ ☐ ☐ ☐ ☐ ____
r.   Other _____

22. (continued)

	NA	Current Activities		Under consideration		Data insufficient at	Attachment No. &
		Yes	No	Yes	No	headquarters	Page No.

Company voluntarily finances

		NA	Yes	No	Yes	No	headquarters	Page No.
s.	Afforestation efforts on corporate property	☐	☐	☐	☐	☐	☐	____
t.	Epidemiological studies	☐	☐	☐	☐	☐	☐	____
u.	Waste technologies	☐	☐	☐	☐	☐	☐	____
v.	Environmental organizations	☐	☐	☐	☐	☐	☐	____
w.	Plant sites in rural areas	☐	☐	☐	☐	☐	☐	____
x.	Other _____							

23. State-of-the-art environmental management practices:

   a. Which are the most innovative environmental management practices currently in use in your company's main sectors of operation? Attachment No. ____

   b. Which are the most innovative environmental management practices currently in use in your major sectors operation by other companies? Attachment No. ____

   c. Which companies are implementing these practices?

24. In your view, which international activities of the United Nations system would best further the environmental objectives of your company? Please rank the three most important activities in your company's view

   ____ a. Setting international policy guidelines
   ____ b. Setting international technical standards
   ____ c. Assisting in review of voluntary corporate "performance" standards
   ____ d. Creating/strengthening national regulatory systems in developing countries
   ____ e. Creating/strengthening national inspection systems in developing countries
   ____ f. Reducing differences in environmental rules and regulations of industrialized countries
   ____ g. Reporting on corporate leadership and their achievements
   ____ h. Establishing norms and procedures for public disclosure
   ____ i. Mediating between corporations and governments on environmental conflicts
   ____ j. Compiling national environmental laws and regulations
   ____ k. Other (specify or explain)_____

Please return survey to:

Harris Gleckman
Chief, Environment Unit
United Nations Centre on Transnational Corporations
Two United Nations Plaza, Room DC2-1202
New York, NY 10017

Telephone:	(212) 963-3162/4689
Fax:	(212) 963-2146
Telex:	661062 UNCTNC

ANNEX B:
METHODOLOGY

A. STATISTICS

The statistical processing of the material for this report has used the Cross-tabulations and Frequencies features of the Statistical Package for the Social Sciences. The Frequencies function tabulates the distribution of cases on a single variable. The Cross-tabulations function gives statistical correlations useful for understanding the relationships between two variables.

The cross-tabulations have been limited to the following independent variables: "region", "size of firm" (sales), and "sector". The analysis has focused on two-dimensional cross-tabulations, and no control for a third variable has been made. To measure the strength of a correlation between variables, the statistical measure R^2 or the level of significance was utilized. Usually a low level of significance (for example, 0.01) indicates that the distribution difference can reasonably be attributed to non-chance factors such as the variables being tested. For the purpose of this study, it was decided that a level of significance of less than 0.05 should be considered satisfactory.

B. VALIDITY OF THE RESULTS

Even if relations between variables are found significant, conclusions have to be made with a certain degree of caution. Thus the strength of the conclusions derived from the Benchmark Survey depends on the careful assessment of the possibility of coincidental or systematical errors that can occur in the data-collecting and data-processing process. Three potential sources affecting the validity of the conclusions will discussed in this section: (a) reliability of the data; (b) representativeness of the sample; and (c) problems related to the operationalization of the variables and hypothesis.

1. Reliability

The reliability of the data might have been affected in at least three dimensions: (a) the collection of data; (b) the precision of the data-entry process; and (c) the characteristics of the respondents.

One thousand TNCs with annual sales over $1 billion were selected from the Lotus One-Source Database. The database provided information on the name, address and telephone numbers of the chief executive officer of each corporation. Based on the database, a mailing list was established and the senior environmental official, whenever available, was sent a copy of the cover letter and the questionnaire. A number of firms were eliminated from the mailing list when they were found to be affiliates of other corporations or had been acquired by another firm in the mailing list. Eventually, the questionnaire was mailed out to 794 large TNCs with sales above $1 billion. In order to increase the response rate, follow-up telephone calls to the chief environmental official were made by the five regional centers and a follow-up letter was sent out to the non-respondents.

The subjective nature of the Benchmark Survey data could affect the reliability of the data. Thus, there may be notable discrepancies between subjective responses to particular questions and the actual state of environmental affairs in the corporation, resulting from interpretive differences and imprecision of answers. Even questions that appeared to refer to commonly accepted concepts might have been understood differently by the respondents. Interpretation of words such as "environment" (Does it include workers health and safety?), "international guidelines" (Does an European Community respondent consider European Community regulations as international?) or "environmental disclosure" (How much information should be disclosed to call it "disclosure"?), may have varied across regions and sectors, thereby affecting the reliability of the responses. In addition, because of the high degree contentiousness on environmental issues, the social desirability of displaying positive environmental records might have created a systematic bias in favor of environmentally positive answers.

A special problem arose because the analysis of EH&S activities in different regions was divided among five research centres. The way in which these centres interpreted the material varied significantly due to different cultural backgrounds of the researchers.

Another factor affecting the quality of the responses is that the Benchmark Survey was distributed in English only. Non-native English speakers were thus disadvantaged in distinguishing certain nuances in the questions, thereby influencing the precision of their responses. In fact, some TNCs declined to participate in the survey because they did not possess the necessary language skills to complete the questionnaire.

Finally, the survey was addressed to the corporate headquarters of each firm. Given the diversified and widespread operations of many TNCs, an accurate portrayal of all subsidiaries and divisions might not have been possible to make at corporate headquarters. In order to minimize the bias from that source, respondents were provided with the opportunity of answering "data insufficient at headquarters". Still, it is likely that some respondents may have cited home country policies when asked for global policies and programmes, thus overestimating the extent of global policies of the firm.

Most fundamentally, there was no assessment of the "truthfulness" of the responses. The responses and the attachments could, in theory, bear little or no relation to the reality of corporate management. Future studies of corporate management issues should include an evaluation of the actual implementation of corporate policies and programmes.

2. Representativeness

The degree to which the sample represents the total population of TNCs with sales above $1 billion is of crucial importance for making generalizations beyond the sample. The following section will describe the biases of the sample when compared to the 794 corporations originally targeted.

One hundred and sixty-nine firms with sales above $1 billion responded by completing the questionnaire. Another 41 firms chose to send attachments only. A positive response rate of 12-15 per cent for this type of survey is normally considered sufficient for most statistical purposes. Hence a response rate of 25 per cent is a remarkable result, especially when considering the diverse nature of the firms targeted, the high political contentiousness surrounding the issues of TNC environmental management issues, and the fact that the survey covered three major regions and 15 countries with wide cultural and economic disparity. Nonetheless, the sample is likely to be biased in several dimensions:

(i)   Corporations that have a unit dealing specifically with environmental questions or a designated environmental officer would be expected to be more likely to respond than firms that did not have such structures. Corporations with a centralized management structure would probably be more likely to participate than firms with a decentralized management structure. Moreover, where environmental policies are the responsibility of top management, it can be expected that the likelihood of a response to the questionnaire would be higher than from firms where the environmental responsibilities fall lower in the management structure.

(ii)   Firms with a strong commitment to environmental questions would be more inclined to answer than firms that have a weak environmental record, simply to display their progressive environmental record. Therefore, it is likely that the firms in the sample are the leading firms with regard to environmental managerial performance.

(iii)   Numerous corporations declined participating in the survey because they were channeling their activities on sustainable development though other organizations. Some of the corporations most engaged in environmental management such as Dupont, responded that they preferred to work through the Business Council for Sustainable Development.

The response rate among regions was markedly different. In the Asian region, which consists almost exclusively of Japanese TNCs, the response rate was more than one third of the total population of Asian-based TNCs targeted. At the other end of the spectrum was North America with a reply ratio of approximately 15 per cent (see figure 2). One very important bias in the sample is caused by the fact that only one out of eight developing country TNCs responded fully to the survey. It is essential that future research focus more specifically on the specific EH&S problems of developing country TNCs.

With regard to the industrial sectors, it was found that some sectors were more likely to respond than others. In general, TNCs in the extractive sector were more inclined to respond than TNCs from other sectors (see figure 2).

Comparing the respondents' sample with the population originally targeted, another bias was found with regard to sales; the bottom and middle third group of firms were more likely to respond (22 and 22 per cent vs. 17 per cent) than the top third sales group (see figure 2).

3. Operational definitions

Even if the data collected were reliable and representative, there still may be validity problems in the following areas: (a) the operational definition of variables; (b) the operational variable measures; and (c) spurious variable relations.

Problems inherent in making operational definitions of variables can affect the validity of the results. One example is that some respondents might be inappropriately grouped by regions. Australian TNCs were grouped with European TNCs based on an presumption that firms in Australia probably have more in common with European firms than with Japanese firms or North American TNCs.

Another problem of operationalization arises with the definition of "line of business". The Lotus OneSource Database divides the sample into 30 sectors. It was decided to merge those into 4 commonly used categories or industries. Thus "line of business" was defined according to the raw materials used by the firm in its production. This definition lead to the identification of four lines of business; agricultural products processing, extractive products processing, finished products and services. One problem with this definition of sector is that the sectors are extremely broad, covering firms that are markedly different in other respects. A validity problem related to the definition of sectors derives from the fact that many TNCs are diversified.

Although the operational definitions of the regional and sectoral variables were questionable, they all caused strong variations on most questions, resulting in low level of significance. The regional variable caused the strongest variations followed by the sectoral variable. This suggests that an actual quality was captured by the operational definition of these variables.

Another problem related to the operational design of the survey was associated with the fact that the operational definitions used in the survey did not make it possible to distinguish among various degrees of policy and program involvement. A firm with a scant safety training program would answer the same as one with an extensive training system. Similarly, questions pertaining to developing nations did not distinguish between those companies with only a single affiliate in a developing country, and those having extensive operations in multiple locations. In other words, the operational measures were only a rough indicator of the quality of the material analyzed.

One of the central questions regarding the validity of the results concerns the problem of how to interpret measured correlations between variables. Thus it is probable that even if strong correlations between an independent and dependent variable are found, this might be explained by a third variable. Some of the conclusions based on cross-tabulations between one of the independent variables and a given dependent variable in the reports might be accounted for by the influence of one of the other two independent variables, or both. In statistical terms the correlation might be spurious. The possibility of spurious relationships is a warning that conclusions regarding correlations between two variables should be made with caution. Annex figures 1, 2 and 3 indicate how the three independent variables--sales, region and sector--might influence each other. In particular, European corporations are disproportionately in the bottom third sales group; Japanese corporations are disproportionately in the finished products sector; and corporations in the finished products sector are disproportionately in the top third sales group. This warns that conclusions on these three dimensions especially, might be spurious. In order to assess the extent of these problems, a selection of correlations between an independent variable and a dependent variable were controlled for by a second independent variable. In most cases, controlling for a third variable did not eradicate the correlations.

C. CONCLUSION

This section has discussed some of the problems affecting the statistical validity of the results of the survey. Several problems affecting the reliability of the findings were identified. With regard to the representativeness of the sample, it is suggested that generalizations beyond the sample should be made with some caution. However, a very high response rate provided an opportunity for interesting inferences and for recommendations on TNCs and environmental management. Nonetheless, problems related to the operational definitions of some of the variables and the interpretation of some of the correlations suggest that the results in some cases should be carefully evaluated.

ANNEX FIGURES: CORRELATIONS BETWEEN INDEPENDENT VARIABLES

Annex figure B.1.

Primary line of business (LOB)
By   Country or Region (MCTRY)

MCTRY-> LOB	Count Row Pct Col Pct	ASIA ASI	EUROPE EUR	N. AM NAM	Row Total
73 Services		1 6.7 1.8	6 40.0 10.3	8 53.3 14.5	15 8.9
72 Finished		28 46.7 50.0	15 25.0 25.9	17 28.3 30.9	60 35.5
71 Extractives		16 30.2 28.6	19 35.8 32.8	18 34.0 32.7	53 31.4
70 Agricultural		11 26.8 19.6	18 43.9 31.0	12 29.3 21.8	41 24.3
Column Total		56 33.1	58 34.3	55 32.5	169 100.0

Chi-Square	D.F.	Significance	Min E.F.	Cells with E.F.< 5
12.39723	6	.0537	4.882	2 OF 12 (16.7%)

Number of Missing Observations = 0

Annex figure B.2.

Ntiles of sales (nsales)
By   Country or Region (MCTRY)

MCTRY→ NSALES	Count Row Pct Col Pct	ASIA ASI	EUROPE EUR	N. AM NAM	Row Total
TOP THIRD	3	21 37.5 37.5	15 26.8 25.9	20 35.7 36.4	56 33.1
SECOND THIRD	2	21 36.8 37.5	17 29.8 29.3	19 33.3 34.5	57 33.7
BOTTOM THIRD	1	14 25.0 25.0	26 46.4 44.8	16 28.6 29.1	56 33.1
Column Total		56 33.1	58 34.3	55 32.5	169 100.0

Chi-Square	D.F.	Significance	Min E.F.	Cells with E.F.< 5
5.78651	4	.2157	18.225	None

Number of Missing Observations = 0

Annex figure B.3.

Ntiles of sales (nsales)
By   Primary line of business (LOB)

LOB–>	Count Row Pct Col Pct	Agricult ural 70	Extracti ves 71	Finished 72	Services 73	Row Total
NSALES						
TOP THIRD	3	2 3.6 4.9	21 37.5 39.6	30 53.6 50.0	3 5.4 20.0	56 33.1
SECOND THIRD	2	22 38.6 53.7	13 22.8 24.5	18 31.6 30.0	4 7.0 26.7	57 33.7
BOTTOM THIRD	1	17 30.4 41.5	19 33.9 35.8	12 21.4 20.0	8 14.3 53.3	56 33.1
Column Total		41 24.3	53 31.4	60 35.5	15 8.9	169 100.0

Chi-Square	D.F.	Significance	Min E.F.	Cells with E.F.< 5
29.05838	6	.0001	4.970	2 OF 12 (16.7%)

Number of Missing Observations = 0

ANNEX C:
COMPANY PROFILES

COMPANY PROFILE C.1. PROFILE OF COMPANIES COMPLETING THE BENCHMARK SURVEY QUESTIONNAIRE.

Company name	Home country	Net sales (thousands of US$)	Fiscal date	Classification of line of business used in data analysis	Breakdown of the three largest sectors
Alko Ltd.	Finland	1 174 485	31-Dec-88	Food	Ethanol production Feed production Bitechnical products
Alusuisse-Lonza Holding AG	Switzerland	3 990 913	31-Dec-88	Metals	Aluminium Chemicals Packaging
Amoco Corporation	United States	23 966 000	31-Dec-89	Oil/Gas/Coal & Services	Petroleum Petrochemicals
Arvin Industries Inc.	United States	1 540 523	31-Dec-89	Automotive	Automotive original equipment Auto replacement parts Technology
Assi	Sweden	1 116 117	31-Dec-88	Paper	Paper Packaging
Bayer AG	Germany	23 904 448	31-Dec-88	Chemicals	Chemicals (polymers) Health care Agrochemicals
Bayerische Motoren Werke (BMW)	Germany	12 211 345	31-Dec-88	Automotive	Automobiles Motorcycles Engines
Bekeart N.V.	Belgium	1 301 065	31-Dec-88	Metal products	Steelwire Rubber reinforcement wire Industrial equipment
Borden Inc.	United States	7 593 417	31-Dec-89	Food	Dairy Grocery Films & Adhesives
Cargil, Inc.	United States	N/A ᵃ	N/A	Miscellaneous	Commodity marketing Oilseed processing Corn milling
Carl Zeiss	Germany	1 923 106	30-Sep-88	Miscellaneous	

Company name	Home country	Net sales (thousands of US$)	Fiscal date	Classification of line of business used in data analysis	Breakdown of the three largest sectors
Cartiere Burgo S.p.A.	Italy	1 212 203	31-Dec-88	Paper	Coated paper Uncoated Newsprint
Caterpillar, Inc.	United States	10 882 000	31-Dec-89	Construction	Transportation Energy Housing
Charter Medical Corporation	United States	1 009 471	30-Sep-87	Miscellaneous	Health care
Chevron Corporation	United States	25 196 000	31-Dec-88	Oil/Gas/Coal & Services	Oil production Oil refining & marketing Chemicals
Ciba-Geigy Ltd.	Switzerland	11 781 137	31-Dec-88	Chemicals	Pharmaceuticals Agrochemicals Dyestuffs/chemicals
Cockerill Sambre S.A.	Belgium	4 985 695	31-Dec-88	Metal products	Iron and Steel Coated steel products
Cultor Ltd.	Finland	1 149 816	30-Nov-89	Food	Animal feed division Food division Sweetener division
DAF N.V.	The Netherlands	2 725 861	30-Dec-88	Automotive	Commercial vehicles Special products
Deere & Company	United States	7 219 774	31-Oct-89	Machinery & Equipment	Agricultural equipment Ind.\Construction equipment Lawn care
Degussa AG	Germany	8 030 575	30-Sep-88	Metals	Precious metals Chemicals Pharmaceuticals
DMV Campina Melkunie B.V.	The Netherlands	1 418 874	24-Dec-88	Food	Foods Food ingredients Feeds
Ebara Corporation	Japan	1 486 510	31-Dec-88	Metals	Mn-alloys FeSi-alloys Aluminium

Company name	Home country	Net sales (thousands of US$)	Fiscal date	Classification of line of business used in data analysis	Breakdown of the three largest sectors
Enso-Gutzeit OY	Finland	2 449 649	31-Dec-88	Paper	Pulp & Board Publication matters Fine paper
ERCROS S.A.	Spain	2 322 380 b/	..	Oil/Gas/Coal & Services	Oil refining & petrochemicals Fertilizers Mining
Ericsson (L.M.) Telefon AB	Sweden	5 126 449	31-Dec-88	Electrical	Telecommunications Cables Defense products
Gechem/Recticel N.V.	Belgium	1 236 416	31-Dec-88	Chemicals	Flexible PU-foam Rigid PU-foam PUR-RIM foam
Georgia Gulf Corporation	United States	1 060 612	31-Dec-88	Chemicals	SIC code 28 SIC code 30
Georgia-Pacific Corporation	United States	10 171 000	31-Dec-89	Construction	Building products Pulp & Paper
Glaxo Holdings plc	United Kingdom	4 234 075	30-Jun-89	Drugs/Cosmetics/Health	Pharmaceuticals
Hollandsche Beton Groep N.V.	The Netherlands	1 599 514	31-Dec-88	Construction	Building & Civil construction Dredging Industrial services
Huhtamaki OY (Leiras)	Finland	1 109 963	31-Dec-88	Food	Pharmaceuticals
Imperial Chemical Industries plc	United Kingdom	19 274 103	31-Dec-88	Chemicals	
John Labatt Ltd.	Canada	4 151 394	30-Apr-89	Food	Dairy Beer Milling/Baking
Kaiser Aluminum & Chemical Corporation	United States	1 987 200	31-Dec-87	Metals	Bauxite refining - Alumina Primary metal Flat rolled products
KAO Corporation	Japan	3 616 190	31-Mar-89	Drugs/Cosmetics/Health	Laundry & Cleansing products Personal care products Hygiene products

Company name	Home country	Net sales (thousands of US$)	Fiscal date	Classification of line of business used in data analysis	Breakdown of the three largest sectors
Kawasaki Steel Corporation	Japan	7 211 449	31-Mar-89	Metal Products	Steel making Engineering Chemicals
Kemira OY	Finland	2 306 900	31-Dec-88	Chemicals	Fertilizers Titanium dioxides Paints
Kirin Brewery Co., Ltd.	Japan	3 572 057	31-Dec-88	Beverages	Beer
Kymmene Corporation	Finland	2 594 100	31-Dec-88	Paper	Pulp & Paper Mechanical forest industry Paper converting
Linjeflyg AB	Sweden	1 555 000	..	Transportation	Domestic airline Freight Charter
Messerschmitt-Bölkow-Blohm GmbH	Germany	4 205 561	31-Dec-88	Aerospace	Transport aircrafts Defense systems Military aircrafts
Metallgesellschaft AG	Germany	8 999 367	31-Dec-88	Metal Products	Raw materials production Engineering Automobile supply industry
Metsä-Serla OY	Finland	1 899 150	31-Dec-88	Paper	Pulp & Paper Board & Sawmill industry Joinery products
Mitsubishi Paper Mills Ltd.	Japan	1 474 355	31-Mar-89	Paper	Paper Photosensitive materials Pulp
Mo och Domsjö AB	Sweden	3 199 342	31-Dec-88	Paper	Forestry & Forest products
NEC Corporation	Japan	19 421 640	31-Mar-89	Electronics	Computers & Electric systems Communication systems/equipment Electron devices

Company name	Home country	Net sales (thousands of US$)	Fiscal date	Classification of line of business used in data analysis	Breakdown of the three largest sectors
Nippon Steel Corporation	Japan	15 075 804	31-Mar-89	Metal Products	Steelmaking / Engineering / Chemicals
NKK Corporation	Japan	7 234 896	31-Mar-88	Metal Products	Steel / Engineering & Construction / Shipbuilding
Noranda, Inc.	Canada	8 004 300	31-Dec-89	Construction	Forest / Minerals / Energy
Oji Paper Co., Ltd.	Japan	2 658 685	31-Mar-89	Paper	Newsprint mill / pr/wr paper mill / Coated paper mill
Oryx Energy Co.	United States	1 140 000	31-Dec-89	Oil/Gas/Coal & Services	Oil production / Gas production
Petro Canada, Inc.	Canada	3 991 528	31-Dec-88	Oil/Gas/Coal & Services	Oil & Gas production
Pitney Bowes, Inc.	United States	2 875 685	31-Dec-89	Machinery & Equipment	Mailing systems / Financial services / Copier division
Ranks Hovis McDougall plc	United Kingdom	2 942 600	02-Sep-89	Food	Food & Beverage
Rautaruuki OY	Finland	1 307 556	31-Dec-88	Metal Products	Steel plate / Thin plate / Tubes & Profiles
Raychem Corporation	United States	1 083 028	30-Jun-89	Chemicals	Electronics / Telecommunications
Rio Algom Ltd.	Canada	1 691 909	31-Dec-88	Metals	Metal distribution / Uranium mining / Potash mining
Rover Group	United Kingdom	5 101 319	31-Dec-87	Automotive	Motor vehicles manufacturing
Royal Packaging Industries B.V.	The Netherlands	1 419 922	31-Dec-88	Paper	Steel industrial containers / Food packaging / Flexible packaging

Company name	Home country	Net sales (thousands of US$)	Fiscal date	Classification of line of business used in data analysis	Breakdown of the three largest sectors
Ruetgerswerke AG	Germany	1 846 721	31-Dec-88	Chemicals	Chemicals Plastics Construction
Sandoz International Ltd.	Switzerland	6 776 808	31-Dec-88	Chemicals	Pharmaceuticals Chemicals Agrochemicals
Shindler Holding AG	Switzerland	1 466 116	31-Dec-88	Machinery & Equipment	Elevators Escalators Rolling stock
Servistar Corporation	United States	1 072 090	30-Jun-88	Miscellaneous	Hardware distribution Lumber building management Rental
Sonoco Products Company	United States	1 599 751	31-Dec-88	Paper	Paperboard manufacturing Industrial packaging Consumer packaging
Sumitomo Chemical Co., Ltd.	Japan	5 670 715	31-Dec-88	Chemicals	Basic chemicals Fine chemicals Agricultural chemicals
Sun Company, Inc.	United States	8 612 000	31-Dec-88	Oil/Gas/Coal & Services	Petroleum refining Coal mining Petroleum exploration
Texas Instruments, Inc.	United States	6 521 900	31-Dec-89	Electronics	Semiconductors Defense electronics Data processing equipment
Tata Iron & Steel Co., Ltd.	India	15 014 500 *ᵈ*	..	Metals	Steel manufacture Export of minerals Export of food products
Toray Industries, Inc.	Japan	4 997 310	31-Mar-89	Chemicals	Fibers & Textiles Plastics Housing & Engineering

Company name	Home country	Net sales (thousands of US$)	Fiscal date	Classification of line of business used in data analysis	Breakdown of the three largest sectors
Toyota Motor Corporation	Japan	50 692 985	30-Jun-89	Automotive	Vehicles Industrial vehicles Prefabricated housing unit
Union Camp Corporation	United States	2 761 337	31-Dec-89	Paper	Paper & Pulp Chemical manufacture Paper packaging
Unitika Ltd.	Japan	2 091 181	31-Mar-88	Textiles	Synthetic fibers (nylon) Spun textiles Filament textiles
VARTA Batterie AG	Germany	1 159 120	31-Dec-88	Electrical	Portable batteries Starter batteries Industrial batteries
AB Volvo	Sweden	15 829 468	31-Dec-88	Automotive	Automobiles Trucks Buses
Waste Management, Inc.	United States	4 458 904	31-Dec-89	Miscellaneous	Sanitary Service
Westinghouse Electric Corporation	United States	12 844 000	31-Dec-89	Electrical	Electronic systems Commercial Industries
White Consolidated Industries	United States	1 946 203	31-Dec-85	Electrical	Home appliances Garden products Kitchen equipment
Xerox Corporation	United States	16 440 900	31-Dec-88	Machinery & Equipment	SIC 3861 SIC 3577 SIC 7629
Yamaha Corporation	Japan	3 066 065	31-Mar-89	Electronics	Musical instruments Furniture & House products Audio visual products
Yamaha Motor Corporation Ltd.	Japan	3 303 401	31-Mar-89	Automotive	Motorcycles Marine Quality life

(Company profile C.1., cont'd.)

....
a/ Cargil, Inc. is a privately held company and chose not to disclose its net sales.
b/ Net sales figure is in Spanish pesetas.
c/ Net sales figure is in Indian rupees.

COMPANY PROFILE C.2. PROFILE OF COMPANIES SUBMITTING INFORMATIONAL MATERIAL

Company name	Home country	Net sales (thousands of US$)	Fiscal date	Classification of line of business used in data analysis
Air Products & Chemicals, Inc.	United States	2 641 823	30-Sep-89	Chemicals
Akzo N.V.	The Netherlands	9 819 538	31-Dec-89	Chemicals
Allied-Lyons plc	United Kingdom	7 420 340	04-Mar-89	Beverages
Anheuser-Busch Companies, Inc.	United States	9 481 300	31-Dec-89	Beverages
Atlantic Richfield Company	United States	15 351 000	31-Dec-89	Oil/Gas/Coal & Services
B.F. Goodrich Company (The)	United States	24 197 000	31-Dec-89	Chemicals
BASF AG	Germany	25 912 828	31-Dec-88	Chemicals
Boehringer Ingelheim	Germany	2 451 996	31-Dec-88	Chemicals
Bristol-Myers Squibb Co.	United States	9 189 000	31-Dec-89	Drugs/Cosmetics/Health
Coca-Cola Company (The)	United States	8 965 786	31-Dec-89	Beverages
CRA Limited	Australia	4 010 325	31-Dec-88	Metals
Dana Corporation	United States	4 857 325	31-Dec-89	Automotive
Electrolux AB	Sweden	12 114 648	31-Dec-88	Electrical
Euroc Cementa AB	Sweden	1 539 2291	31-Dec-88	Machinery & Equipment
Fried Krupp GmbH	Germany	8 705 376	31-Dec-87	Metal Products
Grand Metropolitan plc	United Kingdom	15 318 455	30-Sep-89	Diversified
Hoechst AG	Germany	24 197 435	31-Dec-88	Chemicals
Inland Steel Industries, Inc.	United States	4 146 698	31-Dec-89	Metals
James River Corporation	United States	5 871 773	31-Dec-88	Paper
Kellog Company	United States	46 517 000	31-Dec-89	Food

Company name	Home country	Net sales (thousands of US$)	Fiscal date	Classification of line of business used in data analysis
Kimberly-Clark Corporation	United States	5 733 600	31-Dec-89	Paper
Lilly (Eli) and Company	United States	4 175 600	31-Dec-89	Drugs/Cosmetics/Health
McCormick & Company, Inc.	United States	1 246 080	30-Nov-89	Food
Murphy Oil Corporation	United States	1 473 595	31-Dec-88	Oil/Gas/Coal & Services
N.V. Philips' Gloeilampenfabrieken	The Netherlands	30 309 264	31-Dec-89	Electronics
Nampak Ltd.	South Africa	1 164 297	30-Sep-89	Paper
Norsk Hydro A/S	Norway	11 299 808	31-Dec-89	Chemicals
Ok Petroleum AB	Sweden	1 382 783	31-Dec-87	Oil/Gas/Coal & Services
Orkla-Borregaard A/S	Norway	1 150 407	31-Dec-88	Food
Pennzoil Company	United States	1 985 144	31-Dec-89	Oil/Gas/Coal & Services
PWA AG	Germany	2 021 865	31-Dec-88	Paper
Quaker Oats Company (The)	United States	5 724 500	30-Jun-89	Food
Scott Paper Company	United States	4 726 400	31-Dec-88	Paper
Shell International Petroleum Co., Ltd.	United Kingdom The Netherlands	28 997 977	31-Dec-88	Oil/Gas/Coal & Services
Stone Container Corporation	United States	3 742 489	31-Dec-88	Paper
T.I. Group plc	United Kingdom	1 579 788	31-Dec-88	Diversified
Tate and Lyle plc	United Kingdom	5 535 435	30-Sep-89	Food
Tenneco, Inc.	United States	13 234 000	31-Dec-88	Diversified
Texaco, Inc.	United States	33 544 000	31-Dec-88	Oil/Gas/Coal & Services
Thorn EMI plc	United Kingdom	5 403 297	31-Mar-89	Electronics
Unilever plc	United Kingdom	10 517 640	31-Dec-88	Food
Union Carbide Corporation	United States	8 324 000	31-Dec-88	Chemicals
United Technologies Corporation	United States	18 000 100	31-Dec-88	Diversified

PROFILE C.3. COMPANIES REQUESTING ANONYMITY[1]

Company Z	United States-based manufacturer in the aerospace, automotive and engineered materials sectors
Company Y	United States-based computer manufacturer
Company X	United States-based diversified company
Company W	United States-based manufacturer in the miscellaneous industry
Company V	United States-based aluminum producer and manufacturer of plastic products
Company U	United States-based oil producer
Company T	United States-based computer manufacturer
Company S	Germany-based chemical company
Company R	Germany-based company in the electrical engineering and electronics sectors
Company Q	United Kingdom-based major international natural resource group
Company P	United States-based integrated forest product company
Company O	Japan-based electronics company
Company N	United States-based manufacturer of household grocery products
Company M	New Zealand-based forestry and construction company
Company L	Japan-based electronics company
Company K	Japan-based electronics company
Company J	Japan-based machinery equipment manufacturer
Company I	Japan-based chemical company
Company H	United States-based plastic recycler
Company G	Japan-based paper company
Company F	United Kingdom-based metals company
Company E	Japan-based machinery and equipment manufacturer

Note:

[1]To protect anonymity, no further breakdown of these corporations is being provided.

PROFILE C.4. TARGETED AND SAMPLE CORPORATIONS

Regions	Firms targeted	Total respondents	Attachment only	Requesting anonymity	Questionnaire
Asia	160	60	1	43	59
Europe	292	72	17	18	55
North America	342	78	23	26	55
total (#)	794	210	41	87	169
Percentage of total (%)		26	5	11	21

Sector	Firms targeted	Total respondents	Attachment only	Requesting anonymity	Questionnaire
Agricultural	193	58	17	17	41
Extractive	165	65	12	28	53
Finished	325	72	12	38	60
Services	111	15	..	6	15
total (#)	794	210	41	89	169
percentage of total (%)		26	5	11	21

Sales	Firms targeted	Total respondents	Attachments only	Requesting anonymity	Questionnaire
Top third	266	65	9	29	56
Second third	262	65	9	35	56
Bottom third	266	80	23	23	57
totals (#)	794	210	41	87	169
percentage of total (%)		26	5	11	21

[1]To protect anonymity, no further breakdown of these corporations is being provided.

ANNEX D:
STATISTICAL TABLES

Annex table D.1. Corporate Policy Priorities: Corporate activities on EH&S and Sustainable Development

Activity	Energy-related activities (higher priority)				Health and safety activities (higher priority)			
	R&D for energy efficient production	Policies for conserving energy supplies	Policies for conserving non-renewable resources	International conservation of energy supplies	Company-wide worker health & safety policies	Company-wide accident prevention policies	Company-wide emergency preparedness policies	Standardized hazard assessment procedures
Total % (number)	70.7 (111)	67.7 (105)	54.4 (81)	54.0 (81)	67.5 (106)	60.3 (94)	58.0 (91)	56.9 (87)
Home-country region: Asia	77.8 (42)	62.3 (33)	49.0 (25)	46.8 (22)	78.2 (43)	64.8 (35)	66.0 (35)	69.1 (38)
Europe	59.6 (31)	55.8 (29)	44.0 (22)	48.1 (25)	51.9 (27)	43.4 (23)	40.4 (21)	34.7 (17)
North America	74.5 (38)	86.0 (43)	70.8 (34)	66.7 (34)	72.0 (36)	73.5 (36)	67.3 (35)	65.3 (32)
Significance level	0.26	0.07	0.18	0.19	0.04	0.01	0.02	0.00
Sector: Agricultural	66.7 (26)	65.7 (23)	50.0 (17)	61.8 (21)	42.1 (16)	42.1 (16)	37.8 (14)	40.5 (15)
Extractive-based	79.6 (39)	68.0 (34)	66.0 (31)	59.1 (26)	78.7 (37)	72.9 (35)	70.8 (34)	66.7 (30)
Finished-goods	70.9 (39)	71.4 (40)	51.9 (28)	50.9 (29)	74.1 (43)	62.1 (36)	61.4 (35)	63.8 (37)
Services	50.0 (7)	57.1 (8)	35.7 (5)	33.3 (5)	71.4 (10)	78.6 (11)	53.3 (8)	38.5 (5)
Significance level	0.02	0.48	0.02	0.30	0.00	0.00	0.02	0.02
Sales size: Top third	88.5 (46)	82.7 (43)	73.5 (36)	71.2 (37)	83.7 (41)	76.0 (38)	74.0 (37)	67.3 (33)
Second third	71.2 (37)	71.2 (37)	50.0 (25)	45.1 (23)	60.0 (33)	52.8 (28)	52.7 (29)	59.3 (32)
Bottom third	52.8 (28)	49.0 (25)	40.0 (20)	44.7 (21)	60.4 (32)	52.8 (28)	48.1 (25)	44.0 (22)
Significance level	0.00	0.04	0.05	0.04	0.04	0.08	0.07	0.15

/...

(annex table D.1. cont'd)

Activity	Traditional environmental activities (higher priorities)				Waste/disposal-related activities			
	Company-wide water quality/pollution policies	Company-wide air quality/pollution policies	Company-wide noise pollution	Company-wide soil quality/pollution policies	Recycling	Standardized waste handling procedures	Company-wide waste disposal policies	Company-wide waste reduction technologies
Total % (number)	48.1 (77)	47.2 (76)	41.1 (65)	31.2 (49)	84.5 (131)	56.3 (89)	51.6 (82)	48.7 (77)
Home-country region: Asia	69.1 (38)	65.5 (36)	63.0 (34)	31.5 (17)	82.7 (43)	74.1 (40)	61.1 (33)	54.7 (29)
Europe	24.1 (13)	29.1 (16)	18.9 (10)	18.9 (10)	75.5 (40)	35.8 (19)	29.6 (16)	27.8 (15)
North America	51.0 (26)	47.1 (24)	41.2 (21)	44.0 (22)	96.0 (48)	58.8 (30)	64.7 (33)	64.7 (33)
Significance level	0.00	0.00	0.00	0.01	0.04	0.00	0.00	0.00
Sector: Agricultural	28.9 (11)	28.2 (11)	32.4 (12)	21.1 (8)	88.2 (30)	37.8 (14)	36.8 (14)	31.6 (12)
Extractive-based	58.3 (28)	60.4 (29)	43.8 (21)	47.9 (23)	88.0 (44)	62.0 (31)	60.4 (29)	60.4 (29)
Finished-goods	59.3 (35)	55.9 (33)	50.0 (29)	26.8 (15)	86.0 (49)	66.7 (38)	58.6 (34)	54.4 (31)
Services	20.0 (3)	20.0 (3)	20.0 (3)	20.0 (3)	57.1 (8)	42.9 (6)	33.3 (5)	33.3 (5)
Significance level	0.00	0.00	0.04	0.03	0.00	0.02	0.00	0.01
Sales size: Top third	60.8 (31)	64.7 (33)	58.0 (29)	44.9 (22)	94.2 (49)	64.7 (33)	69.4 (34)	66.0 (33)
Second third	50.0 (28)	45.6 (26)	41.1 (23)	32.1 (18)	82.7 (43)	58.2 (32)	52.6 (30)	47.3 (26)
Bottom third	34.0 (18)	32.1 (17)	25.0 (13)	17.3 (9)	76.5 (39)	46.2 (24)	34.0 (18)	34.0 (18)
Significance level	0.03	0.01	0.01	0.05	0.13	0.22	0.00	0.01

/...

(annex table D.1. cont'd)

	Genuine sustainable development activities (lower priority areas)					
Activity	Afforestation efforts on corporate property	Company-wide greenhouse gas generation reduction	Use renewable energy resources	Preservation of endangered species	Conservation of biodiversity	Protection of wetlands and rainforests in LDCs
Total % (number)	40.4 (59)	30.1 (46)	22.0 (33)	15.8 (23)	10.1 (15)	9.2 (11)
Home-country region: Asia	56.9 (29)	42.0 (21)	28.8 (15)	4.0 (2)	2.0 (1)	4.4 (2)
Europe	29.8 (14)	21.8 (12)	13.7 (7)	10.4 (5)	8.0 (4)	2.9 (1)
North America	33.3 (16)	27.1 (13)	23.4 (11)	33.3 (16)	20.8 (10)	20.5 (8)
Significance level	0.07	0.11	0.04	0.00	0.09	0.01
Sector: Agricultural	42.4 (14)	15.8 (6)	14.7 (5)	20.0 (7)	14.3 (5)	3.8 (1)
Extractive-based	43.5 (20)	40.9 (18)	21.7 (10)	25.0 (11)	13.3 (6)	15.8 (6)
Finished-goods	37.5 (21)	37.5 (21)	30.4 (17)	5.7 (3)	1.8 (1)	6.7 (3)
Services	36.4 (4)	6.7 (1)	7.1 (1)	14.3 (2)	21.4 (3)	10.0 (1)
Significance level	0.95	0.01	0.01	0.02	0.03	0.70
Sales size: Top third	47.1 (24)	54.2 (26)	36.0 (18)	21.3 (10)	14.3 (7)	15.9 (7)
Second third	46.0 (28)	22.6 (12)	15.7 (8)	20.0 (10)	10.2 (5)	8.1 (3)
Bottom third	26.7 (12)	15.4 (8)	14.3 (7)	6.1 (3)	5.9 (3)	2.6 (1)
Significance level	0.28	0.00	0.02	0.15	0.36	0.27

Annex table D.2. Factors influencing change in corporate environmental policies and programmes

Influencing factor	Changes in home-country legislation	Environment-ally related legal actions involving company	Environmental accidents at other companies	Changes in host-country legislation	Environment-ally related legal actions involving other companies	Environmental accidents at company premises	Consumer-related events	Worker-related events
Total % (number)	62.7 (106)	21.9 (37)	20.1 (34)	18.9 (32)	15.4 (26)	14.2 (24)	8.9 (15)	7.1 (12)
Home-country region:								
Asia	75.0 (42)	17.9 (10)	8.9 (5)	8.9 (5)	7.1 (4)	7.1 (4)	1.8 (1)	5.4 (3)
Europe	44.8 (26)	12.1 (7)	19.0 (11)	15.5 (9)	10.3 (6)	13.8 (8)	12.1 (7)	6.9 (4)
North America	69.1 (38)	36.4 (20)	32.7 (18)	32.7 (18)	29.1 (16)	21.8 (12)	12.7 (7)	9.1 (5)
Significance level	0.00	0.01	0.01	0.00	0.00	0.09	0.07	0.74
Sector:								
Agricultural	53.7 (22)	19.5 (8)	24.4 (10)	22.0 (9)	19.5 (8)	22.0 (9)	17.1 (7)	4.9 (2)
Extractive-based	67.9 (36)	17.0 (9)	24.5 (13)	15.1 (8)	17.0 (9)	11.3 (6)	9.4 (5)	9.4 (5)
Finished-goods	66.7 (40)	28.3 (17)	15.0 (9)	21.7 (13)	11.7 (7)	11.7 (7)	3.3 (2)	6.7 (4)
Services	53.3 (8)	20.0 (3)	13.3 (2)	13.3 (2)	13.3 (2)	13.3 (2)	6.7 (1)	6.7 (1)
Significance level	0.39	0.50	0.47	0.72	0.72	0.44	0.12	0.86
Sales size:								
Top third	71.4 (40)	21.4 (12)	25.0 (14)	25.0 (14)	19.6 (11)	10.7 (6)	8.9 (5)	10.7 (6)
Second third	54.4 (31)	22.8 (13)	19.3 (11)	17.5 (10)	12.3 (7)	15.8 (9)	7.0 (4)	5.3 (3)
Bottom third	62.5 (35)	21.4 (12)	16.1 (9)	14.3 (8)	14.3 (8)	16.1 (9)	10.7 (6)	5.4 (1)
Significance level	0.17	0.98	0.49	0.33	0.53	0.66	0.79	0.44

Annex table D.3. Voluntary international environmental guidelines

Guideline	Sectorial trade association guidelines	CMA's Responsible CARE	ICC environmental guidelines	ISO technical environmental standards	UNEP's environmental guidelines	ILO's code of practice on accident prevention
Total % (number)	19.7 (25)	18.7 (25)	17.3 (24)	13.0 (17)	9.4 (13)	7.5 (10)
Home-country region:						
Asia	..	5.0 (2)	2.4 (1)	2.4 (4)	9.1 (4)	7.3 (3)
Europe	29.3 (12)	8.9 (4)	32.7 (16)	28.9 (13)	13.0 (6)	13.0 (6)
North America	28.9 (13)	38.8 (19)	14.3 (7)	6.7 (3)	6.3 (3)	2.1 (1)
Significance level	0.00	0.00	0.00	0.00	0.37	0.00
Sector:						
Agricultural	16.1 (5)	12.9 (4)	17.1 (6)	9.4 (3)	12.1 (4)	6.1 (2)
Extractive-based	31.6 (12)	40.0 (16)	25.0 (10)	10.8 (4)	5.1 (2)	5.3 (2)
Finished-goods	8.3 (4)	4.0 (2)	13.5 (7)	16.0 (8)	11.1 (6)	11.8 (6)
Services	40.0 (4)	23.1 (3)	8.3 (1)	16.7 (2)	8.3 (1)	..
Significance level	0.09	0.00	0.34	0.56	0.63	0.57
Sales size:						
Top third	20.0 (8)	26.7 (12)	27.3 (12)	14.3 (6)	16.3 (7)	9.5 (4)
Second third	16.3 (7)	24.4 (11)	12.5 (6)	11.4 (5)	8.3 (4)	6.4 (3)
Bottom third	22.7 (10)	4.5 (2)	12.8 (6)	13.3 (6)	4.3 (2)	6.7 (3)
Significance level	0.73	0.03	0.19	0.28	0.11	0.63

/...

(annex table D.3. cont'd) Guideline	CEFIC guidelines for the safe storage of chemicals	OECD guidelines on multinational enterprises	ILO tripartite agreement on multinational enterprises	CEFIC guidelines for the safe transfer of technology	FAO's code for the safe marketing & use of pesticides	UNEP's APPEL programme
Total % (number)	6.3 (8)	6.1 (8)	4.5 (6)	3.8 (5)	3.6 (5)	3.0 (4)
Home-country region: Asia	..	2.5 (1)	7.5 (3)	..	4.8 (2)	..
Europe	14.0 (6)	8.9 (4)	2.2 (1)	6.5 (3)	6.3 (3)	4.4 (2)
North America	4.5 (2)	6.5 (3)	4.3 (2)	4.3 (2)	..	4.2 (2)
Significance level	0.00	0.03	0.01	0.08	0.10	0.16
Sector: Agricultural	9.4 (3)	3.1 (1)	..	3.0 (1)	..	..
Extractive-based	9.1 (3)	5.6 (2)	5.3 (2)	11.1 (4)	12.5 (5)	10.0 (4)
Finished-goods	4.1 (2)	7.8 (4)	7.8 (4)	..	..	..
Services	..	8.3 (1)	..	..	..	..
Significance level	0.75	0.66	0.42	0.02	0.03	0.06
Sales size: Top third	10.3 9 (4)	11.9 (5)	4.7 (2)	7.3 (3)	6.8 (3)	7.0 (3)
Second third	4.5 (2)	4.3 (2)	4.3 (2)	2.1 (1)	..	2.2 (1)
Bottom third	4.7 (2)	2.3 (1)	4.5 (2)	2.3 (1)	4.3 (2)	..
Significance level	0.10	0.09	0.58	0.15	0.43	0.15

Annex table D.4. Corporate preferences for United Nations' role in environmental activities

Preference	Reducing differences in env. rules & regulations of industrialized countries	Setting international policy guidelines	Setting international technical standards	Compiling national environmental laws and regulations	Strengthening/-creating national regulatory systems LDCs
Total % (number)	62.1 (105)	52.7 (89)	45.6 (77)	34.9 (59)	20.1 (34)
Home-country region: Asia	48.2 (27)	60.7 (34)	44.6 (25)	42.9 (24)	26.8 (15)
Europe	69.0 (40)	53.4 (31)	60.3 (35)	19.0 (11)	12.1 (7)
North America	69.1 (38)	43.6 (24)	30.9 (17)	43.6 (24)	21.8 (12)
Significance level	0.03	0.20	0.01	0.01	0.14
Sector: Agricultural	61.0 (25)	58.5 (24)	39.0 (16)	29.3 (12)	17.1 (34)
Extractive-based	62.3 (33)	37.7 (20)	37.7 (20)	35.8 (19)	18.9 (43)
Finished-goods	61.7 (37)	60.0 (36)	46.7 (28)	38.3 (23)	26.7 (44)
Services	66.7 (10)	60.0 (9)	86.7 (13)	33.3 (5)	6.7 (14)
Significance level	0.98	0.07	0.01	0.82	0.31
Sales size: Top third	60.7 (34)	53.6 (30)	42.9 (24)	37.5 (21)	26.8 (15)
Second third	57.9 (33)	54.4 (31)	43.9 (25)	38.6 (22)	15.8 (9)
Bottom third	67.9 (38)	50.0 (28)	50.0 (28)	28.6 (16)	17.9 (10)
Significance level	0.53	0.88	0.71	0.47	0.30

Preference	Reporting on corporate leadership & their achievements	Assisting in review of voluntary corporate "performance" standards	Mediating between corporations & governments on environmental conflicts	Strengthening/creating national regulatory inspection in LDCs	Establishing norms & procedures for public disclosure
Total % (number)	17.2 (29)	11.2 (19)	10.7 (18)	9.5 (16)	5.9 (10)
Home-country region: Asia	16.1 (9)	10.7 (6)	7.1 (4)	12.5 (7)	7.1 (4)
Europe	6.9 (4)	8.6 (4)	10.3 (6)	10.3 (6)	6.9 (4)
North America	29.1 (16)	29.1 (16)	14.5 (8)	5.5 (3)	3.6 (2)
Significance level	0.01	0.60	0.45	0.43	0.68
Sector: Agricultural	14.6 (6)	12.2 (5)	4.9 (2)	17.1 (7)	7.3 (3)
Extractive-based	15.1 (8)	15.1 (8)	15.1 (8)	9.4 (5)	7.5 (4)
Finished-goods	23.3 (14)	6.7 (4)	10.0 (6)	3.3 (3)	3.3 (2)
Services	6.7 (1)	13.3 (2)	13.3 (2)	13.3 (2)	6.7 (1)
Significance level	0.37	0.54	0.44	0.13	0.77
Sales size: Top third	25.0 (14)	5.4 (3)	16.1 (9)	5.4 (3)	7.1 (4)
Second third	12.3 (7)	3.5 (2)	7.0 (4)	14.0 (8)	8.8 (5)
Bottom third	14.3 (8)	25.0 (14)	8.9 (5)	8.9 (5)	1.8 (1)
Significance level	0.16	0.00	0.29	0.29	0.26

Annex table D.5. Corporate functional areas involved in initiating environmental programmes

Division/Function	Top management	Strategic planning	R&D	Public relations	Production	Market research	Marketing	Human resources	Accounting
Total % (number)	77.3 (126)	55.4 (87)	51.6 (82)	38.0 (60)	31.7 (51)	25.0 (37)	24.3 (37)	20.6 (32)	11.2 (17)
Home-country region: Asia	85.2 (46)	85.2 (46)	55.6 (30)	47.3 (26)	36.4 (20)	44.2 (23)	32.7 (17)	32.1 (17)	26.9 (14)
Europe	72.7 (40)	45.6 (24)	53.8 (28)	32.7 (16)	29.6 (16)	21.7 (10)	22.9 (11)	16.3 (8)	4.3 (2)
North America	74.1 (40)	33.3 (17)	45.3 (24)	33.3 (18)	28.8 (15)	8.0 (4)	17.3 (9)	13.2 (7)	1.9 (1)
Significance level	0.17	0.00	0.03	0.13	0.37	0.00	0.32	0.03	0.00
Sector: Agricultural	74.4 (29)	50.0 (18)	51.3 (20)	39.5 (15)	35.0 (14)	30.3 (10)	24.2 (8)	8.8 (3)	5.9 (2)
Extractive-based	84.0 (42)	62.5 (30)	63.3 (31)	46.9 (23)	49.0 (24)	37.2 (16)	36.2 (17)	23.4 (11)	15.2 (7)
Finished-goods	75.0 (45)	55.0 (33)	44.1 (26)	32.8 (19)	16.7 (10)	16.9 (10)	15.3 (9)	23.3 (14)	13.6 (8)
Services	71.4 (10)	46.2 (6)	41.7 (5)	23.1 (3)	25.0 (3)	7.7 (1)	23.1 (3)	28.6 (4)	..
Significance level	0.31	0.16	0.06	0.26	0.00	0.18	0.06	0.14	0.21
Sales size: Top third	81.1 (43)	66.0 (35)	61.5 (32)	51.0 (26)	32.1 (17)	29.4 (15)	30.8 (16)	23.1 (12)	15.7 (8)
Second third	81.5 (44)	56.0 (28)	53.7 (29)	31.5 (17)	26.4 (14)	27.1 (13)	24.0 (12)	19.6 (10)	9.8 (5)
Bottom third	69.6 (39)	44.4 (24)	39.6 (21)	32.1 (17)	36.4 (20)	18.4 (9)	18.0 (9)	19.2 (10)	8.0 (4)
Significance level	0.32	0.03	0.26	0.03	0.27	0.26	0.54	0.31	0.00

Annex table D.. Corporate mana ement of s bsidiaries

Formal arrangement		Between head uarters and subsidiaries	Between head uarters and uncontrolled affiliates
Total % (number)		44.9 (66)	14.5 (20)
Home-country region:	Asia	31.9 (15)	8.3 (4)
	Europe	45.1 (23)	16.3 (7)
	North America	57.1 (28)	19.1 (9)
Significance level		0.05	0.46
Sector:	Agricultural	42.9 (15)	6.5 (2)
	Extractive-based	47.8 (22)	30.2 (13)
	Finished-goods	42.6 (23)	5.7 (3)
	Services	50.0 (6)	18.2 (2)
Significance level		0.93	0.00
Sales size:	Top third	56.0 (28)	20.4 (10)
	Second third	40.0 (20)	6.8 (3)
	Bottom third	38.3 (18)	15.6 (7)
Significance level		0.15	0.11

Annex table D.7. Corporate environmental data collection

Programme/procedure	Higher-priority issues				
	Standardized safety audit procedures	International safety and environmental audits	Standardized hazard assessment procedures	Monitoring hazard waste-disposal procedures in developing countries	Environmental bulletin for company managers
Total % (number)	64.7 (101)	64.7 (99)	57.8 (93)	47.8 (54)	44.4 (72)
Home-country region: Asia	81.8 (45)	53.1 (26)	61.8 (34)	45.5 (20)	56.4 (31)
Europe	42.0 (21)	59.3 (32)	37.0 (20)	39.4 (13)	30.4 (17)
North America	68.6 (35)	82.0 (41)	75.0 (39)	58.3 (21)	47.1 (24)
Significance level	0.00	0.04	0.00	0.36	0.02
Sector: Agricultural	51.4 (19)	65.8 (25)	44.7 (17)	42.3 (11)	31.6 (12)
Extractive-based	69.6 (32)	69.8 (30)	65.3 (32)	45.7 (16)	58.0 (29)
Finished-goods	66.7 (40)	59.6 (34)	64.4 (38)	51.1 (23)	41.7 (25)
Services	76.9 (10)	66.7 (10)	40.0 (6)	57.1 (4)	42.9 (6)
Significance level	0.42	0.26	0.03	0.60	0.09
Sales size: Top third	64.7 (33)	76.5 (39)	74.5 (38)	63.4 (26)	56.6 (30)
Second third	58.2 (32)	60.8 (31)	55.4 (31)	40.5 (15)	44.4 (24)
Bottom third	46.2 (24)	56.9 (29)	44.4 (24)	37.1 (13)	32.7 (18)
Significance level	0.22	0.26	0.02	0.14	0.04

/...

(annex table D.7. cont'd)

Programme/procedure		Standard pollution-monitoring techniques	Standard env. impact assessment procedures	Separate annual env. statement for corporate board	Company-wide env. impact assessment	Monitors stacks for air-emission components in LDCs	Int'l env. accounting	Survey on biological species on underdeveloped lands in LDCs
					Lower-priority issues			
Total % (number)		39.9 (63)	39.6 (63)	37.8 (62)	37.2 (58)	36.6 (41)	29.7 (41)	8.7 (10)
Home-country region:	Asia	61.8 (34)	50.9 (28)	30.9 (17)	45.3 (24)	39.1 (18)	50.9 (28)	12.2 (5)
	Europe	23.1 (12)	25.9 (14)	39.3 (22)	22.6 (12)	30.3 (3)	25.9 (14)	8.1 (3)
	North America	33.3 (17)	42.0 (21)	43.4 (23)	44.0 (22)	39.4 (13)	42.0 (21)	5.4 (2)
Significance level		0.00	0.48	0.39	0.09	0.48	0.12	0.87
Sector:	Agricultural	29.7 (11)	24.3 (9)	31.7 (13)	21.1 (8)	20.8 (5)	25.0 (8)	4.0 (1)
	Extractive-based	45.8 (22)	51.1 (24)	46.9 (23)	53.2 (25)	48.5 (16)	39.0 (16)	18.4 (7)
	Finished-goods	44.1 (26)	40.0 (24)	35.6 (23)	37.5 (21)	34.8 (16)	27.4 (15)	4.7 (2)
	Services	28.6 (4)	40.0 (6)	33.3 (5)	26.7 (4)	44.4 (4)	14.3 (2)	..
Significance level		0.07	0.07	0.45	0.00	0.33	0.55	0.15
Sales size:	Top third	49.0 (25)	58.8 (30)	53.8 (28)	61.2 (30)	59.5 (25)	46.7 (21)	6.7 (3)
	Second third	42.9 (24)	32.1 (18)	33.3 (19)	32.1 (18)	16.7 (6)	27.1 (13)	11.8 (4)
	Bottom third	27.5 (14)	28.8 (15)	27.3 (15)	19.6 (10)	29.4 (10)	15.6 (7)	8.3 (3)
Significance level		0.11	0.01	0.01	0.00	0.00	0.02	0.59

Annex table D.8. Corporate public relations activities

Activity	Higher-priority activities							
	Contents of MSDS	Contents of prod. labels & safety guides	Int'l community join in emergency planning	Voluntary financing of env. organizations	Annual meeting HQs/local env. organizations	Separate env. section in annual report	Contribute to local env. societies	Formal published int'l policy programmes
Total % (number)	63.7 (100)	51.4 (74)	51.4 (74)	51.0 (74)	50.3 (74)	47.2 (77)	46.1 (65)	43.1 (72)
Home-country region: Asia	69.6 (39)	58.2 (32)	37.8 (17)	62.0 (31)	50.0 (24)	21.8 (12)	43.2 (19)	18.2 (10)
Europe	53.1 (26)	42.9 (21)	54.2 (26)	34.0 (16)	56.9 (29)	53.6 (30)	42.9 (21)	41.4 (24)
North America	67.3 (35)	54.9 (28)	60.8 (31)	56.3 (27)	44.0 (22)	67.3 (35)	52.1 (25)	70.4 (38)
Significance level	0.02	0.01	0.08	0.09	0.09	0.00	0.35	0.00
Sector: Agricultural	44.4 (16)	38.9 (14)	46.9 (15)	46.9 (15)	38.2 (13)	51.3 (20)	50.0 (16)	45.5 (17)
Extractive-based	78.7 (37)	63.0 (29)	65.9 (29)	57.4 (27)	68.2 (30)	66.0 (33)	59.1 (26)	58.5 (31)
Finished-goods	66.1 (39)	53.4 (31)	42.6 (23)	50.9 (28)	48.3 (28)	30.5 (18)	35.8 (19)	30.5 (18)
Services	53.3 (8)	46.7 (7)	50.0 (7)	36.4 (4)	30.8 (4)	40.0 (6)	33.3 (4)	40.0 (6)
Significance level	0.02	0.14	0.34	0.53	0.06	0.00	0.18	0.03
Sales size: Top third	78.0 (39)	58.0 (29)	60.0 (30)	74.0 (37)	62.0 (31)	60.4 (32)	55.3 (26)	58.2 (32)
Second third	58.2 (32)	49.1 (27)	37.5 (18)	42.0 (21)	41.2 (21)	45.5 (25)	43.8 (21)	41.1 (23)
Bottom third	55.8 (29)	50.0 (25)	56.5 (26)	35.6 (16)	47.9 (23)	36.4 (20)	39.1 (18)	30.4 (17)
Significance level	0.11	0.62	0.21	0.02	0.34	0.04	0.45	0.01

/...

(annex table D.8. cont'd)

Activity	Higher-priority Toxic education progs. for work-force in LDCs	Lower-priority activities Special public brochure on env. performance	Separate annual env. report for corporate board	Company policy for disclosure of product-risk info.	Company policy for disclosure of process-risk info.	Public access to env. R&D results	Public access to corporate lands for walks	Green labelling
Total % (number)	40.5 (45)	38.5 (65)	37.8 (62)	32.7 (51)	28.5 (43)	27.2 (43)	25.2 (39)	12.3 (17)
Home-country region: Asia	45.5 (20)	42.9 (65)	30.9 (17)	27.8 (15)	22.6 (12)	28.3 (15)	24.5 (13)	18.2 (8)
Europe	27.3 (9)	31.0 (18)	39.3 (22)	25.5 (13)	23.1 (12)	24.1 (13)	19.2 (10)	10.2 (5)
North America	47.1 (16)	41.8 (23)	43.4 (23)	45.1 (23)	41.3 (19)	29.4 (15)	32.0 (16)	8.9 (4)
Significance level	0.38	0.07	0.39	0.05	0.05	0.06	0.04	0.22
Sector: Agricultural	21.7 (5)	34.1 (14)	31.7 (13)	15.8 (6)	13.9 (5)	23.7 (9)	34.2 (13)	12.1 (4)
Extractive-based	51.4 (18)	35.8 (19)	46.9 (23)	52.2 (24)	50.0 (22)	34.0 (17)	22.9 (11)	14.6 (6)
Finished-goods	45.5 (20)	46.7 (28)	35.6 (21)	31.6 (18)	26.8 (145)	25.0 (14)	17.9 (10)	14.0 (7)
Services	22.2 (2)	26.7 (4)	33.3 (5)	20.0 (3)	6.7 (1)	21.4 (3)	38.5 (5)	..
Significance level	0.07	0.34	0.45	0.00	0.00	0.78	0.29	0.65
Sales size: Top third	65.1 (28)	60.7 (34)	53.8 (28)	46.0 (23)	46.9 (23)	40.4 (21)	33.3 (17)	19.0 (8)
Second third	29.4 (10)	35.1 (20)	33.3 (19)	20.0 (11)	15.4 (8)	24.1 (13)	20.4 (11)	6.1 (3)
Bottom third	20.6 (7)	19.6 (11)	27.3 (15)	33.3 (17)	24.0 (12)	17.3 (9)	22.0 (11)	12.8 (6)
Significance level	0.00	0.00	0.01	0.08	0.00	0.11	0.50	0.30

Annex table D.9. Corporate labor relations activities

Activity	EHS part of employees' job description	Educating staff on environmental impact of firm's operations	Env. performance & safety records part of staff evaluation	Worker's participation in setting EH&S int'l committees	Worker health and safety a company-wide policy	Standardized worker-safety training programmes
			Higher priority activities			
Total % (number)	82.3 (130)	68.6 (105)	68.6 (107)	67.8 (101)	67.5 (106)	67.3 (105)
Home-country region:						
Asia	90.4 (47)	70.8 (34)	78.4 (40)	68.1 (32)	78.2 (43)	89.3 (50)
Europe	85.2 (46)	60.4 (32)	58.5 (31)	74.5 (38)	51.9 (27)	44.9 (22)
North America	71.2 (37)	75.0 (39)	69.2 (36)	60.8 (31)	72.0 (36)	64.7 (33)
Significance level	0.04	0.13	0.14	0.02	0.04	0.00
Sector:						
Agricultural	83.8 (31)	61.1 (22)	70.3 (26)	58.8 (20)	42.1 (16)	47.4 (18)
Extractive-based	90.2 (46)	78.3 (36)	76.0 (38)	79.1 (34)	78.7 (37)	73.3 (33)
Finished-goods	73.2 (41)	67.9 (38)	60.0 (33)	64.9 (37)	74.1 (43)	78.0 (46)
Services	85.7 (12)	60.0 (9)	71.4 (10)	66.7 (10)	71.4 (10)	57.1 (8)
Significance level	0.37	0.24	0.53	0.19	0.00	0.01
Sales size:						
Top third	82.7 (43)	82.7 (43)	74.5 (38)	72.5 (37)	83.7 (41)	83.3 (40)
Second third	80.8 (42)	64.7 (33)	74.5 (38)	64.2 (34)	60.0 (33)	64.8 (35)
Bottom third	83.3 (45)	58.0 (29)	57.4 (31)	66.7 (30)	60.4 (32)	55.6 (30)
Significance level	0.68	0.09	0.20	0.80	0.04	0.02

/...

(annex table D.9. cont'd)

Activity	Higher priority activities			Lower priority activities		
	Standardized contents of MSDS	Standardized management safety-training programmes	Incentive schemes for staff contribution to company's env. goals	ILO's code of practice on accident prevention	Worker-related events impacting overall company env. policy	ILO tripartite agreement on multinational enterprises
Total % (number)	63.7 (100)	58.2 (92)	47.4 (74)	7.5 (10)	7.1 (12)	4.5 (6)
Home-country region: Asia	69.6 (39)	75.0 (42)	58.5 (31)	7.3 (3)	5.4 (3)	7.5 (3)
Europe	53.1 (26)	37.3 (19)	48.1 (25)	13.0 (6)	6.9 (4)	2.2 (1)
North America	67.3 (35)	60.8 (31)	35.3 (18)	2.1 (1)	9.1 (5)	4.3 (2)
Significance level	0.02	0.00	0.06	0.00	0.88	0.01
Sector: Agricultural	44.4 (16)	43.2 (16)	45.7 (17)	6.1 (2)	4.9 (2)	..
Extractive-based	78.7 (37)	68.8 (33)	52.1 (25)	5.3 (2)	9.4 (5)	5.3 (2)
Finished-goods	66.1 (39)	62.7 (37)	49.1 (28)	11.8 (6)	6.7 (4)	7.8 (4)
Services	53.3 (8)	42.9 (6)	28.6 (4)	..	6.7 (1)	..
Significance level	0.02	0.01	0.47	0.57	0.33	0.42
Sales size: Top third	78.0 (39)	74.5 (38)	58.8 (30)	9.5 (4)	10.7 (6)	4.7 (2)
Second third	58.2 (32)	50.0 (27)	46.2 (24)	6.4 (3)	5.3 (3)	4.3 (2)
Bottom third	55.8 (29)	50.9 (27)	37.7 (20)	6.7 (3)	5.3 (3)	4.5 (2)
Significance level	0.11	0.06	0.10	0.63	0.27	0.58

Annex table D.10. Transnational Corporations and the UNCED themes (the themes of relevant importance to the respondents)

Theme	Protection of the atmosphere	Environmentally sound management of toxic wastes & chemicals	Protection of freshwater resources	Protection and management of land resources	Protection of oceans	Environmentally sound management of biotechnology	Conservation of biodiversity
Total % (number)	91.7 (155)	82.8 (140)	79.9 (135)	53.3 (90)	35.5 (60)	17.2 (29)	9.5 (16)
Home-country region:							
Asia	96.4 (54)	83.9 (47)	80.4 (45)	46.4 (26)	55.4 (31)	26.8 (15)	5.4 (3)
Europe	84.5 (49)	77.6 (45)	70.7 (41)	37.9 (22)	29.3 (17)	20.7 (12)	12.1 (7)
North America	94.5 (52)	87.3 (48)	89.1 (49)	76.4 (42)	21.8 (12)	3.6 (2)	10.9 (6)
Significance level	0.04	0.38	0.05	0.00	0.00	0.00	0.43
Sector:							
Agricultural	90.2 (37)	65.9 (27)	82.9 (34)	53.7 (22)	36.6 (15)	39.0 (16)	14.6 (6)
Extractive-based	90.6 (48)	90.6 (48)	77.4 (41)	52.8 (28)	34.0 (18)	13.2 (7)	3.8 (2)
Finished-goods	96.7 (58)	90.0 (54)	81.7 (49)	51.7 (31)	36.7 (22)	8.3 (5)	10.0 (6)
Services	80.0 (12)	73.3 (11)	73.3 (11)	60.0 (9)	33.3 (5)	6.7 (1)	13.3 (2)
Significance level	0.18	0.00	0.81	0.95	0.99	0.00	0.31
Sales size:							
Top third	94.6 (53)	87.5 (49)	82.1 (46)	62.5 (35)	28.6 (16)	10.7 (6)	7.1 (4)
Second third	87.7 (50)	82.5 (47)	78.9 (45)	47.4 (27)	40.4 (23)	21.1 (12)	19.3 (11)
Bottom third	92.9 (52)	78.6 (44)	78.6 (44)	50.0 (28)	37.5 (21)	19.6 (11)	1.8 (1)
Significance level	0.38	0.45	0.87	0.23	0.40	0.29	0.00

Annex table D.11. Transnational corporations and protection of the atmosphere
(respondents who have activities and/or use materials hazardous to the atmosphere)

Activity and emission	Activities		Hazardous materials used and/or discharged			
	Use CFCs & related materials in manufacturing	Products containing CFCs	Oxides of nitrogen	Volatile Organic Compounds	Oxides of sulphur	Asbestos
Total % (number)	48.0 (59)	24.4 (38)	66.9 (105)	66.9 (105)	60.9 (96)	18.9 (32)
Home-country region:						
Asia	60.9 (28)	24.1 (13)	76.4 (42)	61.8 (34)	74.5 (41)	23.2 (13)
Europe	33.3 (13)	21.2 (11)	63.0 (34)	64.2 (34)	52.7 (29)	12.1 (7)
North America	47.4 (18)	28.0 (14)	60.4 (29)	75.5 (37)	53.1 (26)	21.8 (12)
Significance level	0.05	0.96	0.17	0.64	0.07	0.08
Sector:						
Agricultural	16.7 (5)	10.8 (4)	64.1 (25)	48.7 (19)	52.5 (21)	..
Extractive-based	41.2 (14)	21.3 (10)	72.9 (35)	79.2 (38)	79.2 (38)	26.4 (14)
Finished-goods	75.0 (39)	41.4 (24)	69.0 (40)	72.4 (42)	56.9 (33)	30.0 (18)
Services	14.3 (1)	..	41.7 (5)	50.0 (6)	30.8 (4)	..
Significance level	0.00	0.00	0.39	0.07	0.03	0.05
Sales size:						
Top third	67.4 (29)	42.3 (22)	74.0 (37)	79.6 (39)	70.6 (36)	25.0 (14)
Second third	46.3 (19)	19.6 (10)	67.9 (36)	64.8 (35)	61.1 (38)	19.3 (11)
Bottom third	28.2 (11)	11.3 (6)	59.3 (32)	57.4 (31)	50.0 (27)	12.5 (7)
Significance level	0.00	0.00	0.13	0.00	0.09	0.05

Annex table D.12. Corporate policies/programmes for the protection of the atmosphere.

Policy/Programme	Air quality	Reduction of greenhouse-gas generation	R&D for greenhouse-gas generation reduction	Energy conservation	Energy supplies
Total % (number)	47.2 (76)	30.1 (46)	39.0 (60)	54.0 (81)	67.7 (105)
Home-country region:					
Asia	65.5 (36)	42.0 (21)	39.6 (21)	46.8 (22)	62.3 (33)
Europe	29.1 (16)	21.8 (12)	43.1 (22)	48.1 (25)	55.8 (29)
North America	47.1 (24)	27.1 (13)	34.0 (17)	66.7 (34)	86.0 (43)
Significance level	0.00	0.11	0.09	0.19	0.07
Sectors:					
Agricultural	28.2 (11)	15.8 (6)	22.9 (8)	61.8 (21)	65.7 (23)
Extractive-based	60.4 (29)	40.9 (18)	36.7 (18)	59.1 (26)	68.0 (34)
Finished-goods	55.9 (33)	37.5 (21)	52.6 (30)	50.9 (29)	71.4 (40)
Services	20.0 (3)	6.7 (1)	30.8 (4)	33.3 (5)	57.1 (8)
Significance level	0.00	0.01	0.00	0.30	0.48
Sales size:					
Top third	64.7 (33)	54.2 (26)	55.8 (14)	71.2 (37)	82.7 (43)
Second third	45.6 (26)	22.6 (12)	33.3 (17)	45.1 (23)	71.2 (37)
Bottom third	32.1 (17)	15.4 (8)	27.5 (29)	44.7 (21)	49.0 (25)
Significance level	0.01	0.00	0.00	0.04	0.37

Annex table D.13. Corporate sustainable development programmes related to protection of the atmosphere

Programme or policy		Env.-oriented R&D for energy-efficiency production methods	Use of renewable energy sources
Total % (number)		70.7 (111)	22.0 (33)
Home-country region:	Asia	77.8 (42)	28.8 (15)
	Europe	59.6 (31)	13.7 (7)
	North America	74.5 (38)	23.4 (11)
Significance level		0.26	0.04
Sectors:	Agricultural	66.7 (26)	14.7 (5)
	Extractive-based	79.6 (39)	21.7 (10)
	Finished-goods	70.9 (39)	30.4 (17)
	Services	50.0 (7)	7.1 (1)
Significance level		0.17	0.01
Sales size:	Top third	88.5 (46)	36.0 (18)
	Second third	71.2 (37)	15.7 (8)
	Bottom third	52.8 (28)	14.3 (7)
Significance level		0.10	0.02

Annex table D.14. Corporate developing country policies/practices on protection of the atmosphere

Programme or policy		Use CFCs or related products at plants in developing countries	Monitor stacks for air-emission components in developing countries
Total % (number)		27.4 (32)	36.6 (41)
Home-country region:	Asia	31.8 (14)	39.1 (18)
	Europe	14.7 (5)	30.3 (10)
	North America	33.3 (13)	39.4 (13)
Significance level		0.17	0.48
Sectors:	Agricultural	10.7 (3)	20.8 (5)
	Extractive-based	28.6 (10)	48.5 (16)
	Finished-goods	43.2 (19)	34.8 (16)
	Services	..	44.4 (4)
Significance level		0.15	0.33
Sales size:	Top third	42.9 (18)	59.5 (25)
	Second third	27.0 (10)	16.7 (6)
	Bottom third	10.5 (4)	29.4 (10)
Significance level		0.02	0.00

Annex table D.15. Corporate activities involving toxic chemicals and hazardous wastes

Activity	Carcinogens in manufacturing	Radioactive wastes	PCB waste & emissions	Dioxin wastes and emissions	Disposal of waste outside the country of origin
Total % (number)	43.9 (69)	20.8 (32)	29.3 (46)	14.2 (22)	13.8 (22)
Home-country region:					
Asia	36.4 (20)	20.0 (11)	12.7 (7)	5.5 (3)	3.6 (2)
Europe	36.5 (19)	11.8 (6)	25.0 (13)	19.2 (10)	16.7 (9)
North America	60.0 (30)	31.3 (15)	52.0 (26)	18.8 (9)	22.0 (11)
Significance level	0.01	0.17	0.00	0.17	0.02
Sectors:					
Agricultural	30.0 (12)	17.5 (7)	12.5 (5)	25.6 (10)	5.0 (2)
Extractive-based	64.6 (31)	33.3 (15)	43.5 (20)	14.9 (7)	21.3 (10)
Finished-goods	42.1 (24)	14.0 (8)	31.0 (18)	5.3 (3)	13.6 (8)
Services	16.7 (2)	16.7 (2)	23.1 (3)	16.7 (2)	15.4 (2)
Significance level	0.01	0.00	0.01	0.14	0.25
Sales size:					
Top third	60.0 (30)	19.1 (9)	36.7 (18)	16.3 (8)	25.5 (13)
Second third	35.2 (19)	26.4 (14)	24.1 (13)	17.0 (9)	11.1 (6)
Bottom third	37.7 (20)	16.7 (9)	27.8 (15)	9.4 (5)	5.6 (3)
Significance level	0.03	0.02	0.33	0.12	0.04

Annex table D.16. Corporate policies and procedures related to environmentally sound management of toxic wastes and chemicals

Policy & procedure	Company-wide policy going beyond national regulation				Procedure/programme standardized for use throughout the firm			
	Toxic substances in general	Specific hazardous compounds	Waste disposal	Waste reduction/ technologies	Waste handling	Contents of MSDS	Worker Safety	Voluntarily finances waste technologies
Total % (number)	47.8 (76)	46.7 (75)	51.6 (82)	48.7 (77)	56.3 (89)	63.7 (100)	67.3 (105)	58.3 (88)
Home-country region: Asia	53.7 (29)	48.1 (26)	61.1 (33)	54.7 (29)	74.1 (40)	69.6 (39)	89.3 (50)	65.4 (34)
Europe	32.7 (18)	31.5 (17)	29.6 (16)	27.8 (15)	35.8 (19)	53.1 (26)	44.9 (22)	51.0 (25)
North America	58.0 (29)	61.5 (37)	64.7 (33)	64.7 (33)	58.8 (30)	67.3 (35)	64.7 (33)	58.0 (29)
Significance level	0.02	0.01	0.00	0.00	0.00	0.02	0.00	0.33
Sectors: Agricultural	32.4 (12)	31.6 (12)	36.8 (14)	31.6 (12)	37.8 (14)	44.4 (16)	47.4 (18)	51.4 (18)
Extractive-based	62.5 (30)	59.2 (29)	60.4 (29)	60.4 (29)	62.0 (31)	78.7 (37)	73.3 (33)	63.8 (30)
Finished-goods	50.8 (30)	50.0 (29)	58.6 (34)	54.4 (31)	66.7 (38)	66.1 (39)	78.0 (46)	60.7 (34)
Services	26.7 (4)	33.3 (5)	33.3 (5)	33.3 (5)	42.9 (6)	53.3 (8)	57.1 (8)	46.2 (6)
Significance level	0.02	0.00	0.00	0.01	0.02	0.02	0.01	0.69
Sales size: Top third	60.8 (31)	62.0 (31)	69.4 (34)	66.0 (33)	64.7 (33)	78.0 (39)	83.3 (40)	78.4 (40)
Second third	51.8 (29)	47.4 (27)	52.6 (30)	47.3 (26)	58.2 (32)	58.2 (32)	64.8 (35)	48.1 (25)
Bottom third	30.8 (16)	32.1 (17)	34.0 (18)	34.0 (18)	46.2 (24)	55.8 (29)	55.6 (30)	47.9 (23)
Significance level	0.04	0.03	0.00	0.01	0.22	0.11	0.02	0.04

Annex table D.17. Developing country issues pertaining to environmentally sound management of toxic wastes and chemicals

Activity		Monitors disposal of hazardous wastes generated in plants	Has toxic education programmes for workforce etc.
Total % (number)		47.8 (54)	40.5 (45)
Home-country region:	Asia	45.5 (20)	45.5 (20)
	Europe	39.4 (13)	27.3 (9)
	North America	58.3 (21)	47.1 (16)
Significance level		0.36	0.38
Sectors:	Agricultural	42.3 (11)	21.7 (5)
	Extractive-based	45.7 (16)	51.4 (18)
	Finished-goods	51.1 (23)	45.5 (20)
	Services	57.1 (4)	22.2 (2)
Significance level		0.60	0.07
Sales size:	Top third	63.4 (26)	65.1 (28)
	Second third	40.5 (15)	29.4 (10)
	Bottom third	37.1 (13)	20.6 (7)
Significance level		0.14	0.00

Annex table D.18. Corporate activities with potential deleterious impact on water resources

Activity	Emissions of heavy metals (e.g. cadmium)	Use of large below ground storage tanks
Total % (number)	55.6 (89)	38.9 (61)
Home-country region: Asia	43.6 (24)	23.2 (13)
Europe	49.1 (27)	30.0 (15)
North America	76.0 (38)	64.7 (33)
Significance level	0.01	0.00
Sectors: Agricultural	30.0 (12)	35.9 (14)
Extractive-based	64.6 (31)	37.5 (18)
Finished-goods	69.5 (41)	38.6 (22)
Services	38.5 (5)	53.8 (7)
Significance level	0.01	0.65
Sales size: Top third	72.5 (37)	53.1 (26)
Second third	50.9 (28)	33.3 (18)
Bottom third	44.4 (24)	31.5 (17)
Significance level	0.01	0.17

Annex table D.19. Corporate issues on freshwater resources in developing countries

Issue	Company's plants located near drinking water supplies in developing countries	Company's products hazardous to drinking water supplies in developing countries
Total % (number)	16.0 (19)	3.4 (4)
Home-country region: Asia	4.3 (2)	2.2 (1)
Europe	17.6 (6)	5.9 (2)
North America	28.2 (11)	2.6 (1)
Significance level	0.00	0.17
Sectors: Agricultural	17.9 (5)	3.7 (1)
Extractive-based	22.2 (8)	8.3 (3)
Finished-goods	10.9 (5)	..
Services	11.1 (1)	..
Significance level	0.44	0.51
Sales size: Top third	20.9 (9)	7.0 (3)
Second third	10.8 (4)	..
Bottom third	15.4 (6)	2.6 (1)
Significance level	0.33	0.42

Annex table D.20. Corporate programmes for the protection of water resources

Policy and programme		Company-wide water quality/pollution programmes	Company-wide storage tank programmes
Total % (number)		48.1 (77)	39.9 (63)
Home-country region:	Asia	69.1 (38)	44.4 (24)
	Europe	24.1 (13)	20.4 (11)
	North America	51.0 (26)	56.0 (28)
Significance level		0.00	0.00
Sectors:	Agricultural	28.9 (11)	26.3 (10)
	Extractive-based	58.3 (28)	48.9 (23)
	Finished-goods	59.3 (35)	43.1 (25)
	Services	20.0 (3)	33.3 (5)
Significance level		0.00	0.39
Sales size:	Top third	60.8 (31)	58.0 (29)
	Second third	50.0 (28)	35.7 (20)
	Bottom third	34.0 (18)	26.9 (14)
Significance level		0.03	0.02

Annex table D.21. Corporate sustainable development programmes for water resources

Practice		Conservation of water resources
Total % (number)		67.9 (106)
Home-country region:	Asia	60.4 (32)
	Europe	62.3 (33)
	North America	82.0 (41)
Significance level		0.17
Sectors:	Agricultural	62.2 (23)
	Extractive-based	71.4 (35)
	Finished-goods	73.2 (41)
	Services	50.0 (7)
Significance level		0.54
Sales size:	Top third	86.3 (44)
	Second third	63.0 (34)
	Bottom third	54.9 (28)
Significance level		0.01

Annex table D.22. Transnational corporations and land pollutants.
(number of respondents who use or dispose of selected pollutants)

Waste and emission		Heavy Metals	PCBs	Dioxins	Radioactive Materials
Totals% (number)		55.6 (89)	29.3 (46)	14.2 (22)	20.8 (32)
Home-country region:	Asia	43.6 (24)	12.7 (7)	5.5 (3)	20.0 (11)
	Europe	49.1 (27)	25.0 (13)	19.2 (10)	11.8 (6)
	North America	76.0 (38)	52.0 (26)	18.8 (9)	31.3 (15)
Significance level		0.01	0.00	0.17	0.17
Sectors:	Agricultural	30.0 (12)	12.5 (5)	25.6 (10)	17.5 7
	Extractive-based	64.6 (31)	43.5 (20)	14.9 (7)	33.3 (15)
	Finished-goods	69.5 (41)	31.0 (18)	5.3 (3)	14.0 (8)
	Services	38.5 (5)	23.1 (3)	16.7 (2)	16.7 (2)
Significance Level		0.01	0.01	0.14	0.00
Sales size:	Top third	72.5 (37)	36.7 (18)	16.3 (8)	19.1 (9)
	Second third	50.9 (28)	24.1 (13)	17.0 (9)	26.4 (14)
	Bottom third	44.4 (24)	27.8 (15)	9.4 (5)	16.7 (9)
Significance level		0.01	0.33	0.12	0.02

Annex table D.23. Corporate land policies and programmes.
(number of respondents who have selected international land-based policies)

Policy/Programme		Land/soil quality	Site selection	Land transport	Land reclamation/- rehabilitation
Total % (number)		31.9 (49)	34.0 (52)	24.3 (37)	21.6 (33)
Home-country region:	Asia	31.5 (17)	31.5 (17)	21.2 (11)	21.6 (11)
	Europe	18.9 (10)	17.3 (9)	16.0 (8)	9.4 (5)
	North America	44.0 (22)	55.3 (26)	36.0 (18)	34.7 (17)
Significance level		0.01	0.00	0.00	0.03
Sectors:	Agricultural	21.1 (8)	24.3 (9)	11.1 (4)	10.8 (4)
	Extractive-based	47.9 (23)	45.7 (21)	42.2 (19)	29.5 (13)
	Finished-goods	26.8 (15)	32.7 (18)	21.4 (12)	21.1 (12)
	Services	20.0 (3)	26.7 (4)	13.3 (2)	26.7 (4)
Significance level		0.03	0.15	0.00	0.03
Sales size:	Top third	44.9 (22)	45.8 (22)	39.6 (19)	33.8 (19)
	Second third	32.1 (18)	29.6 (16)	21.8 (12)	18.9 (10)
	Bottom third	17.3 (9)	27.5 (14)	12.2 (6)	7.8 (4)
Significance level		0.05	0.26	0.01	0.00

Annex table D.24. Sustainable development activities for land resources

Activity	Afforestation on corporate land	Integrated pest management
Total % (number)	40.4 (59)	11.9 (18)
Home-country region: Asia	56.9 (29)	13.5 (7)
Europe	29.8 (14)	7.8 (4)
North America	33.3 (16)	14.6 (7)
Significance level	0.07	0.79
Sectors: Agricultural	42.4 (14)	17.6 (6)
Extractive-based	43.5 (20)	10.6 (5)
Finished-goods	37.5 (21)	10.7 (6)
Services	36.4 (4)	7.1 (1)
Significance level	0.95	0.67
Sales size: Top third	47.1 (24)	16.0 (8)
Second third	46.0 (23)	9.6 (5)
Bottom third	26.7 (12)	10.2 (5)
Significance level	0.28	0.55

Annex table D.25. Corporate land-based programmes in developing countries

Activity/Programme	Hold land for safety zones	Wetland & rainforest protection
Total % (number)	13.6 (16)	9.2 (11)
Home-country region: Asia	24.4 (11)	4.4 (2)
Europe	11.4 (4)	2.9 (1)
North America	2.6 (1)	20.5 (8)
Significance level	0.01	0.01
Sectors: Agricultural	11.1 (3)	3.8 (1)
Extractive-based	24.3 (9)	15.8 (6)
Finished-goods	8.9 (4)	6.7 (3)
Services	..	10.0 (1)
Significance level	0.36	0.69
Sales size: Top third	19.0 (8)	15.9 (7)
Second third	13.2 (5)	8.1 (3)
Bottom third	7.9 (3)	2.6 (1)
Significance level	0.18	0.27

Annex table D.26. Corporate activities impacting oceans

Activity	Ocean disposal of wastes	Oil shipping (specific sector)
Total % (number)	9.6 (15)	13.1 (20)
Home-country region: Asia	9.1 (5)	12.5 (7)
Europe	9.6 (5)	4.2 (2)
North America	10.0 (5)	22.4 (11)
Significance level	0.79	0.05
Sectors: Agricultural	7.5 (3)	10.3 (4)
Extractives	20.8 (10)	22.2 (10)
Finished-goods	1.8 (1)	10.7 (6)
Services	7.7 (1)	..
Significance level	0.13	0.10
Sales size: Top third	14.0 (7)	18.8 (9)
Second third	7.5 (4)	13.2 (7)
Bottom third	7.4 (4)	7.7 (4)
Significance level	0.53	0.58

Annex table D.27. Transnational corporations and protection of oceans

Programme/activity	Company-wide policy for marine transport beyond national regulation	Effluents released into oceans or seawater tributaries off developing countries
Total % (number)	13.8 (21)	14.3 (17)
Home-country region: Asia	17.3 (9)	13.6 (6)
Europe	8.0 (4)	8.8 (3)
North America	16.0 (8)	19.5 (8)
Significance level	0.06	0.61
Sectors: Agricultural	2.6 (1)	7.1 (2)
Extractives	40.9 (18)	35.1 (13)
Finished-goods	3.6 (2)	2.3 (1)
Services	..	10.0 (1)
Significance level	0.00	0.00
Sales size: Top third	21.3 (10)	20.9 (9)
Second third	10.9 (6)	10.5 (4)
Bottom third	10.0 (5)	10.5 (4)
Significance level	0.33	0.56

Annex table D.28. Corporate involvement in biotechnology

Process/activity		Bioengineering process	Products derived from biotechnology	Markets genetically engineered products in developing countries
Total % (number)		17.2 (26)	17.2 (27)	2.6 (3)
Home-country region:	Asia	21.6 (11)	26.8 (15)	..
	Europe	22.0 (11)	18.9 (10)	5.9 (2)
	North America	8.0 (4)	4.2 (2)	2.6 (1)
Significance level		0.12	0.04	0.49
Sectors:	Agricultural	29.7 (11)	27.5 (11)	7.7 (2)
	Extractive-based	23.9 (11)	26.1 (12)	2.7 (1)
	Finished-goods	7.3 (4)	7.0 (4)	..
	Services	..	..	..
Significance level		0.03	0.00	0.27
Sales size:	Top third	22.9 (11)	18.4 (9)	2.3 (1)
	Second third	11.5 (6)	18.9 (10)	5.4 (2)
	Bottom third	17.6 (9)	14.5 (8)	..
Significance level		0.47	0.65	0.70

Annex table D.29. Corporate activities detrimental to biological diversity

Activity		Use mono-crops from developing countries in manufacturing	Drift net fishing as a specific sector	Practice mono-cropping or clear-cutting in developing countries
Total % (number)		2.0 (3)	2.0 (3)	1.7 (2)
Home-country region:	Asia	1.9 (1)	1.8 (1)	..
	Europe	..	2.0 (1)	2.9 (1)
	North America	4.2 (2)	2.1 (1)	2.7 (1)
Significance level		0.36	0.64	0.85
Sectors:	Agricultural	..	2.6 (1)	4.0 (1)
	Extractive-based	6.7 (3)	2.3 (1)	2.6 (1)
	Finished-goods	..	1.8 (1)	..
	Services	..	..	..
Significance level		0.12	0.54	0.90
Sales size:	Top third	2.2 (1)	2.1 (1)	2.4 (1)
	Second third	3.8 (2)	2.0 (1)	..
	Bottom third	..	1.9 (1)	2.7 (1)
Significance level		0.22	0.99	0.85

Annex table D.30. Corporate programmes for the conservation of biodiversity

Programme	Conserve biodiversity	Conserve endangered species	Afforestation efforts on corporate property	Wetlands & rainforest protection in developing countries	Survey on biological species on underdeveloped land in developing countries
Total % (number)	10.1 (15)	15.8 (23)	40.4 (59)	9.2 (11)	8.7 (10)
Home-country region:					
Asia	2.0 (1)	4.0 (2)	56.9 (29)	4.4 (2)	6.7 (3)
Europe	8.0 (4)	10.4 (5)	29.8 (14)	2.9 (1)	11.8 (4)
North America	20.8 (10)	33.3 (16)	33.3 (16)	20.5 (8)	8.3 (3)
Significance level	0.09	0.00	0.07	0.01	0.59
Sectors:					
Agricultural	14.3 (5)	20.0 (7)	42.4 (14)	3.8 (1)	4.0 (1)
Extractive-based	13.3 (6)	25.0 (11)	43.5 (20)	15.8 (6)	18.4 (7)
Finished-goods	1.8 (1)	5.7 (3)	37.5 (21)	6.7 (3)	4.7 (2)
Services	21.4 (3)	14.3 (2)	36.4 (4)	10.0 (1)	..
Significance level	0.03	0.02	0.95	0.69	0.15
Sales size:					
Top third	14.3 (7)	21.3 (10)	47.1 (24)	15.9 (7)	12.2 (5)
Second third	10.2 (5)	20.0 (10)	46.0 (23)	8.1 (3)	8.1 (3)
Bottom third	5.9 (3)	6.1 (3)	26.7 (12)	2.6 (1)	5.4 (2)
Significance level	0.36	0.15	0.28	0.27	0.87

255

ANNEX E:
AGENDA 21 - BUSINESS & INDUSTRY

AGENDA 21, CHAPTER 30
STRENGTHENING THE ROLE OF BUSINESS AND INDUSTRY 1/

INTRODUCTION

30.1. Business and industry, including transnational corporations, play a crucial role in the social and economic development of a country. A stable policy regime enables and encourages business and industry to operate responsibly and efficiently and to implement longer-term policies. Increasing prosperity, a major goal of the development process, is contributed primarily by the activities of business and industry. Business enterprises, large and small, formal and informal, provide major trading, employment and livelihood opportunities. Business opportunities available to women are contributing towards their professional development, strengthening their economic role and transforming social systems. Business and industry, including transnational corporations, and their representative organizations should be full participants in the implementation and evaluation of activities related to Agenda 21.

30.2. Through more efficient production processes, preventive strategies, cleaner production technologies and procedures throughout the product life cycle, hence minimizing or avoiding wastes, the policies and operations of business and industry, including transnational corporations, can play a major role in reducing impacts on resource use and the environment. Technological innovations, development, applications, transfer and the more comprehensive aspects of partnership and cooperation are to a very large extent within the province of business and industry.

30.3. Business and industry, including transnational corporations, should recognize environmental management as among the highest corporate priorities and as a key determinant to sustainable development. Some enlightened leaders of enterprises are already implementing "responsible care" and product stewardship policies and programmes, fostering openness and dialogue with employees and the public and carrying out environmental audits and assessments of compliance. These leaders in business and industry, including transnational corporations, are increasingly taking voluntary initiatives, promoting and implementing self-regulations and greater responsibilities in ensuring their activities have minimal impacts on human health and the environment. The regulatory regimes introduced in many countries and the growing consciousness of consumers and the general public and enlightened leaders of business and industry, including transnational corporations, have all contributed to this. A positive contribution of business and industry, including transnational corporations, to sustainable development can increasingly be achieved by using economic instruments such as free market mechanisms in which the prices of goods and services should increasingly reflect the environmental costs of their input, production, use, recycling and disposal subject to country-specific conditions.

30.4. The improvement of production systems through technologies and processes that utilize resources more efficiently and at the same time produce less wastes - achieving more with less - is an important pathway towards sustainability for business and industry. Similarly, facilitating and encouraging inventiveness, competitiveness and voluntary initiatives are necessary for stimulating more varied, effecient and effective options. To address these major requirements and strengthen further the role of business and industry, including transnational corporations, the following two programmes are proposed.

PROGRAMME AREAS

A. Promoting cleaner production

Basis for action

30.5. There is increasing recognition that production,technology and management that use resources inefficiently form residues that are not reused, discharge wastes that have adverse impacts on human health and the environment and manufacture products that when used have further impacts and are difficult to recycle, need to be replaced with technologies, good engineering and management practices and know-how that would minimize waste throughout the product life cycle. The concept of cleaner production implies striving for optimal efficiencies at every stage of the product life cycle. A result would be the improvement of the overall competitiveness of the enterprise. The need for a transition towards cleaner production policies was recognized at the UNIDO-organized Ministerial-level Conference on Ecologically Sustainable Industrial Development, held at Copenhagen in October 1991.2/

Objectives

30.6. Governments, business and industry, including transnational corporations, should aim to increase the efficiency of resource utilization, including increasing the reuse and recycling of residues, and to reduce the quantity of waste discharge per unit of economic output.

Activities

30.7. Governments, business and industry, including transnational corporations, should strengthen partnerships to implement the principles and criteria for sustainable development.

30.8. Governments should identify and implement an appropriate mix of economic instruments and normative measures such as laws, legislations and standards, in consultation with business and industry, including transnational corporations, that will promote the use of cleaner production, with special consideration for small and medium-sized enterprises. Voluntary private initiatives should also be encouraged.

30.9. Governments, business and industry, including transnational corporations, academia and international organizations, should work towards the development and implementation of concepts and

methodologies for the internalization of environmental costs into accounting and
pricing mechanisms.

30.10. Business and industry, including transnational corporations, should be encouraged:

    (a)   To report annually on their environmental records, as well as on their
use of energy and natural resources;

    (b)   To adopt and report on the implementation of codes of conduct
promoting best environmental practice, such as the International Chamber
of Commerce's Business Charter on Sustainable Development and the
chemical industry's responsible care initiative.

30.11. Governments should promote technological and know-how cooperation between enterprises,
encompassing identification, assessment, research and development, management marketing and
application of cleaner production.

30.12. Industry should incorporate cleaner production policies in its operations and investments, taking
also into account its influence on suppliers and consumers.

30.13. Industry and business associations should cooperate with workers and trade unions to continuously
improve the knowledge and skills for implementing sustainable development operations.

30.14. Industry and business associations should encourage individual companies to undertake
programmes for improved environmental awareness and responsibility at all levels to make these
enterprises dedicated to the task of improving environmental performance based on internationally
accepted management practices.

30.15. International organizations should increase education, training and awareness activities relating to
cleaner production, in collaboration with industry, academia and relevant national and local authorities.

30.16. International and non-governmental organizations, including trade and scientific associations,
should strengthen cleaner production information dissemination by expanding existing databases such as
the UNEP, International Cleaner Production Clearing House (ICPIC), the UNIDO Industrial and
Technological Information Bank (INTIB) and the ICC/IEB, as well as forge networking of national and
international information systems.

B. Promoting responsible entrepreneurship

Basis for action

30.17. Entrepreneurship is one of the most important driving forces for innovations, increasing market
efficiencies and responding to challenges and opportunities. Small and medium-sized entrepreneurs, in
particular, play a very important role in the social and economic development of a country. Often, they

are the major means for rural development, increasing off-farm employment and providing the transitional means for improving the livelihoods of women. Responsible entrepreneurship can play a major role in improving the efficiency of resource use, reducing risks and hazards, minimizing wastes and safeguarding environmental qualities.

Objectives

30.18. The following objectives are proposed:

(a)   To encourage the concept of stewardship in themanagement and utilization of natural resources by entrepreneurs;

(b)   To increase the number of entrepreneurs engaged in enterprises that subscribe to and implement sustainable development policies.

Activities

30.19. Governments should encourage the establishment and operations of sustainably managed enterprises. The mix would include regulatory measures, economic incentives and streamlining of administrative procedures to assure maximum efficiency in dealing with applications for approval in order to facilitate investment decisions, advice and assistance with information, infrastructural support and stewardship responsibilities.

30.20. Governments should encourage, in cooperation with the private sector, the establishment of venture capital funds for sustainable development projects and programmes.

30.21. In collaboration with business, industry, academia and international organizations, Governments should support training in the environmental aspects of enterprise management. Attention should also be directed towards apprenticeship schemes for youth.

30.22. Business and industry, including transnational corporations, should be encouraged to establish world-wide corporate policies on sustainable development, arrange for environmentally sound technologies to be available to affiliates owned substantially by their parent company in developing countries without extra external charges, encourage overseas affiliates to modify procedures in order to reflect local ecological conditions and share experiences with local authorities, Governments and international organizations.

30.23. Large business and industry, including transnational corporations, should consider establishing partnership schemes with small and medium-sized enterprises to help facilitate the exchange of experience in managerial skills, market development and technological know-how, where appropriate, with the assistance of international organizations.

30.24. Business and industry should establish national councils for sustainable development and help promote entrepreneurship in the formal and informal sectors. The inclusion of women entrepreneurs should be facilitated.

30.25. Business and industry, including transnational corporations, should increase research and development of environmentally sound technologies and environmental management systems, in collaboration with academia and the scientific/engineering establishments, drawing upon indigenous knowledge, where appropriate.

30.26. Business and industry, including transnational corporations, should ensure responsible and ethical management of products and processes from the point of view of health, safety and environmental aspects. Towards this end, business and industry should increase self-regulation, guided by appropriate codes, charters and initiatives integrated into all elements of business planning and decision-making, and fostering openness and dialogue with employees and the public.

30.27. Multilateral and bilateral financial aid institutions should continue to encourage and support small- and medium-scale entrepreneurs engaged in sustainable development activities.

30.28. United Nations organizations and agencies should improve mechanisms for business and industry inputs, policy and strategy formulation processes, to ensure that environmental aspects are strengthened in foreign investment.

30.29. International organizations should increase support for research and development on improving the technological and managerial requirements for sustainable development, in particular for small and medium-sized enterprises in developing countries.

Means of implementation

Financing and cost evaluation

30.30. The activities included under this programme area are mostly changes in the orientation of existing activities and additional costs are not expected to be significant. The cost of activities by Governments and international organizations are already included in other programme areas.

Notes

1/   This is a final, advanced version of chapter 30 of Agenda 21, as adopted by the Plenary in Rio de Janeiro, on June 14, 1992. This document will be further edited, translated into the official languages, and published by the United Nations (forthcoming April 1993).

2/   See A/CONF.151/PC/125.

How to obtain United Nations Publications
*For more information on how to obtain
United Nations Publications, or to receive a
copy of our most recent catalogue,
please write to:*

United Nations Publications
United Nations
Room DC2-0853, Dept. 600
New York, New York 10017
Fax No. (212) 963-4116, *or:*

United Nations Publications
Sales Section
Palais des Nations
1211 Geneva 10
Switzerland

Litho in United Nations, New York
93-52910—October 1993—3,825
ISBN 92-1-104422-7

United Nations publication
Sales No. E.94.II.A.2
ST/CTC/149